A GERMAN REFERENCE GRAMMAR

R. Hammond

Revised Impression

Oxford University Press

Oxford University Press, Walton Street, Oxford OX2 6DP

Oxford New York Toronto
Delhi Bombay Calcutta Madras Karachi
Kuala Lumpur Singapore Hong Kong Tokyo
Nairobi Dar es Salaam Cape Town
Melbourne Auckland Madrid

and associated companies in
Berlin Ibadan

Oxford is a trade mark of Oxford University Press

© Oxford University Press 1981
First published 1981
Reprinted 1981, 1987, 1992, 1993

ISBN 0 19 912048 X

Phototypeset by Tradespools Limited, Frome, Somerset
Printed in Hong Kong

Preface

A German Reference Grammar is primarily aimed at university
and A-level students, or those at the equivalent level in English-
speaking countries, as well as adults studying German at an advanced
level. It is assumed that anyone who consults a reference grammar is
either in doubt about a particular point, or is uncertain of the way in
which a particular aspect of grammar functions. Every attempt has
therefore been made to keep to simple explanations, and to ensure that
the examples are simple, clear, modern, and relevant. Involved
grammatical terminology and elaborate examples from modern
literature have been avoided so that students are better able to
concentrate on the particular grammatical point involved. It is hoped
that the better GCSE students will also begin to find the book useful,
and go on using it in their later studies.

It is no longer possible to assume that students will have had a good
grounding in the grammar of their mother tongue, and for many the
first contact with grammatical terminology is in the studying of a
foreign language. Comments and statements of a simple analytical
nature have therefore been inserted into the text, as and when these
might appear to be necessary or useful. There is also a special glossary
at the end of the book. The main grammatical terms are defined in the
glossary, and after each definition a paragraph number is given,
indicating where the student can find examples of the definition in
practical use. It is strongly recommended that glossary and text should
be used together. Many students find it easier to understand grammar
through examples rather than by working from general statements to
particular instances, from theory to practice. **A German Reference
Grammar** is therefore rich in examples, each one of which is
designed to bring out an additional grammatical, lexical, or semantic
point. This work is therefore more than a plain reference grammar, in
that it contains many useful words and phrases.

English translations of the German examples have been given in almost
all paragraphs, as the user of the reference grammar may not always
have a dictionary immediately available. The author has given the
translations which he believes to be the best, or at least the most
understandable, but alternative translations are sometimes possible
without altering a word of the German original. Perhaps only the
professional translator knows the enormous problems of translating
one culture into another, for translation is an art and not a science.

Specific translation problems encountered when working from English into German are dealt with in an appendix at the back of the book.

There is a one-page list of contents which is designed to give an overall view of the reference book, but the highly detailed list of contents is, in fact, the index itself. It is therefore placed before the main text, in line with the Oxford **A French Reference Grammar**. Users should in any case consult the index, as the systematic division and classification of grammar for the purpose of analytical description conceals the fact that grammar is indivisible. There are always points which have to be considered under several aspects and yet for reasons of space are only handled in the text under one heading. The unity of grammar is only reestablished in the index as a whole.

German is the mother tongue of some 100 million people, living mainly in reunited Germany, in Austria, and in Switzerland. It is very much a living and expanding language, open to outside influences from north, south, east, and west. The post-war years have been ones of considerable social change, brought about by the great movements of population, and by the subsequent presence of many foreign cultures on the soil of all three main German-speaking countries. With other cultures have come other linguistic influences, which are communicated to the indigenous population almost entirely by means of the spoken word and only to a very limited extent in writing. The overwhelming means of communication for the transplanted or incoming populations is therefore spoken German, so that the spoken language has assumed an unexpected social importance. It is therefore understandable that the post-war years have been years of considerable linguistic change.

The changes, however, have been mainly in the lexical field, and not so much in the field of grammar. The most obvious academic effort has been the greatly enhanced study of the spoken language. In the post-war years it has become possible for everyone to record, to store, and to retrieve at will the spoken word. The accurate recording of speech has become a precise study rather than a hopeful feat of memory. The present work, therefore, is not only based on written material, but also on the careful analysis of spoken German. Much of the detailed work and most of the examples are original, and are based on both spoken and written German.

There are minor differences in the grammar of the spoken and the written languages; for example, in the order of adverbs of place and manner, or in the use (misuse) of the subjunctive or indicative in reported speech. Attention has been called to such differences throughout the work. Since many of the examples have been taken from the spoken language, the author hopes that they have the directness of speech and are thereby simple, clear, modern, and relevant. The chapter on punctuation on the other hand has been based largely on written sources or on adaptations of written material and not on transcriptions.

Five works have been of particular help: the companion volume, Ferrar's **A French Reference Grammar** (Oxford University Press), in the planning stage, Thompson & Martinet's latest edition of **A Practical English Grammar** (Oxford University Press) for its many insights into grammar; Quirk's **A Grammar of Contemporary English** (Longman) for its modern analysis and terminology; **The Concise Oxford-Duden German Dictionary** for the occasional translation, and **Der Große Duden**. It has been comforting to have one's own findings confirmed by cross-checking with one of the ten volumes of that great work.

No work such as **A German Reference Grammar** can be completed without the critical help of native speakers. The author wishes to express his grateful thanks to Karin Lenz and Walburga Freund-Spork, teachers of English and German respectively, and to their husbands Willi Lenz and Dr. Winfried Freund, Professor of Modern German Literature, all of whom were most helpful in suggesting improvements in the German examples and in the prevention of errors. Karin Lenz also ensured that the examples really match the English text and translate back accurately into German, whilst Professor Freund, who is himself author of many articles of literary criticism and books on modern German literature, and his wife, who has written articles on the teaching of German literature, were particularly helpful in assessing trends and changes in modern German. My wife was my preliminary critic and she typed the whole manuscript, some parts of it several times. To all of them my thanks.

Abbreviations

The following abbreviations are used:

acc.	= accusative	N.B.	= (nota bene) note well
cond.	= conditional	nom.	= nominative
dat.	= dative	pl.	= plural
e.g.	= for example	sing.	= singular
etc.	= and so on	subj.	= subjunctive
et seq.	= (et sequentia) and the following	usw.	= (und so weiter) and so on
f.	= feminine	v.i.	= verb intransitive
gen.	= genitive	v.t.	= verb transitive
m.	= masculine	v.t. & i.	= verb transitive and intransitive
n.	= neuter	z.B.	= (zum Beispiel) for example

The special abbreviations used in paragraphs 90 and 98 are explained in those paragraphs, and are not listed above.

Square brackets ['blaibn] are used for phonetic transcriptions. Double oblique strokes /a/ are used for phonetic symbols. Single oblique strokes (I shall/will go) indicate alternative forms. Round brackets (good and evil) are used for English translations within texts, for cross-references, and for words which may either be included or excluded.

Contents

Numbers in dark type refer to paragraphs.
Numbers in italic refer to pages.

Index

Numbers refer to paragraphs.

Index

Spelling and pronunciation

1 The International Phonetic Alphabet

The phonetic alphabet used in dictionaries such as The Concise Oxford–Duden German Dictionary is taken from the Alphabet of the International Phonetic Association.

The sounds normally used in German are reduced to standard sounds which are recognizable in all German-speaking regions. The '*Deutsche Bühnenaussprache*' worked out by Theodor Siebs and his colleagues in Berlin at the end of the 19th century has served as the written norm of the spoken word for more than half a century. In 1974 the Duden Verlag published a new edition of the *Aussprachewöterbuch*, in which the results of long research in both parts of Germany were reduced to a modern standard pronunciation (*Standardaussprache*). Briefly, the *Bühnenaussprache* was found to be a slightly exaggerated form of speech.

2 Pronunciation

The problem of reducing spoken sound to a written form remains. The following table gives the main sounds used in German, together with the phonetic symbol and German examples. To the specialist these are phonemes and not allophones, or (less clearly expressed) approximations and not precise sounds. The phonetic transcriptions are in square brackets.

Vowels

/a/	hat	['hat]	/œ/	Löffel	['lœfl]
/a:/	Vater	['fa:tɐ]	/ɐ/	oder	['o:dɐ]
/ɛ/	besser	['bɛsɐ]	/ʊ/	und	['ʊnt]
/ɛ:/	Tüter	['tɛ:tɐ]	/u:/	gut	['gu:t]
/e:/	See	['ze:]	/ɣ/	würde	['vɣrdə]
/ə/	alte	['altə]	/y:/	müde	['my:də]
/ɪ/	mit	['mɪt]	/ɔ/	Bonn	['bɔn]
/i:/	bieten	['bi:tn]	/ai/	ein	['ain]
/o:/	Mode	['mo:də]	/au/	Haus	['haus]
/ø:/	mögen	['ˊmø:gn]	/ɔy/	treu	['trɔy]

There are fewer diphthongs in German than in English.

Foreign words taken into the German language are often spoken in the same way as in the foreign language. For example, from the French, **Bonjour** [bõ'ʒu:r], **Parfum** [par'fœ̃:], and from the

English, **Band** ['bɛnt] or ['bænd], **O.K.** [oˈkeː] or [oʊˈkei]. The list includes the main sounds in German.

Consonants

/p/	Paß	['pas]	/s/	West	['vɛst]
/b/	bitter	['bɪtɐ]	/z/	sollen	['zɔlən]
/t/	Taxi	['taksi]	/ʃ/	Shop	['ʃɔp]
/d/	Doktor	['dɔktɔr]	/ʒ/	Genie	[ʒeˈniː]
/k/	kahl	['kaːl]	/ç/	ich	['ɪç]
/g/	gehen	['geːən]	/j/	ja	['jaː]
/m/	muß	['mʊs]	/x/	Dach	['dax]
/n/	nein	['nain]	/h/	hoch	['hoːx]
/ŋ/	lang	['laŋ]	/pf/	Pfanne	['pfanə]
/l/	Liebe	['liːbə]	/ts/	zehn	['tseːn]
/r/	reif	['raif]	/tʃ/	Kaffeeklatsch	['kafeˈklatʃ]
/f/	fast	['fast]	/dʒ/	Gin	['dʒɪn]
/v/	wie	['viː]			

The three sounds which are not commonly used in the English language are [ts], [ç] and [x]. The Scottish pronunciation of 'loch' is often [lɔx]. The pronunciation of these – and other – sounds is best learned by listening to native speakers. When once the sounds are clearly in the memory the above tables can be used successfully in conjunction with a good dictionary which gives the phonetic transcription (as in the square brackets). A word of warning. Certain sounds like the **a** in **Vater** and the English *father* are not the same. The phonetic transcriptions are ['faːtɐ] and ['fɑːðə].

3 Intonation

German, like English, is a rhythmic language when spoken well, and the voice rises and falls on a musical scale. The rhythm of a sentence depends on a number of factors, such as the mood of the speaker, his or her range of vocabulary, and above all on the choice of words. Long compound words, for example, tend to disturb the rhythm.

Spoken German is divided into lengths of connected speech, which usually – but not necessarily – coincide with punctuation in the written language. The breathing habits of a speaker may determine the actual spoken lengths. German intonation is best studied from recordings of native speakers, and preferably studied length by length of connected speech.

The following observations may be helpful, but are certainly not to be regarded as rules of speech:

(**a**) A listener hears the stressed syllables more clearly than the unstressed, and is therefore more likely to deduce the meaning from the stressed syllables.

(**b**) Stress for meaning may be achieved by slow and clear diction, or by extra loudness.

(**c**) In a simple statement the voice rises slowly, and falls sharply at the end. For example: **Er machte das Buch zu**.

(**d**) The voice may fall sharply just before the end of a simple statement, but it then remains low. For example:
Sie ist eine Berlinerin.

(**e**) A genuine question or enquiry leads to a sharp rise in the voice near or at the end of the sentence. For example:
Hast du schon gegessen?

(**f**) The preliminary verb in a command is stressed, and the voice may then rise or fall slightly. For example:
Geh mal schnell zur Post!
Fahren Sie links ab an der nächsten Kreuzung!

(**g**) Complex or multiple sentences are spoken in lengths of connected speech. The speaker usually stresses one particular length. For example:
Es ist mir nicht klar, / ob ich überhaupt in der Lage bin, / mein Ziel zu erreichen.
Ist es Ihnen klar, / ob Sie überhaupt in der Lage sind, / Ihr Ziel zu erreichen?

(**h**) German is often spoken more loudly than English.

Intonation is seldom a planned technique, and so much depends on the intention of the speaker that the formation of simple general rules is not possible.

4 The accentuation of words

Words, on the other hand, are always spoken with the stress on a certain syllable. The particular accentuation depends on a generally accepted manner of speech. The following observations may help:

(**a**) In basic words of two syllables the stress falls on the first syllable. For example:
Vater ['faːtɐ], **Mutter** ['mʊtɐ], **Winter** ['vɪntɐ], **Tafel** ['taːfl], **Erde** ['cːɐdə], **Besen** ['bcːzn]. The stress mark (') is always placed before the syllable to be stressed.

(**b**) The stress is usually on the first syllable of simple derivatives. For example:

Büchlein ['by:çlain], **Mädchen** ['mɛ:tçən], **wunderbar** ['vʊndɐba:ɐ], **Möglichkeit** ['mø:klıçkait), **langsam** ['laŋza:m]

(**c**) The stress is also on the first syllable of most basic compound words. For example:

Mondschein ['mo:ntʃain], **Mundart** ['mʊnta:ɐt], **altmodisch** ['altmo:dıʃ], **neunzehn** ['nɔyntse:n]

(**d**) In compound words consisting of two parts the first part is usually stressed, but the second part may also be partly stressed if the meaning requires it. For example:

Staatsmann ['ʃta:ts͵man], **Regierungssprecher** (re'gi:ruŋs͵ʃprɛçɐ], **Lampenlicht** ['lampn͵lıçt], **Straßenkarte** ['ʃtra:sn͵kartə]

The mark (') denotes full stress, and (͵) part stress.

(**e**) In compound words of three parts the first part usually has the most stress, but the secondary stress may come on the second or third part of the word. This often depends on the meaning. For example:

Landeshauptstadt ['landəs'hauptʃtat],
Grenzübergang ['grɛnts͵y:bɐgaŋ],
but **Bahnsteigkarte** ['ba:nʃtaig͵kartə],
Fußballtrainer ['fu:sbal͵trɛ:nɐ].

(**f**) The prefixes **be-**, **emp-**, **ent-**, **er-**, **ge-**, **ver-**, and **zer-** are not stressed. For example:

beginnen [bə'gınən], **erwarten** [ɛɐ'vartn], **gegessen** [gə'gɛsn]

(**g**) The prefixes or particles **ab-**, **an-**, **aus-**, **bei-**, **ein-**, **nach-** and **wieder-** are mostly stressed. For example:

ausgehen ['ausge:ən], **beisitzen** ['baizıtsn], **wiedergeben** ['vi:dɐge:bn]

(**h**) The prefixes or particles **da-**, **dar-**, **durch-**, **her-**, **hier-**, **hin-**, **hinter-**, **in-**, **miß**, **ob-**, **über-**, **um-**, **un-**, **voll-**, **vor-**, **wider-**, **zu-** are sometimes stressed and sometimes not stressed. For example:

hingehen ['hınge:ən], **hingegen** [hın'ge:gn], **durchgehen** (to go or pass through) ['dʊrçge:ən], **durchgehen** (to examine, check) [dʊrç'ge:ən], **übergehen** (to go or pass over) [y:bɐ'ge:ən], **übergehen** (to overlook, pass over) ['y:bɐge:ən], **vormittags** ['fo:ɐmıta:ks], **Widerspruch** ['vi:dɐʃprʊx], **widerstreben** [vidɐ'ʃtre:bn]

(i) The suffixes **-ei** and **-ieren** are stressed. For example:
Polizei [poli'tsai], **Schlägerei** [ʃlɛːgɐ'rai], **buchstabieren**
[buːxʃtaˈbiːrən], **sich rasieren** [zɪç raˈziːrən]

(j) If a speaker is speaking emotionally each syllable may be
stressed. For example:
furchtbar ['fʊrçtbaːɐ], but also ['fʊrçt'baːɐ],
so ein Idiot [zoː ain iˈdɪoːt] but also ['zoː 'ain ɪ'diˌoːt]

(k) All parts of composite expressions tend to be stressed. For
example:
das Hin- und Hergehen [das 'hɪn ʊnt 'heːɐ'geːən],
Für- und Nachsorge ['fyːɐ ʊnt 'naːx'zɔrgə]

(l) Abbreviations are usually stressed on the last syllable. For
example:
CDU [tseːdeːˈjuː], **GB** [geːˈbeː], **USA** [uːɛsˈaː]

5 Notes on German spelling

(a) The vowels **ä** [ɛː], **ö** [ø], and **ü** [yː] are separate vowels, and
always have the umlaut. Information printed by the computer
prints these vowels as **ae**, **oe**, **ue**. For example: **schoen**, **fuer**,
laenger.

(b) The diphthong **ei**, and **ie** are quite different in sound. For
example: **bleiben** ['blaibn] and **blieben** ['bliːbn]. Care should be
taken in the spelling.

(c) The diphthongs **eu** and **äu**, on the other hand, cannot be
distinguished by sound ([ɔy] and [ɔy]). The spelling of particular
words has to be learned. For example: **neu**, **teuer**, **Häuser**,
äußerlich. It helps to know the singular of a word like **Häuser**,
namely **Haus**.

(d) Of the other diphthongs **au** is common, and **ai** is not common.
Examples: **Haus**, **Mauer**, **kaum**, **Airbus**, **Mais** (*maize*), **Mainz**.

(e) The consonant **c** is little used in German except in the
combinations **ch**, **ck**, and **sch**. Words which begin with **c** are
almost all from English or a language of Latin or Greek origin. For
example: **City**, **Country-Music**, **Clique**, **Christus**. Most words
spoken with a hard **c** in English are spelt with a **k** in German. For
example: **Katalog**, **Kategorie**, **kalt**, **Keks**, **Klasse**.

(f) The English sound of **sh**[ʃ] as in *show* or *shape* is written with **sch**
in German.

(**g**) The letter **ß** is written and printed in German rather than the two letters **ss**. The letter **ß** is spoken ['ɛs'tsɛt]. Many nouns which end in **ß** change this consonant to **-ss-** in the genitive singular and all cases in the plural. For example: **der Fluß, des Flusses, die Flüsse; die Nuß, (pl.) die Nüsse; muß** but **müssen**.

(**h**) It is not desirable in handwriting to split a word up, but to begin the given word on a new line. This may not always be possible, and then these simple guide-lines should be followed. Basic words are split according to the way they are spoken. For example: **Wa/gen, wei/ter, Schu/le, schrift/lich, Er/de, ge/hen**. The inadvisability of splitting these words can be seen from the examples. The problem is more likely to arise when the typewriter is used. The printer has a more difficult problem, and all words in Duden's **Rechtschreibung** are shown in the above manner. In the case of compound words the obvious split is between the parts of the compound. Thereafter the further split occurs as for basic words. For example: **Schreib/ma/schi/nen/pa/pier, Fuß/ball/fa/na/ti/ker, Farb/fern/seh/ka/me/ra**. All these divisions are possible, but only a few are reasonable in handwriting or when the typewriter is used.

6 The use of capitals

(**a**) All nouns begin with a capital letter. For example: **das neue Auto, die rote Farbe, der junge Mann**.

(**b**) All words which are used as nouns also begin with a capital letter. For example: **Sie ist eine Bekannte von mir**. (She is someone I know.) **Das Gute und das Böse** (good and evil). **Ich möchte Verschiedenes mit Ihnen besprechen**. (I would like to discuss various things with you.) **Die Ampel zeigt Grün**. (The traffic lights are at green.) **Er bekam eine Eins**. (He got a one.) **Das Für und Wider** (the for and against).

(**c**) Of course, the first word in a sentence begins with a capital letter.

(**d**) The first word of a quotation, the name of a book, a newspaper, the title of a song, etc. also begins with a capital letter. For example: **Er liest „Die Welt"**. **Mutter sagte: „Heute abend essen wir warm."** **Sie sangen „Stille Nacht, heilige Nacht"**.

(**e**) When the infinitive of a word is used as a noun it begins with a capital. For example: **das Sitzen und Stehen, das Lesen und Schreiben.**

(**f**) Adjectives immediately following these words also have a capital: **etwas, nichts, alles, allerlei, genug, viel, wenig**. For example: **etwas Gutes**, **nichts Neues**, **alles Gute**, **wenig Wichtiges**.

(**g**) The familiar **du** is written with a capital in a letter to a relative or to a close friend, in a written communication from a teacher to a pupil to whom he/she says **du**, and on certain inscriptions and dedications to a close friend. The words connected with **du**, such as **dein**, **deinetwegen**, **dich**, **ihr**, **euch**, are also written with capitals under the above circumstances. For example: **Ich danke Dir für Deinen lieben Brief.** (Thank you for your kind letter.) **Lehrer: Du hast Dir viel Mühe gegeben, aber Deine Arbeit ist nie fehlerfrei.** (Teacher: You have taken plenty of trouble, but your work is never free of mistakes.) **Habt Ihr Eure Eltern informiert?** (Have you informed your parents?) **Herzlichen Glückwunsch zu Deinem Geburtstag senden Dir Robin und Lisa.** (All best wishes for your birthday from Robin and Lisa.) These examples show that **du** is only written with a capital to a person with whom the writer is on a **du**-basis. On the other hand text-books, reference grammars, advertisements, brochures, etc. normally use small letters.

(**h**) The words **Sie** (you), **Ihrer**, **Ihre** (your), etc. are written with a capital, as they are polite forms of address. For example: **Können Sie sich an Ihre Deutschlandreise erinnern?** (Can you remember your trip to Germany?). Note: the reflexive pronoun **sich** is always written with a small letter.

(**i**) Christian or first names, family names, geographical place names, street names, as well as names of particular universities, colleges or schools, and so on, are all written with capitals as in English.

(**j**) Titles are also in capitals. For example: **Karl der Große**, **Ihre Königliche Hoheit**, **Eure Majestät**.

7 The use of small letters

It is equally important to know the occasions on which words are written with small letters, although logically the use of capitals might be expected. The main points are:

(**a**) In certain fixed phrases, provided they are not declined. For example: **im großen und ganzen**, **auf dem laufenden sein**, **durch dick und dünn**, **alt und jung**, **arm und reich**, **groß und klein**.

(**b**) Adverbs of time such as: **morgens**, **nachmittags**, **abends**, **mittwochs**, **samstags**, **wochentags**.

(**c**) Adverbs of manner such as: **wegen, trotz, dank, statt, laut, angesichts**.

(**d**) Indefinite numbers such as: **ein paar** (a few), **ein bißchen**, (a little).

(**e**) Certain fixed expressions which have the force of a verb, such as: **angst machen, schuld haben, schuld sein, leid tun, weh tun, instand halten, schade sein**.

(**f**) Certain expressions used adverbially, such as: **vor kurzem, im allgemeinen, vor allem, am besten, im voraus, trotz allem, (ein Mädchen) für alles**.

(**g**) Adjectives are not written with capitals if the following noun is clearly understood from the context, even though the noun is not written. For example: **Der Schuldirektor sprach mit den großen und den kleinen (Schülern). Er war der beste (seiner Schüler)**, but **Er wa der Beste**. (He was the best of all.)

(**h**) Note: **die beiden, wir beide, wir zwei, der eine sowie der andere, die übrigen, die ersten fünf, etwas anderes, allerlei anderes, alle fünf, alles auf einmal, alles in allem, alles oder nichts, alle bis auf einen**.

(**i**) Special problems include: **Er schreibt auf deutsch** (used adverbially), but **Er spricht Deutsch** (used as a noun), **in bezug auf** (with reference to) but **mit Bezug auf** (with reference to), **aufgrund** but **auf Grund** (on the basis of), **anhand** but **an Hand** (by means of), **hundert Leute** (a hundred people) but **Er zählte Hunderte** (He counted hundreds), **tausend Zuschauer** (a thousand spectators) but **Er sah mehrere Tausende** (He saw several thousands), **100 Kilometer je Stunde** but **100 km/st, ein Kilogramm** but **1000 g, drei Meter breit** but **3 m breit, zehn vom Hundert** (ten percent), **x-fach** (any number of times – used adverbially) but **das X-fache, Er hat O-Beine/X-Beine, radfahren** but **Sie fährt Rad, Auto fahren** and **Er fährt Auto**.

It can be seen from the many examples in this section that the subject of capitals and/or small letters is much more complicated than in English. It is therefore not surprising that there is disagreement on certain borderline expressions and words, as between Austria, German-speaking Switzerland, and the two Germanies, or between language specialists within a country.

8 Compound words and separable words

The German language is capable of enriching itself in a number of ways, especially in the making of compound words; and the limit of all reasonable combinations is still not in sight. At its best this leads to clear and compact expressions such as: **eine Bahnsteigkarte** (a platform ticket), **ein Fußballfan** (a football fan), **eine Bushaltestelle** (a bus stop), **ein Skilift** (a ski lift). These are clear concepts which can be translated neatly into English by the use of two words instead of one. Some compound words may not be so easy to translate even though their meanings are clear. For example: **eine Umsteig(e)karte** (a ticket which permits the holder to change train, bus, S-Bahn, etc.), **ein Tatverdächtiger** (a man suspected of a crime), **Alleinherrschaft** (rule by one person alone), **Rechthaberei** (the desire to be always in the right).

The gender is always that of the last word. For example: **der Bahnsteig**, **die Karte**, **die Bahnsteigkarte**.

9 The separation of compound words

A further feature of the German language is the separation of compound words. The unity of thought in the German language is disturbed under certain circumstances by the need to separate verbs, for example, whereby one part is withheld until the end of the sentence. The seasoned reader or the native speaker often manages to anticipate the 'missing' particle, whereas the learner has to carry the missing part of the word in the head, or connect up the particle visually or in the memory, and take it back to the main verb. This can be distracting, and disturb the easy flow of language and sense in the reader's or listener's mind.

There are many verbs which are formed with a prefix. They are mainly separable, but there are important exceptions. The following rules may be helpful:

(**a**) Verbs formed with the unstressed prefixes **be-**, **emp-**, **ent-**, **er-**, **ge-**, **ver-**, and **zer-** (see 3 (**f**) above) are inseparable.
N.B.: None of these prefixes can be used as separate parts of speech.

(**b**) Verbs beginning with prefixes such as **ab-**, **an-**, **auf-**, **aus-**, **bei-**, **ein-**, **entgegen-**, **fort-**, **gegen-**, **her-**, **hin-**, **hinaus-**, **hinein-**, **hinunter-**, **hinzu-**, **mit-**, **nach-**, **vor-**, **weg-**, **zu-**, **zusammen-**, and **zwischen-** are separable. N.B.: All of these prefixes can be used as separate parts of speech.

(**c**) The following prefixes are separable or inseparable according to the meaning of the verb: **durch-**, **miß-**, **über-**, **um-**, and **unter-**. For example: '**durchgehen** (to go or pass through), **durch'gehen** (to walk through), '**umgehen** (to go round, circulate), **um'gehen** (to evade, dodge). The stressed prefixes are separable and the unstressed prefixes (in the second of each pair of words) are inseparable.

The use of separable and inseparable verbs is to be found in paras. 120–3.

10 Problems concerning the separation or joining of words

There is a general lack of clarity and uniformity on the separation or joining of words other than the composite verbs and the compound nouns already mentioned. Duden gives two general pieces of advice:

1. If the first part of a combination is to be stressed, then join the words, but if the second part is to be stressed, then write the words separately.
2. When in doubt, write the words separately.

A number of examples will serve to bring out the problems:

(a) **Er kann gut schreiben.** (He can write well.) **Die Bank wird diese Summe gutschreiben.** (The bank will put this sum to (your) credit.)

(b) **Sie hat die neue Sekretärin mit dem Manager bekannt gemacht.** (She introduced the new secretary to the manager.) **Diese Nachricht wurde bekanntgemacht.** (This piece of news was announced.)

(c) **Wir müssen stehen bleiben.** (We must remain standing.) **Die Uhr wird bald stehenbleiben.** (The clock will soon stop.)

(d) The infinitives of certain composite verbs are inseparable, although the parts become separable when the verb is conjugated. For example: **kennenlernen** (to get to know) and **spazierengehen** (to go for a walk). **Er lernte sie kennen. Er ging spazieren.**

(e) **Auto fahren** but **radfahren**, **Ski laufen** but **das Skilaufen**, **Karten spielen** but **das Kartenspielen**.

(f) **an Hand** (or **anhand**) **von Beweismaterial** (with the aid of the (pieces of) evidence), **auf Grund** (or **aufgrund**) **der Evidenz** (by virtue of the evidence), **Taten an Stelle** (or **anstelle**) **von Worten** (deeds not words).

(g) **Der Saal war gut besetzt.** (The hall was well filled.) **ein gutbesetzter Saal** (a well-filled hall). **Der Spieler wurde leicht verletzt.** (The player was slightly injured.) **ein leichtverletzter Spieler** (a slightly injured player). **Seine Sprache ist schwer**

verständlich. (His speech is hard to understand.) **eine schwerverständliche Sprache** (a language difficult to understand).

(h) Das Buch ist schwer zu lesen. (The book is difficult to read.) **Er war schwer zu verstehen.** (It was difficult to understand him.) **Sie fing an zu laufen.** (She began to run.)

(i) Es freut mich, Sie kennenzulernen. (I am pleased to get to know you.) **Ich habe Ihnen gute Nachrichten mitzuteilen.** (I have good news to tell you.) **Sie brauchen nicht wegzulaufen!** (You needn't run away!)

(j) Karl-Heinz but also **Karlheinz**, **Anne Marie** but more likely **Annemarie**, **Hans** and **Hansjoachim**, also in a derogatory sense **ein Hanswurst** (a nobody, an insignificant person).

(k) Geographical names are made into compound nouns where reasonable. For example: **das Saarland, das Sauerland**, but **das Paderborner Land**; **die Nordsee** but **der Vierwaldstätter See**; **Ostwestfalen** but **Rheinland-Pfalz, Schloßstraße** but **die Konrad-Adenauer-Allee**.

The main problems are illustrated by the above examples. It is not possible to formulate general rules which are both simple and logical. There would be exceptions to almost every rule. A close study of the examples is therefore recommended.

Conjugation of verbs

11 Strong, irregular, and weak verbs – definitions

Strong verbs are those which change the stem vowel in the past tense and the past participle. Weak verbs are those which do not change the stem in the past tense and the past participle. Irregular verbs have features of both strong and weak verbs. The vowel in the stem is changed but the endings are those of weak verbs. The stem of a verb is found by taking off the ending. For example:

lern/en, tu/n, ähnel/n, ruinier/en.

12 Conjugation of strong, irregular, and weak verbs: active – indicative

Present tense

Strong	*Irregular*	*Weak*
ich rufe	ich kenne	ich mache
du rufst	du kennst	du machst
er, sie, es ruft	er, sie, es kennt	er, sie, es macht
wir rufen	wir kennen	wir machen
ihr ruft	ihr kennt	ihr macht
sie rufen	sie kennen	sie machen

Past tense

ich rief	ich kannte	ich machte
du riefst	du kanntest	du machtest
er, sie, es rief	er, sie, es kannte	er, sie, es machte
wir riefen	wir kannten	wir machten
ihr rieft	ihr kanntet	ihr machtet
sie riefen	sie kannten	sie machten

Perfect tense

ich habe gerufen	ich habe gekannt	ich habe gemacht
du hast gerufen	du hast gekannt	du hast gemacht
er, sie, es	er, sie, es	er, sie, es
hat gerufen	hat gekannt	hat gemacht
wir haben gerufen	wir haben gekannt	wir haben gemacht
ihr habt gerufen	ihr habt gekannt	ihr habt gemacht
sie haben gerufen	sie haben gekannt	sie haben gemacht

A number of frequently used strong verbs form the perfect tense with **sein**. For example:

ich bin gegangen
du bist gegangen
er, sie, es ist gegangen

wir sind gegangen
ihr seid gegangen
sie sind gegangen

Pluperfect tense

ich hatte gerufen
du hattest gerufen
er, sie, es
  hatte gerufen
wir hatten gerufen
ihr hattet gerufen
sie hatten gerufen

ich hatte gekannt
du hattest gekannt
er, sie, es
  hatte gekannt
wir hatten gekannt
ihr hattet gekannt
sie hatten gekannt

ich hatte gemacht
du hattest gemacht
er, sie, es
  hatte gemacht
wir hatten gemacht
ihr hattet gemacht
sie hatten gemacht

ich war gegangen
du warst gegangen
er, sie, es war gegangen

wir waren gegangen
ihr war(e)t gegangen
sie waren gegangen

Future tense

ich werde rufen
du wirst rufen
er, sie, es
  wird rufen
wir werden rufen
ihr werdet rufen
sie werden rufen

ich werde kennen
du wirst kennen
er, sie, es
  wird kennen
wir werden kennen
ihr werdet kennen
sie werden kennen

ich werde machen
du wirst machen
er, sie, es
  wird machen
wir werden machen
ihr werdet machen
sie werden machen

Future perfect

Theoretical examples of this tense are given below. Note: only the auxiliary verb **werden** changes. Most of the forms are, however, very seldom used.

ich werde gemacht haben
du wirst gemacht haben
er, sie, es wird gemacht haben
wir werden gemacht haben
ihr werdet gemacht haben
sie werden gemacht haben

ich werde gegangen sein
du wirst gegangen sein
er, sie, es wird gegangen sein
wir werden gegangen sein
ihr werdet gegangen sein
sie werden gegangen sein

The verbs **rufen** and **kennen** are conjugated like **machen**.

13 Conjugation of strong, irregular, and weak verbs: active – subjunctive

Present tense – subjunctive

(ich rufe)
(du rufest)
  er, sie, es rufe

(ich kenne)
(du kennest)
  er, sie, es kenne

(ich mache)
(du machest)
  er, sie, es mache

(wir rufen)	(wir kennen)	(wir machen)
(ihr rufet)	(ihr kennet)	(ihr machet)
(sie rufen)	(sie kennen)	(sie machen)

The forms in brackets are very seldom used.

Past tense – subjunctive

ich riefe	ich kannte	ich machte
du rief(e)st	du kanntest	du machtest
er, sie, es riefe	er, sie, es kannte	er, sie, es machte
wir riefen	wir kannten	wir machten
ihr rief(e)t	ihr kanntet	ihr machtet
sie riefen	sie kannten	sie machten

Perfect tense – subjunctive

ich habe gerufen	ich habe gekannt	ich habe gemacht
(du habest gerufen)	(du habest gekannt)	(du habest gemacht)
er, sie, es	er, sie, es	er, sie, es
habe gerufen	habe gekannt	habe gemacht
wir haben gerufen	wir haben gekannt	wir haben gemacht
(ihr habet gerufen)	(ihr habet gekannt)	(ihr habet gemacht)
sie haben gerufen	sie haben gekannt	sie haben gemacht

ich sei gegangen	wir seien gegangen
(du sei(e)st gegangen)	(ihr seiet gegangen)
er, sie, es sei gegangen	sie seien gegangen

The forms in brackets are very seldom used.
The perfect subjunctive and the pluperfect subjunctive are most likely to be used in reported speech. The word order would therefore be changed to: **daß ich gerufen habe, daß ich gegangen sei, daß ich gerufen hätte, daß ich gegangen wäre,** etc.

Pluperfect – subjunctive

ich hätte gerufen	ich hätte gekannt	ich hätte gemacht
du hättest gerufen	du hättest gekannt	du hättest gemacht
er, sie, es	er, sie, es	er, sie, es
hätte gerufen	hätte gekannt	hätte gemacht
wir hätten gerufen	wir hätten gekannt	wir hätten gemacht
ihr hättet gerufen	ihr hättet gekannt	ihr hättet gemacht
sie hätten gerufen	sie hätten gekannt	sie hätten gemacht

ich wäre gegangen	wir wären gegangen
du wär(e)st gegangen	ihr wär(e)t gegangen
er, sie, es wäre gegangen	sie wären gegangen

Werden + infinitive (first conditional)

ich würde	rufen, gehen, kennen, machen
du würdest	rufen, gehen, kennen, machen
er, sie, es würde	rufen, gehen, kennen, machen
wir würden	rufen, gehen, kennen, machen
ihr würdet	rufen, gehen, kennen, machen
sie würden	rufen, gehen, kennen, machen

This tense is often used instead of the past subjunctive and the perfect subjunctive.

Werden + past participle + haben or sein (second conditional)

ich würde	gerufen/gekannt/gemacht haben
du würdest	gerufen/gekannt/gemacht haben
er, sie, es würde	gerufen/gekannt/gemacht haben
wir würden	gerufen/gekannt/gemacht haben
ihr würdet	gerufen/gekannt/gemacht haben
sie würden	gerufen/gekannt/gemacht haben

ich würde gegangen sein	wir würden gegangen sein
du würdest gegangen sein	ihr würdet gegangen sein
er, sie, es würde gegangen sein	sie würden gegangen sein

Some of the forms are not often used.

Imperative

Singular:	ruf(e)!	geh(e)!	mach(e)!
Plural:	ruft!	geht!	macht!

Infinitive

Present:	rufen	gehen	machen
Past:	gerufen haben	gegangen sein	gemacht haben

14 Conjugation of 'haben', 'sein', and 'werden'

Present tense – indicative

ich habe	ich bin	ich werde
du hast	du bist	du wirst
er, sie, es hat	er, sie, es ist	er, sie, es wird
wir haben	wir sind	wir werden
ihr habt	ihr seid	ihr werdet
sie haben	sie sind	sie werden

Present tense – subjunctive

ich habe	ich sei	ich werde
(du habest)	(du sei(e)st)	(du werdest)
er, sie, es habe	er, sie, es sei	er, sie, es werde
wir haben	wir seien	wir werden
(ihr habet)	(ihr seiet)	(ihr werdet)
sie haben	sie seien	sie werden

The forms in brackets are very seldom used.

Past tense – indicative

ich hatte	ich war	ich wurde
du hattest	du warst	du wurdest
er, sie, es hatte	er, sie, es war	er, sie, es wurde
wir hatten	wir waren	wir wurden
ihr hattet	ihr wart	ihr wurdet
sie hatten	sie waren	sie wurden

Past tense – subjunctive

ich hätte	ich wäre	ich würde
du hättest	du wär(e)st	du würdest
er, sie, es hätte	er, sie, es wäre	er, sie, es würde
wir hätten	wir wären	wir würden
ihr hättet	ihr wär(e)t	ihr würdet
sie hätten	sie wären	sie würden

Perfect tense – indicative

ich habe gehabt	ich bin gewesen	ich bin geworden
du hast gehabt	du bist gewesen	du bist geworden
er, sie, es	er, sie, es	er, sie, es
hat gehabt	ist gewesen	ist geworden
wir haben gehabt	wir sind gewesen	wir sind geworden
ihr habt gehabt	ihr seid gewesen	ihr seid geworden
sie haben gehabt	sie sind gewesen	sie sind geworden

Perfect tense – subjunctive

ich habe gehabt	(ich sei gewesen)	(ich sei geworden)
(du habest gehabt)	(du sei(e)st gewesen)	(du sei(e)st geworden)
er, sie, es	(er, sie, es	(er, sie, es
habe gehabt	sei gewesen)	sei geworden)
wir haben gehabt	(wir seien gewesen)	(wir seien geworden)
(ihr habet gehabt)	(ihr seiet gewesen)	(ihr seiet geworden)
sie haben gehabt	(sie seien gewesen)	(sie seien geworden)

The forms in brackets are seldom used.

Pluperfect tense – indicative

ich hatte gehabt	ich war gewesen	ich war geworden
du hattest gehabt	du warst gewesen	du warst geworden
er, sie, es	er, sie, es	er, sie, es
hatte gehabt	war gewesen	war geworden
wir hatten gehabt	wir waren gewesen	wir waren geworden
ihr hattet gehabt	ihr wart gewesen	ihr wart geworden
sie hatten gehabt	sie waren gewesen	sie waren geworden

Pluperfect tense – subjunctive

ich hätte gehabt	ich wäre gewesen	ich wäre geworden
etc.	etc.	etc.

Future tense

Indicative	Subjunctive
ich werde haben, (sein), (werden)	ich werde haben, (sein), (werden)
du wirst haben	(du werdest haben)
er, sie, es wird haben	er, sie, es werde haben
wir werden haben	wir werden haben
ihr werdet haben	ihr werdet haben
sie werden haben	sie werden haben

Future perfect

Indicative	Subjunctive
er (sie, es) wird gehabt haben	(er (sie, es) werde gehabt haben)
er (sie, es) wird gewesen sein	(er (sie, es) werde gewesen sein)
er (sie, es) wird geworden sein	(er (sie, es) werde geworden sein)

The other forms, such as the first and second persons, singular and plural, are very seldom used.

The future perfect subjunctive is theoretically possible, but in practice the forms **er würde gehabt haben, er würde gewesen sein, er würde geworden sein**, would almost certainly be used in place of the future perfect subjunctive.

Imperative

Singular:	habe!	sei!	werde!
Plural:	habt!	seid!	werdet!

Infinitive

Present:	haben	sein	werden
Past:	gehabt haben	gewesen sein	geworden sein

15 The passive

The passive of all verbs is formed with the aid of two auxiliary verbs, **werden** and **sein**. The appropriate forms of these two verbs have been fully conjugated above, so that it is not necessary to display each tense in detail. The present and past tenses are, however, given in full. Otherwise only the third person singular is given, as it is the form which is most often used.

Present tense – passive

Indicative	Subjunctive
ich werde gefragt	ich werde gefragt
du wirst gefragt	du werdest gefragt
er, sie, es wird gefragt	er, sie, es werde gefragt
wir werden gefragt	wir werden gefragt
ihr werdet gefragt	ihr werdet gefragt
sie werden gefragt	sie werden gefragt

Past tense – passive

Indicative	Subjunctive
ich wurde gefragt	ich würde gefragt
du wurdest gefragt	du würdest gefragt
er, sie, es wurde gefragt	er, sie, es würde gefragt
wir wurden gefragt	wir würden gefragt
ihr wurdet gefragt	ihr würdet gefragt
sie wurden gefragt	sie würden gefragt

Perfect tense – passive

er, sie, es ist gefragt worden   er, sie, es sei gefragt worden

Pluperfect tense – passive

er, sie, es war gefragt worden   er, sie, es wäre gefragt worden

Future tense – passive

er, sie, es wird gefragt werden   er, sie, es werde gefragt werden

First conditional – passive

er würde gefragt werden

Second conditional – passive

er würde gefragt worden sein

Imperative (very rarely used)

Singular: werde gefragt   Plural: werdet gefragt

Infinitive

Present: gefragt werden   Past: gefragt worden sein

Not all forms of the passive are meaningful. For example: **Ich wurde erfahren** from **erfahren** (to experience, get to know) does not make sense. There are, however, other means of expressing the passive than the above tables, and these means are explained in the separate section on the passive.

16 Verbs with 'sein', and verbs with 'sein' or 'haben'

(**a**) The following common verbs always form the perfect and pluperfect tenses, etc. with **sein**:

bleiben	to remain	**schleichen**	to crawl
fallen	to fall	**schmelzen**	to melt
fließen	to flow	(**schrecken**	to frighten)
gehen	to go	**schreiten**	to stride
gelingen	to succeed	**schwinden**	to dwindle
geschehen	to happen	**sein**	to be
gleiten	to glide	**sinken**	to sink
kommen	to come	**springen**	to spring
kriechen	to creep	**steigen**	to climb
laufen	to run	**sterben**	to die
(**löschen**	to put out)	**wachsen**	to grow
mißlingen	to fail	**weichen**	to yield
rennen	to run	**werden**	to become

With the exception of the verbs **bleiben**, **gelingen**, **mißlingen**, **sein**, and possibly **werden**, all of these verbs indicate movement of a person or of matter. It is not correct, however, to say that all verbs of motion are conjugated with **sein**. The above list consists of strong verbs, but a few weak verbs like **tanzen**, **segeln**, **reisen** may also be conjugated with **sein**.

The perfect and pluperfect of **löschen** and **schrecken** are seldom used.

(**b**) Note: All compounds of the above verbs are also conjugated with **sein**. For example:

zurückfallen	to fall back	**verschwinden**	to disappear
fortgehen	to go away	**nachkommen**	to follow on
auslaufen	to run out	**ausweichen**	to turn aside

(**c**) The following common verbs form the perfect and pluperfect tense with **haben** or **sein** according to the meaning:

biegen	to bend	**schießen**	to shoot
brechen	to break	**schwimmen**	to swim
dringen	to urge	**sitzen**	to sit
fahren	to drive	**stehen**	to stand

fliegen	to fly	**stoßen**	to push
fliehen	to flee	**streichen**	to stroke
liegen	to lie	**treiben**	to set in motion
reißen	to tear	**treten**	to tread
reiten	to ride	**verderben**	to spoil
schneiden	to cut	**ziehen**	to pull

This also applies to the compounds like **ausreißen** (to pull out), **zurücktreten** (to step back), **vorziehen** (to prefer).

(**d**) Examples of the use of **haben** or **sein**:

Er hat einen Jumbo geflogen (als Pilot).
He flew a Jumbo (as a pilot).
Er ist mit der Lufthansa geflogen (als Passagier).
He flew by Lufthansa (as a passenger).
Sie hat den Ärmelkanal zweimal durchschwommen.
She swam the Channel twice.
Sie ist von Küste zu Küste geschwommen.
She swam from coast to coast.
Er hat schon den neuen Mercedes gefahren.
He has already driven the new Mercedes.
Er ist nach Berlin gefahren.
He has driven to Berlin.

(**e**) The trend is towards the use of **sein** rather than **haben**, in cases of doubt. Generally, though, the verbs **sein** and **haben** have specific uses, as in the following examples:

Sie ist durch das Einkaufszentrum gebummelt.
She dawdled through the shopping centre.
Sie hat beim Einkaufen gebummelt.
She dawdled whilst shopping.

(**f**) Duden calls attention to a difference in usage in North and South Germany of three verbs: **liegen**, **sitzen**, **stehen**.

North Germany: **Er hat gelegen, gesessen, gestanden.**
South Germany: **Er ist gelegen, gesessen, gestanden.**

17 List of strong verbs

The most commonly used strong verbs are listed below. Most verbs form compounds, and the compounds are conjugated like the simple verb. For example: **ausgleichen** like **gleichen**, **durchbrechen** like **brechen**. The form of the present, past and perfect tenses which is given is always that of the third person, singular. The past subjunctive is given in brackets. So is the auxiliary verb helping to form the perfect tense.

Infinitive	*Present*	*Past (and past subjunctive)*	*(Perfect and) past participle*
befehlen	befiehlt	befahl (befähle)	(hat) befohlen
beginnen	beginnt	begann (begänne)	(hat) begonnen
beißen	beißt	biß (bisse)	(hat) gebissen
bersten	birst	barst (bärste)	(hat) geborsten
biegen	biegt	bog (böge)	(hat/ist) gebogen
bieten	bietet	bot (böte)	(hat) geboten
binden	bindet	band (bände)	(hat) gebunden
bitten	bittet	bat (bäte)	(hat) gebeten
blasen	bläst	blies (bliese)	(hat) geblasen
bleiben	bleibt	blieb (bliebe)	(ist) geblieben
brechen	bricht	brach (bräche)	(ist/hat) gebrochen
dringen	dringt	drang (dränge)	(hat/ist) gedrungen
empfehlen	empfiehlt	empfahl (empfähle)	(hat) empfohlen
essen	ißt	aß (äße)	(hat) gegessen
fahren	fährt	fuhr (führe)	(ist) gefahren
fallen	fällt	fiel (fiele)	(ist) gefallen
fangen	fängt	fing (finge)	(hat) gefangen
fechten	ficht	focht (föchte)	(hat) gefochten
finden	findet	fand (fände)	(hat) gefunden
fliegen	fliegt	flog (flöge)	(ist/hat) geflogen
fliehen	flieht	floh (flöhe)	(ist/hat) geflohen
fließen	fließt	floß (flösse)	(ist) geflossen
fressen	frißt	fraß (fräße)	(hat) gefressen
gebären	gebiert	gebar (gebäre)	(ist/hat) geboren
geben	gibt	gab (gäbe)	(hat) gegeben
gehen	geht	ging (ginge)	(ist) gegangen
gelingen	gelingt	gelang (gelänge)	(ist) gelungen
gelten	gilt	galt (gälte)	(hat) gegolten
genießen	genießt	genoß (genösse)	(hat) genossen
geschehen	geschieht	geschah (geschähe)	(ist) geschchen
gewinnen	gewinnt	gewann (gewönne)	(hat) gewonnen
gießen	gießt	goß (gösse)	(hat) gegossen
gleichen	gleicht	glich (gliche)	(hat) geglichen
gleiten	gleitet	glitt (glitte)	(ist) geglitten
graben	gräbt	grub (grübe)	(hat) gegraben
greifen	greift	griff (griffe)	(hat) gegriffen
halten	hält	hielt (hielte)	(hat) gehalten
hängen	hängt	hing (hinge)	(hat) gehangen
heben	hebt	hob (höbe)	(hat) gehoben
heißen	heißt	hieß (hieße)	(hat) geheißen
helfen	hilft	half (hälfe)	(hat) geholfen
klingen	klingt	klang (klänge)	(hat) geklungen

17 Conjugation of verbs

Infinitive	Present	Past (and past subjunctive)	(Perfect and) past participle
kommen	kommt	kam (käme)	(ist) gekommen
kriechen	kriecht	kroch (kröche)	(ist) gekrochen
laden	lädt	lud (lüde)	(hat) geladen
lassen	läßt	ließ (ließe)	(hat) gelassen
laufen	läuft	lief (liefe)	(ist/hat) gelaufen
leiden	leidet	litt (litte)	(hat) gelitten
leihen	leiht	lieh (liehe)	(hat) geliehen
lesen	liest	las (läse)	(hat) gelesen
liegen	liegt	lag (läge)	(hat/ist) gelegen
löschen	löscht	losch (lösche)	(ist) geloschen
lügen	lügt	log (löge)	(hat) gelogen
meiden	meidet	mied (miede)	(hat) gemieden
melken	melkt	melkte/molk (melkte/mölkte)	(hat) gemolken
messen	mißt	maß (mäße)	(hat) gemessen
mißlingen	mißlingt	mißlang (mißlänge)	(ist) mißlungen
nehmen	nimmt	nahm (nähme)	(hat) genommen
pfeifen	pfeift	pfiff (pfiffe)	(hat) gepfiffen
pflegen	pflegt	pflog (pflöge)	(hat) gepflogen
raten	rät	riet (riete)	(hat) geraten
reiben	reibt	rieb (riebe)	(hat) gerieben
reißen	reißt	riß (risse)	(hat/ist) gerissen
reiten	reitet	ritt (ritte)	(hat/ist) geritten
riechen	riecht	roch (röche)	(hat) gerochen
rufen	ruft	rief (riefe)	(hat) gerufen
saufen	säuft	soff (söffe)	(hat) gesoffen
saugen	saugt	sog (söge)	(hat) gesogen
schaffen	schafft	schuf (schüfe)	(hat) geschaffen
scheiden	scheidet	schied (schiede)	(hat/ist) geschieden
scheinen	scheint	schien (schiene)	(hat) geschienen
schieben	schiebt	schob (schöbe)	(hat) geschoben
schießen	schießt	schoß (schösse)	(hat/ist) geschossen
schlafen	schläft	schlief (schliefe)	(hat) geschlafen
schlagen	schlägt	schlug (schlüge)	(hat) geschlagen
schleichen	schleicht	schlich (schliche)	(ist) geschlichen
schließen	schließt	schloß (schlösse)	(hat) geschlossen
schneiden	schneidet	schnitt (schnitte)	(hat) geschnitten
schreiben	schreibt	schrieb (schriebe)	(hat) geschrieben
schreien	schreit	schrie (schrie)	(hat) geschrie(e)n
schweigen	schweigt	schwieg (schwiege)	(hat) geschwiegen
schwimmen	schwimmt	schwamm (schwömme)	(hat/ist) geschwommen

Infinitive	*Present*	*Past (and past subjunctive)*	*(Perfect and) past participle*
schwinden	schwindet	schwand (schwände)	(ist) geschwunden
schwören	schwört	schwor (schwöre)	(hat) geschworen
sehen	sieht	sah (sähe)	(hat) gesehen
singen	singt	sang (sänge)	(hat) gesungen
sinken	sinkt	sank (sänke)	(ist) gesunken
sinnen	sinnt	sann (sänne)	(hat) gesonnen
sitzen	sitzt	saß (säße)	(hat) gesessen
spinnen	spinnt	spann (spänne/ spönne)	(hat) gesponnen
sprechen	spricht	sprach (spräche)	(hat) gesprochen
springen	springt	sprang (spränge)	(hat) gesprungen
stehen	steht	stand (stände)	(hat) gestanden
stehlen	stiehlt	stahl (stähle)	(hat) gestohlen
sterben	stirbt	starb (stürbe)	(ist) gestorben
stoßen	stößt	stieß (stieße)	(ist/hat) gestoßen
streiten	streitet	stritt (stritte)	(hat) gestritten
tragen	trägt	trug (trüge)	(hat) getragen
treffen	trifft	traf (träfe)	(hat) getroffen
treiben	treibt	trieb (triebe)	(hat/ist) getrieben
treten	tritt	trat (träte)	(hat/ist) getreten
trinken	trinkt	trank (tränke)	(hat) getrunken
tun	tut	tat (täte)	(hat) getan
verderben	verdirbt	verdarb (verdürbe)	(hat/ist) verdorben
vergessen	vergißt	vergaß (vergäße)	(hat) vergessen
verlieren	verliert	verlor (verlöre)	(hat) verloren
wachsen	wächst	wuchs (wüchse)	(ist) gewachsen
waschen	wäscht	wusch (wüsche)	(hat) gewaschen
weisen	weist	wies (wiese)	(hat) gewiesen
werben	wirbt	warb (würbe)	(hat) geworben
werden	wird	wurde (würde)	(ist) geworden
werfen	wirft	warf (würfe)	(hat) geworfen
wiegen	wiegt	wog (wöge)	(hat) gewogen
winden	windet	wand (wände)	(hat) gewunden
zeihen	zeiht	zieh (ziehe)	(hat) geziehen
ziehen	zieht	zog (zöge)	(hat/ist) gezogen
zwingen	zwingt	zwang (zwänge)	(hat) gezwungen

Not all forms are in common use, and not all strong verbs are given. Compound verbs are sometimes more common than the simple verbs given above. For example: **verzeihen** (to forgive) rather than **zeihen** (to accuse a person of a thing).

18 List of irregular verbs

Infinitive	Present	Past (and past subjunctive)	(Perfect and) past participle
backen	backt/bäckt	backte (backte)	(hat) gebacken/gebackt
brennen	brennt	brannte (brannte)	(hat) gebrannt
bringen	bringt	brachte (brächte)	(hat) gebracht
denken	denkt	dachte (dächte)	(hat) gedacht
dürfen	darf	durfte (dürfte)	(hat) gedurft
haben	hat	hatte (hätte)	(hat) gehabt
kennen	kennt	kannte (kannte)	(hat) gekannt
können	kann	konnte (könnte)	(hat) gekonnt
mögen	mag	mochte (möchte)	(hat) gemocht
müssen	muß	mußte (müßte)	(hat) gemußt
nennen	nennt	nannte (nannte)	(hat) genannt
rennen	rennt	rannte (rannte)	(ist) gerannt
sein	ist	war (wäre)	(ist) gewesen
senden	sendet	sandte/sendete (sandte/sendete)	(hat) gesandt/gesendet
sollen	soll	sollte (sollte)	(hat) gesollt
wenden	wendet	wandte/wendete (wandte/wendete)	(hat) gewandt/ (hat) gewendet
wissen	weiß	wußte (wüßte)	(hat) gewußt
wollen	will	wollte (wollte)	(hat) gewollt

The irregular verbs in the above list, with the exception of **sein**, take on the form of a weak verb in the past tense and also in the perfect tense (but see **backen**). There is usually a vowel change.

19 Special points on the form of verbs

(a) The **du**-form of the present tense of a strong verb can always be formed from the third person singular, which is given in the above lists. Replace the last letter (**t**) by (**st**). For example: **er ruft / du rufst**, **er läuft / du läufst**, **er hilft / du hilfst**.

(b) The following exceptions should be noted:

du bist	er ist	du mußt	er muß
du ißt	er ißt	du weißt	er weiß
du läßt	er läßt	du mißt	er mißt
du liest	er liest	du stößt	er stößt
du wächst	er wächst	du vergißt	er vergißt
du bläst	er bläst	du reißt	er reißt
du schießt	er schießt	du schließt	er schließt

(c) If the stem of a weak or strong verb ends in **d** or **t**, an **e** is inserted after the stem in the second and third persons singular, and in the second person plural of the present tense. For example:

du sendest	du streitest	du achtest
er sendet	er streitet	er achtet
ihr sendet	ihr streitet	ihr achtet

(**d**) Note, however, the forms of the second persons, singular and plural, of similar verbs in the past tense:

du tat(e)st	du fand(e)st	du achtetest
ihr tatet	ihr fandet	ihr achtetet

The **du**-form without the **e** is more common, if a choice of forms exists, as in **tat(e)st** and **fand(e)st**. The sound of a word may be decisive in making the choice, as in the case of **achtetest**.

(**e**) The **e** is also inserted where the sound of certain consonant combinations makes this necessary. For example:

du zeichnest	du atmest	
er zeichnet	er atmet	es regnet
ihr zeichnet	ihr atmet	

The last letter of the stem in these examples is a nasal **m** or **n**.

20 Omission of 'e'

The **e** is sometimes omitted in certain verb forms, particularly in colloquial speech or in poetry.

(**a**) In the imperative. For example: **geh! hör zu!**

(**b**) In the first person singular. For example:

Ich geh' nicht gern allein.   Ich hab' ihn gesehen.
I don't like going alone.   *I've seen him.*

(**c**) In an abbreviation of the pronoun **es** in combination with a verb. For example:

Bald gibt's Regen!   Das war's!
It's going to rain soon!   That's the lot! That's done!

The student is, however, advised to use the **e** in the written forms of the above, unless colloquial speech is being accurately recorded.

21 Vowel changes in the past subjunctive

There is sometimes a vowel change between the past tense and the past subjunctive. For example: **warb/würbe**, **warf/würfe**.

The past subjunctive is mostly used in elevated speech, and the changes are probably due to an attempt to elevate the sound of the words.

Conjugation of modal, impersonal, and reflexive verbs

22 Definitions

A modal verb is one which describes or indicates a mood. This may be a wish, an obligation felt, a liking, or a feeling of ability to do a thing. There are six modal verbs in German: **dürfen** (to be permitted), **können** (to be able to), **mögen** (to want, to like), **müssen** (to have to), **sollen** (to be obliged to), **wollen** (to want to).

An impersonal verb is one whose subject is not specified or is indefinite. For example: **Es regnet.** (It is raining.)

A reflexive verb is one in which a reflex action occurs to the subject. For example: **Er rasiert sich.** (He is shaving.)

23 Conjugation of modal verbs

The modal verbs (**dürfen**, **können**, **mögen**, **müssen**, **sollen**, **wollen**), like the auxiliaries (**haben**, **sein**, **werden**) can be used on their own, or to form verb groups. The present and past tenses, indicative and subjunctive, are in common use. They are listed below:

Present tense – indicative

darf	kann	mag	muß	soll	will
darfst	kannst	magst	mußt	sollst	willst
darf	kann	mag	muß	soll	will
dürfen	können	mögen	müssen	sollen	wollen
dürft	könnt	mögt	müßt	sollt	wollt
dürfen	können	mögen	müssen	sollen	wollen

Past tense – indicative

durfte	konnte	mochte	mußte	sollte	wollte
durftest	konntest	mochtest	mußtest	solltest	wolltest
durfte	konnte	mochte	mußte	sollte	wollte
durften	konnten	mochten	mußten	sollten	wollten
durftet	konntet	mochtet	mußtet	solltet	wolltet
durften	konnten	mochten	mußten	sollten	wollten

Present tense – subjunctive

dürfe	könne	möge	müsse	solle	wolle
(dürfest)	(könnest)	(mögest)	(müssest)	(sollest)	(wollest)
dürfe	könne	möge	müsse	solle	wolle
dürfen	können	mögen	müssen	sollen	wollen
(dürfet)	(könnet)	(möget)	(müsset)	(sollet)	(wollet)
dürfen	können	mögen	müssen	sollen	wollen

The forms in brackets are very seldom used.

Past tense – subjunctive

dürfte	könnte	möchte	müßte	sollte	wollte
dürftest	könntest	möchtest	müßtest	solltest	wolltest
dürfte	könnte	möchte	müßte	sollte	wollte
dürften	könnten	möchten	müßten	sollten	wollten
dürftet	könntet	möchtet	müßtet	solltet	wolltet
dürften	könnten	möchten	müßten	sollten	wollten

Perfect tense – indicative

ich habe   gedurft, gekonnt, gemocht, gemußt, gesollt, gewollt
du hast
er, sie, es hat
wir haben
ihr habt
sie haben

The past tense of the modal verbs is often preferred to the perfect tense.

The perfect tense – subjunctive is the same as above, except that the verb **haben** is in the subjunctive.

There is also a future tense which is conjugated as above, but with **werden**. This tense is also to be avoided. Only the present and past tenses are in common use.

24 Conjugation of impersonal verbs

The verbs are, in fact, not impersonal, although this label is given for grammatical convenience, but are used with the impersonal subject **es**. The pronoun **es** refers neither to a definite person nor to a specific thing. For example: **es regnet** (it is raining), **es tut mir leid** (I'm sorry, I regret). The verbs are conjugated as in paras. 12 and 13, but only in the third person, singular and plural.

25 Conjugation of reflexive verbs

The verbs are conjugated as in para 12. The reflexive pronouns are written with small letters: **mich**, **dich**, **sich**, **uns**, **euch**, **sich**. (But see para. 6 (**g**).)

Two examples are: **sich erinnern** (to remember), **sich durchsetzen** (to succeed).

Present tense	Perfect tense
ich erinnere mich	ich habe mich durchgesetzt
du erinnerst dich	du hast dich durchgesetzt
er, sie, es erinnert sich	er, sie, es hat sich durchgesetzt
wir erinnern uns	wir haben uns durchgesetzt
ihr erinnert euch	ihr habt euch durchgesetzt
Sie erinnern sich	Sie haben sich durchgesetzt
sie erinnern sich	sie haben sich durchgesetzt

The use of the indicative tenses

26 Definitions

The indicative mood points out, states, or declares. It is the mood of certainty, especially about facts.

The subjunctive mood expresses a wish, a hope, a thought which may or may not be true, a hypothetical idea, an uncertainty, a supposition, or an action or a state which is not known as a fact.

There are only two moods, indicative and subjunctive. The indicative is dealt with in this section; the subjunctive is considered in paras. 67–79.

27 The present tense

The conjugation of the present tense is given in para. 12. This is the same for all verbs, strong, weak, and irregular, with the exception of the auxiliaries (**haben**, **sein**, **werden**) in para. 14, and the modal verbs (**dürfen**, **können**, **mögen**, **müssen**, **sollen**, **wollen**) in para. 23.

28 Translation of the present tense

In German there is only one present tense, and this can be translated in three different ways. For example:

ich schreibe	I write	I am writing	I do write
du schreibst	you write	you are writing	you do write
er schreibt	he writes	he is writing	he does write
wir schreiben	we write	we are writing	we do write
ihr schreibt	you write	you are writing	you do write
Sie schreiben	you write	you are writing	you do write
sie schreiben	they write	they are writing	they do write

The third way of translation is usually only used if it has been suggested that the opposite is true. For example, if someone suggests that your handwriting is hardly legible, then you protest and say, 'I do write clearly'. The German would be, **'Ich schreibe doch deutlich'.** The emphasis is given by the adverb **doch** (though, however, for all that).

29 Uses of the present tense

The present tense in German is used for actions which are happening now, which are happening round about the present time, which are timeless, and also which are going to take place in the immediate future.
In detail:

(**a**) for an action which is happening now:

Es regnet.   Ich sehe ihn.   Er kommt.
It is raining.   *I see him.*   *He is coming.*

(**b**) for an action which is happening round about now:

Sie trägt ihr neues Kleid.   Sie sehen gerade fern.
She is wearing her new dress.   *They are just watching television.*

(**c**) for an activity which is taking place about this time, but not necessarily at the time of speaking:

Er lernt Deutsch.   Er studiert Germanistik.
He is learning German.   *He is studying German* (at the University).
Sie liest ein Stück von Goethe.
She is reading one of Goethe's plays.

(**d**) for an activity which begins soon at a definite point in time:

Ab 20 Uhr sehe ich das Fußballspiel im Fernsehen.
From 8 o'clock onwards I am (shall be) watching the football match on television.

(**e**) for an activity which is taking place in the near future, or even the not-so-near future:

Morgen früh fahren wir nach München.
We are driving to Munich early tomorrow morning.
Sie gehen bald in Urlaub.
They are going on holiday soon.
Wir fliegen in die Karibik im kommenden Jahr.
We are flying to the West Indies next year.

It should be noted that the future element is given by the adverb, or adverbial phrase, of time: **morgen früh, bald, im kommenden Jahr.**

(**f**) for an activity which is taking place in the immediate future, and where the timing is clear to the speakers:

Wohin fahren Sie?   Wir fahren ins Rheinland.
Where are you driving (going) to?   *We're going to the Rheinland.*

(**g**) for an action which is repeated frequently:

Immer wieder macht er die gleichen Fehler!
He is always making the same mistakes. or
He makes the same mistakes again and again.
Sie sieht immer ängstlich aus.
She is always looking anxious.

(**h**) for a habit:
Sie geht Woche für Woche zum Markt.
She goes to the market week after week.
Sonntags gehen sie in die Kirche.
On Sundays they go to church.

(**i**) for a custom:
Ein Karnevalsumzug findet am Rosenmontag statt.
A carnival procession takes place on the Monday before Lent.
Die Kieler Woche ist gewöhnlich Anfang Juni.
The Kiel Sailing Week is usually at the beginning of June.
Die ganze Familie verbringt Weihnachten zu Hause.
The whole family spends/is spending Christmas at home.

(**j**) to make history more vivid:
Napoleon eilt mit seiner Armee in Richtung Brüssel.
Napoleon hastens with his army in the direction of Brussels.

(**k**) to describe a future plan as if it is in the present:
Wir fahren mit dem Fährschiff von Sheerness nach Vlissingen;
danach fahren wir mit dem Auto durch Holland. Wir erreichen
Düsseldorf am selben Tag.
*We travel by boat from Sheerness to Flushing; then we go by car through
Holland. We reach Düsseldorf the same day.*

(**l**) in time clauses:
Bevor du gehst, möchte ich mit dir sprechen.
I would like to talk to you before you go.
Ich werde so lange warten, bis du kommst.
I will wait until you come.
Sobald du hier bist, können wir anfangen.
As soon as you get here we can begin.

(**m**) to introduce quotations:
Der Major von Tellheim, in Lessings ,,Minna von Barnhelm", sagt:
,,So dacht' ich, so sprach ich, als ich nicht wußte, was ich dachte
und sprach."
*Major von Tellheim, in Lessing's 'Minna von Barnhelm' says, 'I thought
and I spoke in this way when I did not know what I was thinking or
saying.'*

(**n**) to make a happening in the past more vivid in the mind of the narrator and the listeners:

Es war dunkel, furchtbar dunkel, plötzlich kommt mir dieser schreckliche Mann entgegen . . .
It was dark, frightfully dark, suddenly this horrible man comes towards me . . .

30 Interrogative and negative forms of the present tense

(**a**) Questions are asked in German by simply reversing the subject and the verb. For example:

Spielt er?   Wann kommt Ihre Mutter?   Findet das Spiel statt?
Is he playing?   When is your mother coming?   Is the game/match on?

(**b**) However long the subject is, the verb comes before the subject:

Ist der lange, kalte, stürmische Winter endlich vorbei?
Is the long, cold, stormy winter over at last?

(**c**) The verb is usually in the first position in a question sentence, unless one of the question words is used. They include: **wann?** (when), **warum?** (why), **was?** (what), **welcher?** (which), **wer?** (who), **weshalb?** (why), **weswegen?** (why, for what reason), **wie?** (how), **wieso?** (in what way), **wo?** (where), **woher?** (from where), **wohin?** (whence), **womit?** (with what).

(**d**) The word **nicht** (not) or **nie** (never) is used immediately after the verb in the present tense in order to express a negative. For example:

Sie geht nicht.   Der Motor läuft nicht.
She is not going.   The motor is not working.
Meine Uhr geht nicht. Sie läuft nie gut.
My watch is not going.   It never works properly.

31 Interrogative negative form of the present tense

(**a**) The word order of the question-form is reversed, and the verb comes before the subject. The negative **nicht** (not) usually comes after the subject in the interrogative negative form. For example:

Geht er nicht ins Theater?
Isn't he going to the theatre?
Warum geht Ihre Mutter nicht?
Why isn't your mother going?

(**b**) It may happen that the speaker wishes to emphasize the negative aspect, so that **nicht** is placed at the end of a short sentence. For example:

Versteht sie deinen Standpunkt nicht?
Doesn't she see your point of view?
This could also be expressed as in 31 (**a**):
Versteht sie nicht deinen Standpunkt?

Further examples are:

Liest er die Schlagzeilen nicht?	Fährt er den neuen Wagen nicht?
Doesn't he read the headlines?	*Doesn't he drive the new car?*

(**c**) It must be clear that **nicht** at the end of a sentence is one possibility, for emphasis. The most likely way of expressing the above ideas would be:

Liest er keine Schlagzeilen?
Fährt er nicht den neuen Wagen?

32 Problems arising from the translation of the English present tenses

(**a**) It is important to realize that all three forms of the English present tense (we work, we are working, we do work) are translated by the one single tense in German. There are, however, a few ways of bringing out the one form or the other.

(**b**) *Do* and *does* are used to form questions and to make negative statements in the present tense, and do not require special consideration. If, however, *do* and *does* are used for emphasis, then they may be translated by **doch**, **tatsächlich**, or **aber wirklich** in German. For example:

Wir arbeiten doch fleißig.	Er geht aber wirklich steif
We really do work hard.	*He does indeed walk stiffly.*

Sie kommt tatsächlich vom Lande.
She does, in fact, come from the country.

(**c**) Adverbs are often used, as in English, to make the time a little more precise. For example:

Augenblicklich regnet es. / Momentan regnet es.
At the moment it's raining.

Jetzt/nun regnet es.	Es ist gerade fertig.
Now it's raining.	*It is just ready.*

(**d**) The immediate future is also made clear by adverbs, as in English. For example:

Wir fahren sofort.	Wir gehen bald.
We are driving off now (at once).	*We are soon going.*
Jetzt gehen wir aber.	Wir gehen gleich.
Now we are going (at last).	*We are going almost at once.*

(**e**) There are adverbs which express a habit:

Gewöhnlich geht er zu Fuß.   Meistens fährt er mit dem Auto.
He usually goes on foot.   *He mostly goes by car.*
In der Regel trägt er eine Brille.
As a rule he wears glasses.

33 The past tense

The past tense is called the imperfect in some books. The latter term
is misleading, especially to those who are studying French as a first
language.
There is only one form of the past tense in German, and it is
translated into English in three ways, as follows:

ich ging	I went	I was going	I used to go
du gingst	you went	you were going	you used to go
er ging	he went	he was going	he used to go
wir gingen	we went	we were going	we used to go
ihr gingt	you went	you were going	you used to go
Sie gingen	you went	you were going	you used to go
sie gingen	they went	they were going	they used to go

The third way of translating, 'I used to go', etc., is only used to
describe a habit. The other two translations require illustration and
further explanation. See paras. 37–38.

The conjugation of the past tense of strong, irregular, and weak
verbs is given in para. 12. The past tense of the auxiliary verbs and
the modal verbs is given in paras. 14 and 23.

34 The interrogative form of the past tense

As in the present tense, so in the past tense, the subject and the verb
are in the reverse order for a question. For example:

Wartete er lange auf den Zug?   Hieß sie früher Kampmeier?
Did he wait long for the train?   *Was her former name Kampmeier?*

(Note, however, that the perfect tense is much preferred for
questions about the past. E.g.: **Hat er lange auf den Zug
gewartet? Hat sie früher Kampmeier geheißen**?)

35 The negative form of the past tense

The negative word **nicht** (not) or **nie** (never) normally comes after
the verb. For example:

Er arbeitete nicht in den Ferien.   Er ging nie früh ins Bett.
He didn't work during the holidays.   *He never went to bed early.*

The word **nicht** may be put at the end of a short sentence for very special emphasis, especially if someone else says or might think the contrary. For example:

Er arbeitete in den Ferien nicht.

This word order is only likely to occur if someone claims that 'He used to work during the holidays'.

36 The interrogative-negative form of the past tense

The subject of a sentence and the verb are reversed for a question. The words **nicht** (not) and **nie** (never) therefore follow the subject. The order is: verb, subject, **nicht/nie**. For example:

Las er nie ein Buch in seiner Freizeit?
Didn't he ever read a book in his spare time?
Aß sie nicht immer zu viel?
Didn't she always used to eat too much?

(See para. 34. The perfect tense is normally used for interrogative-negative questions.)

37 Uses of the past tense

The past tense must always be considered as the time in the past from the point of view of the speaker or writer. This point is important, for example, in reported speech.

The main uses of the past tense are:

(**a**) When an event or a happening lies clearly in the past in the mind of the narrator. For example:

Der Zug kam mit einer halben Stunde Verspätung an.
The train arrived half an hour late.
Wir genossen die letzten Sommertage.
We enjoyed the last days of summer.
Einst sprach er mit dem Bundeskanzler.
He once spoke with the Bundeskanzler.

(**b**) For a past action when a time is given. For example:

Vorgestern bekamen wir Nachricht aus Deutschland.
We got/received news from Germany the day before yesterday.
Um 6 Uhr stand sie auf.
She got up at six o'clock.

(**c**) For a past action when a period of time is given, which is now ended. For example:

Er studierte fünf Jahre lang.   Eine Zeitlang arbeitete er in Genf.
He studied for five years.   *He worked for a time in Geneva.*

(**d**) To describe a habit. For example:

Er aß immer in den besten Restaurants und trank immer die besten Weine.
He always ate in the best restaurants, and always drank the best wines.
Er arbeitete auf der Schiffswerft, aber jetzt nicht mehr.
He used to work in the shipyard, but no longer does.

(**e**) To describe past actions or occurrences which continued for some time. The time limits may or may not be known. Note: the past continuous is usually used in an English translation. For example:

Es regnete.	Es wurde allmählich hell.
It was raining.	*It was gradually getting light.*

(**f**) When there are two actions in the past, one of which is continuous. Note the use of the past continuous in English. For example:

Das Programm lief schon, als er kam.
The programme was already running when he came.
Als er wegging, weinte sie.
As he went away she was crying.
As he went away she cried.

(**g**) When a particular action continues in the past, and a time reference is given. Note the use of the past continuous in English. For example:

Um 9 Uhr rasierte er sich immer noch.
He was still shaving at nine o'clock.
Zu der bestimmten Zeit telefonierte sie.
She was speaking on the phone at that particular time.

(**h**) In reported speech. Note the use of the past continuous in English. For example:

Sie sagten, sie wohnten in Paderborn.
They said that they were living in Paderborn.
Er sagte, daß sie vor Wut kochte.
He said that she was boiling with rage.

(**i**) In questions. The English translation can be in the past continuous tense. For example:

Was machten Sie gestern?
(more likely: Was haben Sie gestern gemacht?)
What were you doing yesterday?
What did you do yesterday?

38 Problems of translating the English past tenses into German

Since there is only one form of the past tense (**Präteritum**) in German, the fine points in the use of the English past tense and past continuous tense have to be conveyed in a different way.

The use of adverbs and adverbial expressions is a method frequently used. For example:

Sonntags trug er meistens einen dunklen Anzug.
On Sundays he mostly wore a dark suit.
Er ging zweimal in der Woche zur Volkshochschule.
He used to go to the College of Further Education twice a week.

The adverbs **sonntags** and **meistens** and the adverbial phrase **zweimal in der Woche** imply a habit, and are adverbs/an adverbial phrase of time.

Further examples:

Zu diesem Zeitpunkt arbeitete er bei einer Baufirma.
He was working for a building firm at the time.
Als er 19 war, verdiente er schon gutes Geld.
When he was 19 he was already earning good money.
Nach wie vor wirkte er unentschlossen.
As always he appeared indecisive.
Alles in allem machte sie einen guten Eindruck.
All in all she made/created a good impression.

The adverbial phrases **zu diesem Zeitpunkt**, **nach wie vor**, and the adverbial clause **als er 19 war**, are to do with time. The adverbial phrase may just imply time, as in **alles in allem**, which suggests a period of reflection after which an opinion is formed.

Since a tense always reflects a time element, it is not surprising that adverbs of time are used to bring out more detail about the time.

39 The perfect tense

The conjugation of the perfect tense is given in para. 12.
The German perfect tense is translated in three ways:

ich habe gesagt	I said/have said/have been saying
du hast gesagt	you said/have said/have been saying
er hat gesagt	he said/has said/has been saying
wir haben gesagt	we said/have said/have been saying
ihr habt gesagt	you said/have said/have been saying
Sie haben gesagt	you said/have said/have been saying
sie haben gesagt	they said/have said/have been saying

The perfect tense always has some connection with present time. This is symbolized by the use of the present tense of **haben** or **sein** with the past participle of the verb. For example:

Er hat den ganzen Tag daran gearbeitet.
He has been working at it the whole day.

The connection with the present is not always obvious, and it may lie only in the mind of the speaker. For example in answer to a question, or with the subject in mind:

Gestern ist er nach München gefahren.
He drove to Munich yesterday.

It is clear from these remarks and from the examples above and in the following sections, that the perfect tense is more likely to occur in the spoken than in the written language. The differences in use between the perfect tense and the past tense are explained in para. 45.

The position of the past participle should be noted: namely at the end of a simple sentence.

40 The interrogative form of the perfect tense

The subject and the auxiliary verb **haben** or **sein** are reversed in the question–form of the perfect tense. For example:

Hat er Ihren letzten Brief beantwortet?
Has he answered your last letter?

41 The negative form of the perfect tense

The negative word **nicht** (not) or **nie** (never) is placed near the past participle, as this is the part of the verb carrying the meaning. The usual place is next to the past participle. For example:

Nein, er hat den letzten Brief nicht beantwortet.
No, he hasn't answered the last letter.

The German order of words in the above sentence is:
subject, auxiliary verb, direct object, **nicht**, past participle.

Sie hat ihre goldene Armbanduhr nicht gefunden.
She hasn't found her gold wrist-watch.

An adverb which refines the meaning of the past participle may come between **nicht** and the past participle. For example:

Sie hat mich nicht richtig verstanden.
She didn't understand me rightly.
Ihre Arbeit ist nicht wesentlich besser geworden.
Her work has not become noticeably better.

Sie hat meine Bemerkungen nicht übelgenommen.
She didn't take my remarks amiss.

42 The interrogative-negative form of the perfect tense

The following two examples are taken from para. 41, and turned
into questions:

Hat er den letzten Brief nicht beantwortet?
Hasn't he answered the last letter?
Hat sie mich nicht richtig verstanden?
Didn't she understand me correctly?

43 The uses of the perfect tense

Although the perfect tense refers to something happening in the
past, there is always a strong connection with the present. The
perfect tense is used frequently in conversations, in radio and
television, in letters, and in journals. These are forms of personal
communication. The time element is usually somewhat vague and
indefinite.

The main uses of the perfect tense are:

(a) For an action or activity which began in the past and is still
continuing. For example:

Er ist Mitglied unseres Klubs geworden.
He has become a member of our club.
Diese Auffassung hat schon Boden gewonnen.
This point of view has already gained ground.
This point of view has already been gaining ground.

(b) For an action which began in the past and the effects or
consequences of which are still continuing. For example:

Sie hat ihren Mann in Österreich kennengelernt.
She got to know her husband in Austria (and is still married).
Sie hat die Prüfung bestanden.
She (has) passed the examination (and is now continuing with her
career).

(c) For an action which began in the past and ends at the time of
speaking. For example:

Ich habe Sie schon einmal gesehen, nicht wahr?
I've already seen you once before, haven't I?
Er hat diese Arbeit beendet.
He has finished this work.

(**d**) For spoken questions referring to a past action. For example:

Hat er die Stadt verlassen?   Ist sie zum Einkaufszentrum gegangen?
Has he left town?   *Has she gone to the shopping centre?*

(**e**) For an action which took place in the past, and whose only connection with the present is the present enquiry or interest of a speaker. For example:

Ja. Er hat an den Olympischen Spielen teilgenommen.
Yes. He has taken part in the Olympic Games.
Ja. Ich habe den Wagen zur Werkstatt gebracht.
Yes. I (have) brought the car to the garage.
Er hat kürzlich einen Gebrauchtwagen gekauft.
He recently bought a second-hand car.

(**f**) For an activity which is mainly of present interest, but which has an element from the immediate past. For example:

Letzten Sonntag ist sie abgefahren.
(Sorry she is not here)   *She left last Sunday.*
Sie ist noch nicht aus dem Urlaub zurückgekommen.
(Sorry she is not here)   *She hasn't come back from holiday yet.*
Er ist gerade gekommen.
He has just arrived.

(**g**) For a thought in the mind of a speaker when he/she projects himself/herself into the future, and then looks back from the new point in time.

Übermorgen habe ich meine Fahrprüfung schon gemacht.
The day after tomorrow I shall have already taken my driving test.
In einer Stunde habe ich diesen Aufsatz zu Ende geschrieben.
In an hour's time I shall have finished writing this essay.

(**h**) The perfect may be used about the distant past, if the action is likely to be repeated in the present or the future:

Ich bin schon einmal seekrank gewesen.
I've already been sea-sick once.

All the examples in this section have been taken from the spoken language.

44 Problems in the translation of the English perfect tenses

There are two perfect tenses (the perfect and the perfect continuous) in English, and only one form of the perfect in German. For example: **Er hat gesprochen** means *he has spoken* or *he has been speaking*. In English the two tenses are often interchangeable. It can also mean *he spoke*.

The distinction between the two English tenses is made in German by the use of adverbs or adverbial phrases, mostly of time. For example:

Er hat nachts gearbeitet.
He (has) worked at night.
In der letzten Zeit hat er nachts gearbeitet.
Recently he has been working at night.
Er hat schon viel von Brecht gelesen.
He has already read a lot of Brecht.
Neuerdings hat er viel von Brecht gelesen.
He has recently been reading a lot of Brecht.

45 The use of the past tense or the perfect tense

The past tense is used for actions and activities which are past and finished from the point of view of the speaker or the writer. The perfect tense on the other hand concerns the past, but is of present interest to the speaker (or the writer).

(**a**) The past tense is preferred when a definite time or date is given, and the perfect tense is preferred for an indefinite time. For example:

Am Heiligen Abend fuhr er nach Hause.
He drove home on Christmas Eve.
Vor Weihnachten ist er selten nach Hause gefahren.
Before Christmas he seldom drove home.
Um 6 Uhr morgens fuhr der Zug ab.
The train left at 6 o'clock in the morning.
Vor ein paar Tagen ist der Zug mit großer Verspätung abgefahren.
The train left very late a few days ago.

(**b**) The past tense is used for historical statements, and narrative forms about the past. For example:

Die Kaiserkrönung Karls des Großen fand am Weihnachtstag 800 statt.
The coronation of Charlemagne as Emperor took place on Christmas Day in the year 800.
Thomas Mann begann 1897 mit der Niederschrift der ,,Buddenbrooks".
In 1897 Thomas Mann began writing 'Buddenbrooks'.

(**c**) The past tense is used for factual reporting on the past, and for abstract statements:

So wie die Historiker um 400 v.Chr. ihre Aufmerksamkeit auf zeitgeschichtliche Probleme konzentrierten, so taten es auch die Philosophen, nur in anderer Weise.

Just as the historians round about 400 B.C. concentrated their attention on current problems, so did the philosophers too, but in another way.
Zur wirklichen Konfrontation von Philosophie und Theologie kam es erst im christlichen Zeitalter.
A real confrontation between philosophy and theology only came about in the Age of Christianity.

(**d**) The past tense may express certainty and definiteness, whilst the perfect tense may express past certainty, but present uncertainty. For example:

Er war hier.   Er ist hier gewesen.
He was here.   *He was here* (but I don't know where he is now).

(**e**) The perfect tense is used more in conversation, especially when asking questions:

Er ist abgereist.   Hat sie schon angerufen?
He has departed.   *Has she phoned?*

(**f**) Whereas the perfect tense is normally used in colloquial speech, it is sometimes fashionable to use the past tense in speech for social or personal reasons. for example:

Wir gingen schwankend nach Hause und krochen ins Bett.
We went unsteadily home and crawled into bed.

The above notes on the use of the perfect tense or the past tense should be regarded as guide-lines and not as rules. The two tenses are, in fact, often interchangeable.

46 The pluperfect tense

The conjugation of the pluperfect tense, which is sometimes called the past perfect tense, is given in para. 12.
The German pluperfect tense is translated in two ways:

ich hatte gesagt . . .	I had said	I had been saying
du hattest gesagt . . .	you had said	you had been saying
er hatte gesagt . . .	he had said	he had been saying
wir hatten gesagt . . .	we had said	we had been saying
ihr hattet gesagt . . .	you had said	you had been saying
Sie hatten gesagt . . .	you had said	you had been saying
sie hatten gesagt . . .	they had said	they had been saying

The pluperfect is past time before past time. It seldom forms a complete sentence on its own, and is usually used together with the past tense to form a complex sentence. For example:

Nachdem er die Nachricht gehört hatte, unternahm er etwas.
As soon as he had heard the news, he took action.

47 The interrogative form of the pluperfect tense

The subject and the verb are reversed in the question-form of the pluperfect:

Hatte Ihr Freund es richtig überlegt, bevor er diesen klapperigen Gebrauchtwagen kaufte?
Had your friend really thought about it before he bought this rattling old second-hand car?
Hatte er die Arbeit beendet, bevor er ging?
Had he finished the work before he went?

48 The negative form of the pluperfect tense

The negative words like **nicht** (not), **nie** (never), or **nichts** (nothing) are placed before and close to the past participle. For example:

Er hatte in diesem Fall nichts unternommen, als ich ihn traf.
He had done nothing (at all) about this when I met him.

49 The interrogative-negative form of the pluperfect tense

Hatte er nichts unternommen, als Sie ihn trafen?
Hadn't he done anything when you met him?

50 Uses of the pluperfect tense

The pluperfect tense is the past before the past, in which something had happened when something else occurred. It can only be used with reference to some past event or activity. Strictly speaking it cannot be used on its own in a sentence without reference to another past event or activity. A sentence like 'He had finished his breakfast' must be related to something else that happened. Perhaps this is known to the speaker and the listener, and the circumstances need not be put into words. The sentence would then appear to stand on its own, although in fact it would be in a past context.

The pluperfect tense, therefore, is most likely to occur in a complex sentence, in the other part of which there is a past tense.

(a) The pluperfect tense is used in conjunction with the past tense to describe historical events, stories real and imaginary (such as legends), accounts of happenings in the past, etc.:

Schon in den letzten Jahrhunderten v. Chr. hatten die griechischen Philosophen begonnen, sich mit den traditionellen religiösen Vorstellungen auseinanderzusetzen, aber zur wirklichen Konfrontation von Philosophie und Theologie kam es erst im christlichen Zeitalter.

*In the last centuries B.C. the Greek philosophers had already begun to come
to terms with traditional religious ideas, but it only came to a real
confrontation between philosophy and theology in the Age of Christianity.*

(**b**) The pluperfect is also used in conjunction with the past tense to
describe personal happenings which are now completely in the past.

Er hatte einen Brief geschrieben, bevor sie kam.
He had written a letter before she came.

(**c**) The pluperfect may be used with the past tense in order to bring
out the sequence of events in the past:

Nachdem er eine Zeitung gekauft hatte, ging er zur Apotheke.
After he had bought a newspaper he went to the chemist's.

The past tense could equally well be used, provided that the
chronological sequence is clear. For example:

Er kaufte eine Zeitung und ging zur Apotheke.
He bought a newspaper and went to the chemist's.

(**d**) The pluperfect is used in reported speech:

Er sagte, daß er 10 Jahre in Westfalen gewohnt hatte, bevor er die
Leute gut kannte.
*He said that he had lived in Westfalia for 10 years before he knew the
people well.*

Sie meinte, daß er nicht die ganze Wahrheit gesagt hatte.
She was of the opinion that he had not told the whole truth.

(**f**) The pluperfect may be used with the perfect tense, but
preferably only in colloquial speech:

Nachdem er gegessen hatte, ist er in die Stadt gegangen.
After he had eaten, he went to town.

The use of the past tense is to be preferred.

51 The future tense

The conjugation of the future tense is given in para. 12.

The German future tense is translated in two ways:

ich werde gehen	I shall/will go	I shall/will be going
du wirst gehen	you will go	you will be going
er wird gehen	he will go	he will be going
wir werden gehen	we shall/will go	we shall/will be going
ihr werdet gehen	you will go	you will be going
Sie werden gehen	you will go	you will be going
sie werden gehen	they will go	they will be going

The future tense is by no means the only method of expressing the future. The present tense and the modal verbs are frequently used for this purpose. See paras. 29 (**d**)–(**f**) and 83.

52 The interrogative form of the future tense

The subject and the verb are reversed in the question-form:

Wird er in seiner neuen Karriere erfolgreich sein?
Will he be successful in his new career?

53 The negative form of the future tense

In contrast to the negative forms of the tenses which have so far been considered, the negative words such as **nicht** (not) or **nichts** (nothing) when used with the future tense are kept close to the auxiliary verb **werden**. The future element is thereby stressed. For example:

Er wird nicht ins Ausland gehen.
He will not/won't go abroad.
Sie wird nichts aus dem Urlaub mitbringen können.
She won't be able to bring anything with her from the holiday.

54 The interrogative-negative form of the future tense

The negative question-form is:

Wird er nicht bald nach Hause gehen?
Won't he soon go home?

55 Uses of the future tense

Since future action or activity may also be expressed by the present tense and the modal verbs, it is important to note the occasions on which the future tense as described in para. 51 is preferred. Only the uses of this tense are noted here:

(**a**) If a neutral or formal activity is to take place. For example:

Die Sitzung wird im alten Rathaus stattfinden.
The meeting will take place in the old town hall.
Die Konferenz wird erst um neun Uhr abends beginnen.
The conference will only begin at nine o'clock in the evening.

(**b**) If a future happening or prediction is stated, neutrally, without any touch of personal emotion on the part of the speaker or writer. For example:

Morgen wird es wohl mehr Regen geben.
No doubt there will be more rain tomorrow.

Es wird bestimmt bald schneien.
It will definitely snow soon.
Er wird in der nächsten Woche einen Kurzurlaub machen.
He will be taking a short holiday next week.
Es wird wohl überall so sein.
It will be like that everywhere no doubt.

(c) For events in the future which habitually recur, or might recur.
For example:

Bessere Zeiten werden wiederkehren.
Better times will come again.
Die Preise werden bestimmt steigen.
Prices will certainly go up.
Der Winter wird wieder kalt werden.
Winter will be cold again.

(d) To express intention:

Ich werde das Problem überdenken.
I will think about the problem.
Ich werde mich melden, wenn ich in Ihrer Gegend bin.
I'll let you know when I'm in your area.

(e) To express a speaker's believing, doubting, supposing, hoping,
wondering, thinking, knowing, expecting, etc. about the future, as
in the following examples:

Ich glaube, daß er Erfolg haben wird.
I believe that he will be successful.
Ich nehme an, daß Sie kommen werden.
I assume that you will be coming.
Ich denke, daß wir erfolgreich sein werden.
I think that we will be successful.
Ich weiß, daß Sie mitmachen werden.
I know that you will join in.
Er nimmt an, daß wir da sein werden.
He assumes that we shall be there.
Ich zweif(e)le, ob das Wetter sich bessern wird.
I doubt whether the weather will improve.

(f) To express a supposition, after an adverbial clause of condition
or time:

Wenn sie nach Hause kommt, wird sie müde sein.
When she gets home she'll be tired.
Wenn ich eine Million Mark gewinne, werde ich mein Traumhaus
bauen.
If I win a million marks, I'll build the house of my dreams.

Wenn er die Nachricht hört, wird er sich bestimmt freuen.
When he hears the news, he'll certainly be pleased.

(**g**) To express a doubt about the future when used with certain
adverbs of uncertainty, such as **vielleicht**, **möglicherweise**,
wahrscheinlich, **vermutlich**, **sicherlich**, **ohne Zweifel**,
zweifellos, **scheinbar**:

Ich werde möglicherweise Weihnachten zu Hause verbringen.
I shall possibly/probably spend Christmas at home.
Der HSV (Hamburger Sportverein) wird wahrscheinlich
Herbstmeister werden.
*The HSV will probably be at the top of the league table at the halfway
mark.*
Sie werden sich sicherlich darüber freuen.
They'll certainly be pleased about that.
Es wird ohne Zweifel einen harten Winter geben.
No doubt there will be a hard winter.

56 The future perfect tense

The conjugation of the future perfect tense is explained in para. 12.
It is formed with the appropriate form of **werden**, the past
participle of the verb, and the infinitive of **haben** (or **sein**).

Since the question-form, the negative, and the negative question-
form are seldom used, they are not explained here in detail, as they
are similar to the future tense.

57 Use of the future perfect tense

The future perfect tense is used when the speaker (or writer)
projects his/her mind into the future, and then looks back from the
new point in time. For example:

Ende August wird dieses Roggenfeld schon abgeerntet sein.
At the end of August this field of rye will already have been harvested.
In einer Woche werden wir die Verhandlungen beendet haben.
In a week's time we will have ended the negotiations.

58 Future time – the use of the present or future tense

The use of the present tense to express future time is explained in
para. 29 (**e**), (**f**), (**k**). The uses of the future tense are given in para.
55 (**a**)–(**g**). Briefly:

The present tense is more likely to be used in conversation to
express the immediate future.

The future tense is more likely to occur in formal and neutral statements about the future, especially if these occur in the written form. The future tense is also more likely in cases of doubt, uncertainty, and speculation.

59 Different time reactions in German and in English

The preposition **seit** (since, for), with the dative, causes a different time reaction in German and English. This is best explained by examples:

Seit Januar wohnt er hier.
He has been living here since January.
Er wohnt seit einiger Zeit hier.
He has been living here for some time past.

The present tense is used in German, and the perfect or perfect continuous in English.

The passive

60 Definition of the active and passive

The active and passive forms of the verb depend on whether the subject (a person or a thing) is active or passive. If the person or thing does something, perhaps to someone or something else, then the active form of the verb is used. The uses of the active tenses are dealt with in paras. 26–59.

If the subject suffers an action done by someone or something else, then the form of the verb is said to be in the passive. The forms of the verb in the following examples, both of which have **ich** as the subject, illustrate this point:

Active: **Ich fragte.**   (I asked)
Passive: **Ich wurde gefragt.**   (I was asked)

It is the verb which is in the passive form, although, in fact, it is the subject which is passive. In the second sentence **ich** was the subject of questioning by someone else. It is, however, easier to recognize the passive form of the verb than to define it. Students should aim at analysis and recognition.

61 Transitive and intransitive verbs

If a verb can take a direct object (a person or a thing), then it is said to be a transitive verb (v.t.). For example: **Der Mann** (subject) **nahm** (verb) **die Verantwortung** (direct object) **auf sich** (adverbial phrase). *(The man took on the responsibility.)* The verb **nahm** from **nehmen** is a transitive verb. The action of the doer **(Der Mann)** passes by means of the verb over to something else **(die Verantwortung)**.

If, on the other hand, a verb does not take a direct object, then it is said to be an intransitive verb (normally shown as v.i.). For example: **Der Mann** (subject) **schläft** (verb). *(The man is sleeping.)* The verb **schlafen** is an intransitive verb. The action of the doer **(Der Mann)** stops with the verb.

Some verbs like **fahren** (to drive) can be both transitive and intransitive (shown as v.t. & i.). The analysis and recognition in a language is dependent on the meaning of the words, and their use in context. The distinction between transitive and intransitive verbs is significant when the passive form of the verb is considered.

81

62 The passive of transitive verbs

Only transitive verbs can normally be used in the passive.

It is, however, possible to give a passive meaning to an intransitive verb, but in a roundabout way. This is explained in para. 65.

63 The use of the passive

The passive is used to describe what happens or happened to the subject of the sentence. The subject may be either a person, a thing, or an abstract idea. It is a grammatical subject, as seen in the mind's eye of the person who is describing the situation. In every complete sentence the speaker or writer views the subject of the sentence as being either active or passive. In fact we usually use the active in connection with our daily lives and thoughts.

The passive, however, has its uses. It gives distance to what is said and written. It may also be used by a speaker or writer to express a neutral point of view.

The conjugation of the passive is given in para. 15.

The main uses are:

(a) Simply to express what happened to the subject of the sentence. For example:

Das Programm ist zweimal ausgestrahlt worden.
The programme (subject) *was broadcast twice.*
Das Kind wurde grün und blau geschlagen.
The child (subject) *was beaten black and blue.*

(b) To give the impression of being at a certain distance from an event; that is from the point of view of the speaker or writer, even though he or she may be, or may have been, personally involved. For example:

Das Spiel wurde verlängert.   (Passive)
The game went into extra-time.   (Active)
Es wurde in der Dämmerung gespielt.   (Passive)
The game took place in twilight.   (Active)

(c) To express a neutral point of view. For example:

Eine endgültige Entscheidung wurde getroffen.
A final decision was made.
Der Staatsvertrag wurde geschlossen.
The treaty was concluded.

(d) To express a neutral point of view on a matter in which the speaker or writer is personally involved. The interest is thus apparently transferred to someone or something else. For example:

Ich wurde gebeten, Gruppenleiter zu werden.
I was asked to become leader of the group.
An der Grenze wurden wir scharf kontrolliert.
We were subjected to a thorough check at the border.

The interest of the speaker is in the act of becoming **Gruppenleiter**, and in the control at the border, and not in his or her own role, which was a passive one in the two actions.

(**e**) To express non-involvement. For example:

Die Entscheidung wurde ohne mich getroffen.
The decision was taken without me.
Es wurde gewarnt, aber keiner hörte zu.
A warning was given, but nobody listened.

(**f**) To describe historical events, where the main facts are on record, but where all the exact details are not fully known. For example:

Im Jahre 9 nach Chr. wurden drei römische Legionen von Arminius im Teutoburger Wald vernichtet.
In the year 9 A.D. three Roman legions were destroyed by Arminius in the Teutoburger Wald.
Während des Dreißigjährigen Krieges wurde die Vorherrschaft im Ostseeraum hart umkämpft.
During the Thirty Years' War supremacy in the Baltic was the subject of hard fighting.

(**g**) To express a happening when the doer is not known. For example:

Sein Auto wurde gestohlen.   Ein Fenster ist eingeschlagen worden.
His car was stolen.   *A window has been broken.*

(**h**) To express a generality when the exact extent of the supposing, reporting, saying, thinking, knowing, etc. is not known, or when the people cannot be closely identified. For example:

Es ist gesagt worden, er sei vor Gericht gekommen.
It has been said that he came before the court.
Es wird vermutet, daß die Firma Konkurs macht.
It is presumed that the firm is going bankrupt.
Es wird angenommen, daß die Preise regelmäßig steigen werden.
It is assumed that prices will rise steadily.

64 Avoiding the passive

The act of keeping one's distance from events, and of assuming a neutrality towards happenings, are academic virtues which tend to lead towards the use of the passive. This is the voice of reflection, real or assumed. The bustle and the movement of everyday life leads more to the use of the voice of activity. Expressed in terms of grammar, this leads to the avoidance of the passive and the use of the active.

This is achieved in German by, for example, the use of **man** (one), instead of the passive form. The translation of **man** by the English word 'one' is to be avoided, where possible. Usage differs in this respect between German and English. For example:

Man sagt, sie sei verlobt.
It is said that she is engaged (to be married).
Man meint, daß die Wirtschaft einen Aufschwung erlebt.
The general opinion is that the economy is on the up-grade.

Other words than **man** can also be used. For example:

Eine Bauernregel sagt, daß viele rote Beeren einen kalten Winter voraussagen.
There is a country saying that many red berries foretell a cold winter.

65 The passive of intransitive verbs

Intransitive verbs are seldom used in the passive. When they are so used in German, then the language appears to be stiff, unnatural, or too formal. Two examples are sufficient to illustrate this point:

Es wurde getanzt und getrunken.   Es wurde geschlafen.
There was dancing and drinking.   (They) slept.

Neither of the above sentences can be translated into English by using the passive. If the passive of intransitive verbs is used at all in German, then it is usually used deliberately as a kind of word–play, to create the impression of stiffness and formality. The simple way to avoid the passive is to use the indefinite pronoun **man**. The verb is then in the active. This structure is frequently used both in speech and in writing to avoid the passive.

66 Variations on the passive

The general avoidance of the passive has been noted in para. 64. There are a number of ways of avoiding the passive, and the main ones are:

(**a**) By the use of **lassen**. For example:

Dies läßt sich vermeiden.
This can be avoided.
Er läßt sich beraten.
He accepts advice. (He lets himself be advised.)

(**b**) By the use of **bekommen**. For example:

Ich bekam eine bessere Stelle angeboten.
I was offered a better position (job).

(**c**) By the use of **kriegen**, used colloquially. For example:

Sie kriegte einen Diamantring geschenkt.
She was given a diamond ring as a present.

(**d**) By the use of the verbs **bleiben**, **geben** and **sein** + **zu** + the infinitive of the appropriate verb. For example:

Folgendes bleibt zu tun:
The following still has to be done:
Es gibt Folgendes zu überlegen:
The following points have (are) to be considered:
Es geht zu machen.
It can be done.
Es ist kaum zu erwarten, daß er kommt.
It can hardly be expected that he is coming.
The English translations are all in the passive.

(**e**) German verbs can often be used in the reflexive form, whereas their English counterparts cannot be so used. For example:

Es spricht sich herum, daß . . .
(According to gossip) it is said that . . .
Dieses Produkt verkauft sich gut.
This product sells well. (It is sold by virtue of its own merits.)

(**f**) Many transitive verbs can form a kind of passive with the verb **sein** as the auxiliary instead of the verb **werden**. This normally applies only to the present passive and the past passive:

Das Eis ist nach Süden getrieben.   (present passive)
Das Eis war nach Süden getrieben.   (past passive)

The perfect passive, pluperfect passive, and the future passive are usually the normal forms of the passive:

Das Eis ist nach Süden getrieben worden.   (perfect passive)
Das Eis war nach Süden getrieben worden.   (pluperfect passive)
Das Eis wird nach Süden getrieben werden.   (future passive)

The usual forms of the present passive and past passive are:

Das Eis wird nach Süden getrieben.   (present passive)
Das Eis wurde nach Süden getrieben.   (past passive)

All five tenses describe a passive state of affairs in which the activating force is not known or cannot be clearly defined.

The subjunctive: meaning and use

67 The subjunctive

Language is a means of human communication which is dependent on a speaker or writer on the one hand, and a listener or a reader on the other. If the speaker or the writer wishes to communicate a mood of doubt or uncertainty he or she may do so by the apt choice of words or – in German – by the use of the subjunctive. The survivals of the subjunctive in modern English are in words like '*were*' and '*be*' as used in sentences such as, '*If I were you*' or '*So be it*'. The translation of the German subjunctive is therefore subtle and difficult, as there are few traces of the subjunctive left in English.

The subjunctive in German is used to express doubt, uncertainty, supposition, speculation, unreality, conditional events, wishes, desires, and imagined circumstances.

It is also used for reported speech in German, since it can only be hoped and assumed that the indirect or reported speech is correct.

The conjugation of the subjunctive is given in paras. 13–15.

68 The conditional form of the subjunctive

There are two forms of the subjunctive which may be used in German if a condition is stated or implied. These forms are sometimes referred to in English as conditional, or *if*-clauses. In German the first conditional (**werden** + infinitive) is often used, but the second conditional (**werden** + past participle + **haben** or **sein**) is seldom seen and practically never heard. The following examples illustrate these points:

Auch wenn ich etwas sagte, würde nichts geschehen. (past subj. + 1. cond.)
Even if I should say something, nothing would happen.
Ich würde gehen, selbst wenn es regnet. (1. cond. + simple present)
I would go even if it rains (or should rain).
Ginge ich tanzen, würde sie böse auf mich sein. (past subj. + 1. cond.)
If I were to go dancing, she would be angry with me.
Ich würde eine lange Pause einlegen, wenn ich diese komplizierte Arbeit beendet haben würde. (1. conditional + 2. conditional)
I would have a long rest, if I were to have finished this complicated (piece of) work.

The first and second conditional are conjugated in para. 13. It must be stressed, though, that the second conditional is seldom used.

69 Use of the present subjunctive

The main use of the present subjunctive is in indirect or reported speech. Since the words of a third person (not the speaker nor the listener) are to be reported, the forms of the present subjunctive which are used are either the third person, singular, or the third person, plural. All the other forms are theoretically possible, but seldom or never used. The student should therefore concentrate his attention on the third person singular, as this form is different to the third person singular indicative. The third person plural form is the same in the indicative and the subjunctive.

The present subjunctive is also used in certain fixed expressions, and under certain fixed conditions to express a wish or hope, a condition or a concession. These uses are limited, often traditional, and not often used. They are as follows:

(a) To express a wish or hope. For example:
Morgen ist ein Festtag. Möge es schön bleiben!
Tomorrow is a public holiday. Let's hope it remains fine.
Er solle gehen.   Dem sei, wie es wolle.
He should go.   Be that as it may.
Wir wollen das Programm sehen, sei es gut, sei es schlecht.
We want to see the programme, whether it is good or bad.

(b) To give an instruction which it is hoped will be followed. For example:
Man nehme fünf Eier, 50 g Butter, . . .
You take five eggs, 50 grams of butter, . . .
Man nehme zwei Tabletten nach der Mahlzeit.
Take two tablets after the meal.

(c) To express a condition or concession. For example:
Obwohl es gut sei, gefällt es mir nicht.
Although it may be good, I don't like it.

(d) The main use of the present subjunctive, however, is in indirect or reported speech. For example:
Sie sagt, daß sie selten in die Stadt gehe.
She says that she seldom goes to town.

Er meint, er sei krank.
He thinks (that) he is ill.
Er behauptet, daß Bayern München die beste Mannschaft habe.
He maintains that Bayern München has the best team.

In each of the above three examples the reporter expresses some
slight doubt about the truth of the statement by using the present
subjunctive. There is a tendency in colloquial speech to use the
indicative form of the verb where the original statement is believed
to be true, or where there is a wish not to cast doubt on the truth of
the original statement.

70 Use of the present and past subjunctive – a simplified explanation

The present trend is towards the avoidance of the subjunctive,
especially in the use of the spoken word. This avoidance may take
the form of using the ordinary indicative, or it may take the form of
using the subjunctive of a very few common words in conjunction
with the infinitive of others. Provided that one knows the
following: **habe**, **hätte**, **sei**, **wäre**, **würde**, **könnte**, **möchte**,
müßte, **dürfte**, **sollte**, **wollte**, one can practically go through life
without using another verb in the subjunctive. This mini–list may
perhaps satisfy the majority, but not the educated speaker or writer,
who does indeed make use of the subjunctive.

71 Use of the past subjunctive

The conjugation of the past subjunctive is given in paras. 13, 14
(auxiliary verbs), and 23 (modal verbs). The past subjunctive forms
of strong verbs are to be found in para. 17, and of irregular verbs in
para. 18.

The use of the past subjunctive is the sign of the educated speaker or
writer, who is not prepared to make flat statements under
unwarranted circumstances.

The past subjunctive is used to express doubt, uncertainty,
supposition, speculation, unreality, conditional events, wishes,
desires, politeness, vagueness, and imagined circumstances. It is
also used in reported speech. The following examples illustrate
these uses:

(a) To express doubt:
Gäbe es vielleicht keine andere Lösung?
Could it be that there was no other solution?
Ob sie käme oder nicht, war von den Umständen abhängig.
Whether she would come or not depended on the circumstances.

(b) To express uncertainty:

Es war ungewiß, ob sie käme.
It was uncertain whether she would come.
Wenn ich nur eine Antwort wüßte!
If only I knew an answer!

(c) For a supposition:

Er könnte wohl recht gehabt haben.
He could very well have been right.
Es ist gut möglich, daß er die wahre Situation wüßte.
It is quite possible that he knew the real situation.

(d) For speculation:

Es könnte wahr sein.
It could well be true.
Es wäre nicht auszuschließen, daß . . .
It would not be outside the bounds of possibility that . . .

(e) To express unreality:

Es kam mir vor, als wenn ich immer noch auf dem Schiff wäre.
It seemed as if I were still on board ship.
Wenn ich du wäre, würde ich (mir) ein neues Auto kaufen.
If I were you, I would buy (myself) a new car.

(f) For conditional events:

Es wäre gut, wenn . . .
It would be fine if . . .
Wenn sie nur richtig sänge!
If she would only sing in tune!
Wenn er nur sähe, was er verursacht hat.
If only he would see what he has caused.

(g) To express wishes and desires:

Wenn ich nur gut kochen könnte!
If only I could cook well!
Ich würde meinen Urlaub lieber in den Alpen verbringen als an der See.
I would rather spend my holiday in the Alps than by the sea.

(h) As an expression of politeness by which the speaker wishes to indicate that the final decision on a matter would lie, of course, with the other person. For example:

Käme das nicht in Frage?
Would that be out of the question?
Es wäre schön, wenn Sie kommen könnten.
It would be nice if you could come.

(i) To express vagueness:

Wer weiß, was ihr durch den Kopf ginge, wenn sie den Unfall
verursacht hatte.
Who knows what went through her mind when she had caused the accident.

(j) To express imagined circumstances, or flights of the
imagination:

Ich kann mir vorstellen, daß ich mich in sie verliebte.
I can imagine that I could well fall in love with her.
Die Frau konnte nicht sagen, ob es zwei oder drei Einbrecher
wären.
The woman was unable to say whether there were two or three burglars.
Er meint, er hätte eine fliegende Untertasse gesehen.
He thinks he saw a flying saucer.

(k) To report the words used by a third person (the first person
being the writer or speaker, and the second being the reader or
listener). This is indirect or reported speech. The subjunctive is used
if there is the slightest doubt about the accuracy; it may also be used
merely to indicate that it is reported speech. For example:

Man sagte, sie spräche fließend fünf Fremdsprachen.
It was said that she spoke five foreign languages fluently.
Sie behauptet, daß die Medizin ihr nicht gut täte.
She maintains that the medicine didn't do her good.
Sie behauptete, daß sie eine echte Perlenkette besäße.
She maintained that she owned a genuine pearl necklace.

Most of the examples in **(a)**–**(k)** above can be expressed in an
alternative form of the subjunctive using the auxiliary verb forms
hätte, **wäre** and **würde**. These forms are considered in paras. 73
and 75.

72 Use of the perfect subjunctive

The conjugation of the perfect subjunctive is given in para. 13.
Whilst the majority of verbs are conjugated with **haben**, certain
verbs (see para. 16) are conjugated with **sein**.

The use of the perfect subjunctive is practically confined to indirect
or reported speech. The form of the verb mostly to be expected is
the third person singular, and occasionally the third person plural.
For example:

Man sagte mir, er sei angekommen.
I was told that he has arrived.
Sie sagte mir, sie habe gegessen.
She told me she had eaten.

Sie meint, sie habe die Prüfung bestanden.
She is of the opinion that she has passed the test.

73 Use of the pluperfect subjunctive

The conjugation of the pluperfect subjunctive is given in para. 13.
Whilst the majority of verbs are conjugated with **haben**, certain
verbs (see para. 16) are conjugated with **sein**.

The pluperfect subjunctive is a tense in common use to describe
imaginary situations, conditional events, theoretical possibilities, all
in the past, and as a polite way of expressing a wish or desire. In
addition, it is used in indirect or reported speech. The uses in detail
are:

(**a**) In imaginary situations which lie in the past. For example:
Es wäre besser gewesen, wenn sie ihren Beruf früher gewechselt
hätte.
It would have been better had she changed her occupation earlier.
Es ist denkbar, daß sie eher einen Mann gefunden hätte, wenn . . .
It is conceivable that she could have found herself a husband sooner, if . . .

(**b**) For conditional events or circumstances. For example:
Wenn er schneller gefahren wäre, wäre er zur rechten Zeit
angekommen.
If he had driven faster, he would have arrived on time.
Er wäre bestimmt gefallen, wenn er sich nicht festgehalten hätte.
He would definitely have fallen, if he hadn't held tight.

(**c**) For theoretical possibilities which lie in the past. For example:
Wir hätten viel früher Sonnenenergie nutzen sollen.
We ought to have used the sun's energy much earlier.
Sie wären gekommen, wenn sie den Bus nicht verpaßt hätten.
They would have come if they had not missed the bus.
Ein brauchbares Flugzeug wäre schon zur Zeit Leonardo da Vincis
denkbar gewesen.
*A serviceable aircraft would have been conceivable at the time of Leonardo
da Vinci.*

Although the theoretical possibilities lie in the past, they obviously
have a bearing on the present situation in the mind of the writer or
speaker. They are theoretical possibilities about the past.

(**d**) As a polite way of expressing a wish or a desire, which now lies
in the past. For example:
Ich wäre gerne gegangen.
I would have liked to go.
I would like to have gone.

Ich hätte gerne mit ihr gesprochen.
I would have liked to talk with her.
I would like to have talked with her.

(**e**) In indirect or reported speech. For example:

Er sagt(e), er wäre früher gekommen, wenn sein Auto keine Panne gehabt hätte.
He says/said that he would have come earlier, if his car hadn't broken down.

Er behauptete, daß man Diamanten in Südwales gefunden hätte.
He maintained that diamonds had been found in South Wales.

74 Use of the future subjunctive and the future perfect subjunctive

The conjugation of the two tenses is given in para. 13. Whilst the majority of verbs are conjugated with **haben**, certain verbs (see para. 16) are conjugated with **sein**.

The use of the future subjunctive is limited to speculation about the future, or reported speech concerning the future. The use of the future perfect subjunctive is limited to the mind projecting itself forward to look at a situation which would have arisen should the speculations about the future have been realized. The situations are obviously hypothetical, and the future perfect subjunctive is rarely used. The form of both tenses which is most likely to be used is the third person singular.

Examples of the use of the future subjunctive are:

(**a**) To speculate about the future:

Ob er kommen werde, wußte er nicht.
He didn't know whether he would come.

Er bezweifelt, daß Menschen in Frieden leben werden.
He doubts whether people will live in peace.

(**b**) To report on what is said or has been said about the future:

Sie sagte, daß es ihr nicht gelingen werde.
She said that she would not succeed.

Er meinte, eine Wirtschaftskrise werde kommen.
He was of the opinion that an economic crisis may well arise.

The use of the future perfect subjunctive is as follows:

Viele Leute meinen, er werde einige hohe Posten bekleidet haben, bevor er 60 Jahre alt sei.
Many people think (that) he will have held several high offices before he is 60 years old.

75 Use of the first conditional

The conjugation of the first conditional tense (e.g. **er würde gehen**) is given in para. 13. The tense is often used in German as an alternative form of the subjunctive.

The first conditional is used in connection with the future, often the immediate future. It may indicate a hypothetical or imagined situation, a supposition, a theoretical possibility, a suggestion as to future conduct, or a tentative idea. It is also used in indirect or reported speech. The main uses are:

(**a**) To describe a hypothetical or imaginary situation in the future. For example:

Ich würde vorschlagen, daß wir eine andere Straße nehmen sollten.
I (would) suggest that we ought to take another route.
Sie würde gerne ein größeres Haus besitzen.
She would like to own a bigger house.
Er würde gern Premierminister werden.
He would like to become Prime Minister.
Wenn doch die Preise nicht immer steigen würden!
If only the prices didn't always rise!

(**b**) For a supposition:

Vielleicht würde er meinen Vorschlag annehmen.
Perhaps he would accept my suggestion.
Es würde besser sein, wenn eine Begegnung vermieden würde.
It would be better if an encounter were to be avoided.

(**c**) To describe a theoretical possibility in the future:

Zu dieser Jahreszeit würden orkanartige Winde beträchtliche Schäden verursachen.
At this time of the year hurricane-type winds would cause considerable damage.
Zwei Punkte würden dem l.F.C. Köln reichen, um Meister zu werden.
Two points would be enough for the l.F.C. Köln to become champions.

(**d**) For speculations about future conduct or behaviour:

Er würde sich darüber freuen.
He would be pleased about that.
Wenn sie nur vernünftig bleiben würde!
If she would only remain sensible!
Sie würde wahrscheinlich froh sein, wenn . . .
She would probably be pleased if . . .

(e) To express a tentative idea about the immediate future:

Ich würde meinen, daß eine andere Lösung denkbar wäre.
I would think that another solution is conceivable.
Es wäre keine schlechte Idee, wenn wir den Konjunktiv von vorne an wiederholen würden.
It wouldn't be a bad idea if we revised the subjunctive from the very beginning.

(f) In indirect or reported speech concerning the future:

Sie sagte, sie würde lieber zu Hause bleiben.
She said that she would rather stay at home.
Sie erklärte, daß sie zu Hause bleiben würde.
She stated that she would stay at home.

76 Use of the second conditional

The conjugation of the second conditional is given in para. 13. The second conditional (e.g. **er würde gegangen sein**) is seldom used. It describes a situation in which the writer or speaker projects his or her mind into the future, and then looks back to describe what will have been accomplished at that point in time. The following examples demonstrate this use:

Er würde am Jahresende die Arbeit beendet haben, wenn er sofort anfangen würde.
He would have finished the job by the end of the year if he were to begin right away.
Wenn er rechtzeitig abfahren würde, würde er um fünf Uhr angekommen sein.
If he were to set off in good time he would have arrived by five o'clock.

77 The subjunctive in the passive

Only transitive verbs form a passive with **werden**. (See para. 62.) Sentences with intransitive verbs can occasionally be reconstructed so that the verb form is in the passive. (See para. 65.) Generally speaking, the subjunctive in the passive is difficult to use and to manage so that its use is usually limited to reported speech. The occasional use to express objectivity or neutrality on the part of the speaker or writer is possible, but the student of the language is advised to concentrate on recognizing these forms, and using them in connection with reported speech.

The conjugation of the passive subjunctive is given in para. 13, but the following table shows the use of the passive subjunctive in reported speech:

Sie sagte, er werde oft angerufen.   (present subj.)
She said he is often rung up.
Sie sagte, er würde oft angerufen.   (past subj.)
She said he was often rung up.
Sie sagte, er sei oft angerufen worden.   (perfect subj.)
She said he has often been rung up.
Sie sagte, er wäre oft angerufen worden.   (pluperfect subj.)
She said he had often been rung up.
Sie sagte, er werde oft angerufen werden.   (future subj.)
She said he will often be rung up.

The following two conditional tenses are grammatically acceptable, though seldom used:

Sie sagt, er würde oft angerufen werden, wenn . . .
She says that he would often be rung up, if . . .
Sie sagt, er würde oft angerufen worden sein, wenn . . .
She says that he would often have been rung up, if . . .

78 Variation of the subjunctive in the passive

In para. 66 (f) a variation of the passive is noted, in which the verb **sein** is used, instead of the verb **werden**. The following forms, which show the variations of the subjunctive in the passive, are given in indirect speech:

Er sagte, das Eis sei nach Süden getrieben.   (present passive subj.)
Er sagte, das Eis wäre nach Süden getrieben.   (past passive subj.)

Students are advised to use the form of the passive with **werden**, until they can distinguish, for example, the amount of movement (or lack of it) between:

Er sagte, das Eis werde nach Süden getrieben
(He said the ice is being driven southwards) and
Er sagte, das Eis sei nach Süden getrieben
(He said the ice is driven southwards).

79 Indirect speech: indicative or subjunctive?

The uncertainty about the use of the indicative or the subjunctive in reported speech is a reflection of the type of modern language research which is not concerned with theoretical standards of language, but which is mainly concerned with the factual description of the spoken language. This approach is based on systematic observation and analysis, and has tended to supersede scholarly interpretation of observable facts and meanings, in which norms were assumed from written sources, often from the literary language. Both approaches have their merits, but also their demerits.

The function of a German reference grammar is, however, not merely to give a description of the language, but also to give advice in clear terms on generally accepted norms (or normal usage). The following brief notes should therefore be considered as advice on a subject in which usage is changing, almost imperceptibly, and is most complex. Simple guide-lines, such as these, also have their limitations.

(**a**) In formal or literary work the subjunctive should be used for indirect speech. The distance in time of the writer from the actual speaking of the words is thereby emphasized. It may also be that the writer did not hear the actual words, but had been told them by a second person; it may be that the memory is not so accurate as to recall everything word for word; or it may be that the writer wishes to cast doubt on the accuracy of the speaker. The use of the subjunctive is recommended under these circumstances.

(**b**) In giving an oral report about a conversation which has just taken place, and when the memory is still fresh, it is now common practice to use the indicative.

(**c**) Indirect speech is concerned with the spoken word. The reporting of speech usually occurs soon after the event, whether it be in spoken form or in written form, such as in a letter. A compromise is often reached in German in which just a few forms of the subjunctive are used, either as verbs on their own, or to help form tenses. These forms are: **sei**, **wäre**, **hätte**, **würde**, **könnte**, **möchte**, **müßte** and **dürfte**. They occur more frequently than all other forms of the subjunctive. It is not uncommon to hear a mixture of the indicative and subjunctive in spontaneous speech. The trend, though, is away from the subjunctive.

(**d**) The use of the subjunctive, together with the use of involved sentence structure and less commonly used words, may also occur when a speaker wishes to show greater learning. This can be a status symbol. There are also speakers and writers who use the subjunctive naturally, and with great delicacy and skill.

Modal verbs: meaning and use

80 Definition of a modal verb

A modal verb is one which reflects a grammatical mood. This may be in the form of a statement or question, a command, a wish or a doubt. The first recorded use of the word 'modal' in English was in the 16th century to describe the possibility or impossibility, the necessity or the chance occurrence of a proposition in logic. The six modal verbs in German, **dürfen**, **können**, **mögen**, **müssen**, **sollen** and **wollen** reflect these aspects.

81 Modal verb + infinitive

A modal verb is always used with the infinitive of another verb, without **zu**. For example:

Er darf gehen.   Er möchte gehen.
He is allowed to go.   *He would like to go.*
Sie will tanzen gehen.   Sie mag gerne tanzen.
She wants to go dancing.   *She likes dancing.*

82 Translations of the modal verbs

There are many possible translations of the German modal verbs, but these can be grouped together under certain headings, which are given in brackets:

dürfen: to be permitted, to be allowed; may, might, can, could, dare. (Permission and possibility)

können: to know, to be skilled in, to understand how to do a thing; can, could, to be able to, to have the right or power to. (Ability, possibility, and permission)

mögen: to want to, to wish to, to like to, to desire to, to be within the bounds of possibility. (Free will and possibility)

müssen: must, to have to, to be obliged to. (Obligation)

sollen: to be obliged to; must, to have to; to be said to, to be supposed to; shall, should, ought to, (are) to. (Obligation)

wollen: will, would, to be willing; to wish to, to want to, to desire to, to like to; to be about to, to intend, to have a mind to. (Free will)

The six German verbs express: permission, possibility, ability, free will, and obligation. Their uses are considered under those headings.

83 Uses of the modal verbs

Permission

The verbs **dürfen** and **können** both express permission, but not in the same way, or to the same extent. They are not interchangeable when a precise meaning is intended. The verb **dürfen** helps to form a plain statement that permission has been granted. There is no doubt about the permission.

The verb **können** is somewhat more vague about the extent of the permission. It brings in the person involved, and gives him or her a certain amount of choice. The following demonstrate the shades of meaning:

Die Kinder dürfen bis 6 Uhr abends draußen spielen.
The children are allowed to play outdoors until 6 in the evening.
Man darf die Straße bei rot nicht überqueren.
It is not permitted to cross the road when the lights are red.
Wir dürfen gehen.   Wir können gehen.
We can go.   *We can go (if we want to).*
Sie können, wenn Sie wollen, den neuen Wagen sofort testen.
You can test the new car at once if you want.
Wir dürfen wohl hoffen, daß er recht hat.
We can only hope that he is right.

Possibility

The verbs **dürfen** and **können** express a certain degree of possibility. When permission has been given, and a possibility thereby exists, then the verb **dürfen** is used. If a possibility arises as the result of knowledge or skill, then **können** is used. The verb **mögen** places the person or thing involved at the centre of the situation, and indicates the possible rightness of a personal judgement on that person or thing. For example:

Sie darf sich Hoffnungen auf eine gute Karriere machen.
She can well permit herself hopes of a good career.
Wir können Preissteigerungen erwarten.
We may well expect rises in prices.
Wir dürfen Besuch erwarten.   Es mag wohl richtig sein.
We can expect visitors.   *It may very well be right.*
Ich kann meine Urlaubszeit selbst wählen.
I can choose the time of my holiday myself.

It should be clear from the above examples that possibility is implied in each case, even if it is not the main thought.

Ability

There is only one modal verb which expresses ability, namely **können**. For example:

Sie kann gut kochen.
She can cook well.
Ich kann Sie verstehen, auch wenn Sie schnell sprechen.
I can understand you even if you speak quickly.

Free will

There are two verbs which express free will, choice of action, or the choice of doing or not doing something. A deliberate action of the will is expressed by **wollen**, whereas a somewhat random action of the will, depending on mood and emotion, is expressed by **mögen**.

Ich will dies unbedingt klarmachen.
I want to make this absolutely clear.
Sie wollte etwas sagen.
She wanted to say something.
Ich möchte gerne nach Hause gehen.
I would like to go home.
Ich mag nicht länger bleiben.
I don't want to stay any longer.

Obligation

The two verbs expressing obligation are **müssen** and **sollen**. The verb **müssen** implies that the obligation is imposed by an authority, a law, or a person above one in status. It could be an older member of the family. It is a firm obligation, which can very well have consequences if not obeyed. The verb **sollen** expresses a moral obligation, or one in which there is still some freedom of choice about doing something, or not. Examples are:

Sämtliche Verkehrszeichen müssen beachtet werden.
All traffic signs must be respected.
Der Gesetzentwurf muß vom Bundestag verabschiedet werden.
The draft law has to be passed by the Bundestag.
Du mußt auf den Verkehr achten.
You must look out for the traffic.
Ich soll einkaufen gehen, aber ich bin zu faul.
I ought to go shopping, but I'm too lazy.
Jeder Fahrer soll Rücksicht auf spielende Kinder nehmen.
Every driver ought to (should) show consideration for children at play.

In the example 'Ich soll einkaufen gehen, aber ich bin zu faul' the verb 'soll' has the sense of 'I have been told to go shopping'. If the form 'sollte' were used, then there is a sense of inner obligation. Both 'soll' and 'sollte' can be translated by 'ought', but the distinction is not clear.

The future
The meanings of the modal verbs are such that they all imply future activity or fulfilment. This may be the result of permission, the fulfilment of a possibility, the result of ability, free will or an obligation. A repetition of some of the examples demonstrates the future aspect: Wir dürfen gehen. Wir können gehen. Wir dürfen Besuch erwarten. Sie kann gut kochen. Ich möchte gerne nach Hause gehen. Du mußt auf den Verkehr achten. Ich will dies unbedingt klarmachen. Sie soll ruhig bleiben.

There are, of course, future forms of modal verbs, such as: 'Wir werden gehen dürfen.' 'Wir werden gehen können.'

Impersonal
and reflexive verbs

84 Definition of impersonal verbs

Impersonal verbs are those verbs whose use is limited to the third person singular, and which follow the impersonal pronoun **es**. For example:

Es regnet.   Es wurde getanzt.
It's raining.   There was dancing.

The subject of impersonal verbs can never be used in the first or second person, singular or plural. Impersonal verbs can be given a personal touch, but the exact meaning of **es** remains vague, although it is implied in the rest of the sentence. For example:

Mir ist es egal.   Es ist mir warm.   Es freut mich.
It's all the same to me.   I'm (feeling) warm.   I'm glad/pleased.

85 Uses of impersonal verbs

Impersonal verbs are used under the following circumstances:

(**a**) For weather conditions:

Gestern regnete es.   Es friert draußen.
It was raining/rained yesterday.   It's freezing outside.
Es hagelt.   Es blitzt und donnert.
It's hailing.   There's thunder and lightning.

(**b**) For noises:

Es klopfte an der Tür.   Es knarrte.
There was a knock on the door.   There was a creaking noise.
Es knallte.   Es poltert in der Küche!
There was a bang.   There's a poltergeist loose in the kitchen!

(**c**) To describe garden and farmyard conditions, etc.:

Es wächst sehr schnell in diesem Frühling.
Everything is growing very quickly this spring.
Es duftet schön.   Es stinkt.
It smells nice.   It stinks.

(**d**) To give an account of a happening or event in which the participants were/are little known to the speaker, or in which the speaker wishes to lay stress on the action rather than on the participants:

Es wurde zwei Stunden lang gespielt.
The game/the music went on for two hours.
Es wird heute abend getanzt und gefeiert.
This evening there's dancing and a celebration.
Es wurde acht Tage lang um diese Stadt gekämpft.
The fighting for this town went on for eight days.

(**e**) To express personal feelings:
Mir ist es unangenehm, mich dafür zu entschuldigen.
I don't like having to excuse myself for that.
Mir ist es egal, ob wir gehen oder nicht.
It's all the same to me whether we go or not.
Es geht mir gut.   Es tut mir leid.
I'm fine.   I'm sorry.
Es freut mich, Sie kennenzulernen.
I'm pleased to meet you.
Es wundert mich, daß du soviel Geld hast.
I'm surprised that you've got so much money.
Es graut mir, wenn ich daran denke.
I shudder to think of it.

(**f**) For general and often vague statements:
Es ist schon dunkel.   Es ist nicht mehr zu ertragen.
It's dark already.   This is no longer bearable.
Es gibt zwei Möglichkeiten: entweder dies oder das.
There are two possibilities – either this or that.
Es gab mehrere Unfälle auf dieser Kreuzung.
There were several accidents at this road crossing.
Es ist der Professor, der das sagt.
It's the professor who says that.
Es ist möglich, daß er nicht kommen kann.
It's possible that he won't be able to come.

The above statements are often deliberately formulated in this way
in order to give an impersonal or distant touch to the meaning.

(**g**) In narration to give a fanciful touch to the story:
Es war einmal ein Jäger.
Once upon a time there was a hunter.
Es kamen zwei aggressiv aussehende Männer auf ihn zu.
Two aggressive-looking men came towards him.

(**h**) With **daß**-clauses:
Es ist allen klar, daß die Mannschaft nicht sehr stark ist.
It's clear to everyone that the team is not very strong.

Es steht fest, daß sie die Meisterschaft nicht gewinnen kann.
It's clear that it can't win the championship.
Es ist schade, daß der Club so viele verletzte Spieler hat.
It's a pity that the club has so many injured players.

(i) With certain verbs which express actions or happenings:

Es gelang ihm nichts.
He didn't succeed at anything.
Es ereignete sich ein Unfall im dichten Verkehr.
There was an accident in the heavy traffic.
Es sieht nach Schnee aus.   Es kommt auf das Wetter an.
It looks as if it is going to snow.   *It depends on the weather.*
Es handelt sich um eine Lotterie. Es geht um viel Geld.
It's a question of a lottery.   *There's much money involved.*

(j) An unusual structure should be noted, in which the singular **es** is apparently used in an impersonal sense with a verb in the plural. In fact, the plural is determined by the plural number of the following noun:

Es kamen zwei Männer.
There came two (unknown) men.
Es sind drei Kinder, die uns beschäftigen.
There are three children who are occupying our attention.

86 Reflexive verbs

The most obvious type of reflexive verb is that in which the action of the subject reflects back on the subject. E.g.:

Ich rasiere mich.   Er wäscht sich.

The reflexive pronoun is not usually translated into English.
E.g.:   *I shave.   He washes.*

Most of the reflexive verbs in German, however, are not obviously reflexive verbs to the English student, and therefore have to be noted and learned. Typical examples are:

Sie freut sich über das Geschenk.
She is pleased with the present.
Sie schämt sich wegen ihres ungepflegten Aussehens.
She is ashamed of her untidy appearance.
Wir befinden uns in einer schwierigen Lage.
We are in a difficult situation.
Er erinnerte sich an die guten alten Zeiten.
He remembered the good old days.

87 Pseudoreflexive verbs

In colloquial speech (*Umgangssprache*) there is a tendency to insert a reflexive pronoun where there is strictly speaking no grammatical justification. The verbs become in these circumstances pseudoreflexive verbs. Two examples are enough to show this point:

Ich kaufte mir einen neuen Anzug.
I bought (myself) a new suit.
Ich sah mir neue Möbel an.
I looked at new furniture.

The purpose is clearly to show the person for whom the items are intended. The first speaker would wish to emphasize that the new furniture would primarily be for her (or his) use. The reflexive pronouns in both sentences are grammatically unnecessary.

The examples are given in the first person singular in order to show that the reflexive pronoun under these circumstances is in the dative.

Students are advised to avoid pseudoreflexive verbs, certainly in writing, and preferably in colloquial speech. Only a few verbs allow themselves to be handled in this way.

88 Position of the reflexive pronoun in the sentence

The reflexive pronoun takes the same position in the sentence as the ordinary direct object. This is immediately after the verb in a main clause. E.g.:

Ich ziehe mich immer sehr schnell um.
I always get changed quickly.
Wir haben uns darüber gewundert.
We wondered about that.

In a subordinate clause the reflexive pronoun comes directly after the subject. E.g.:

Nachdem er sich nochmals verletzt hatte, ging er zum Arzt.
After he had once again injured himself he went to the doctor.
Man sagt, daß er sich darüber sehr amüsierte.
It is said that he was very amused about that.

89 Simple reflexive verbs

A simple reflexive verb is one which can form, together with the subject, a simple sentence. For example: **Ich ziehe mich an** (*I get dressed*) forms a complete sentence. Other words can, of course, be added but they are not necessary to give the sentence a full meaning. Examples of simple reflexive verbs are:

sich anziehen	to get dressed
sich aufhalten	to stop, or stay
sich ausruhen	to rest
sich ausziehen	to undress
sich äußern	to express (an idea)
sich bedanken	to thank a person
sich beeilen	to hurry
sich erholen	to recover (in health)
sich freuen	to be glad
sich hinlegen	to lie down
sich hinsetzen	to sit down
sich setzen	to take a seat
sich täuschen	to be mistaken
sich umsehen	to look around
sich umziehen	to change (clothes)
sich verabschieden	to say goodbye
sich waschen	to wash

A very few reflexive verbs are followed by the genitive case, and
even fewer are followed by the dative case. Examples of each
follow:

with the genitive

sich enthalten	to abstain from
sich vergewissern	to make sure of
sich schämen	to be ashamed of

with the dative

sich anschließen	to attach oneself to
sich nähern	to draw near to

90 Reflexive verbs followed by a preposition

A group of commonly used reflexive verbs often require a
completion of meaning. They are followed by a preposition and a
noun or pronoun. The most common verbs are given in the
following list.
N.B. The abbreviation **j. (jemand)** refers to a p. (person), and **e.
(etwas)** refers to a t. (thing or abstract idea).

sich aufregen über j./e.	to get excited about a p./t.
sich bedanken für e.	to return thanks for a t.
sich befassen mit j./e.	to deal with, concern oneself with a p./t.
sich beklagen über/ wegen j./e.	to complain about a p./t.
sich belustigen über j./e.	to make fun of/laugh at a p./t.

sich beschweren bei j.	to complain to a p.
sich beschweren über e./j.	to complain about a t./p.
sich besinnen auf j./e.	to call to mind/ remember a p./t.
sich beziehen auf j./e.	to refer/ allude to a p./t.
sich distanzieren von j./e.	to move away from and remain aloof from a p./t.
sich einigen mit j./über/ auf e./j.	to agree with a p. about a t./p.
sich einsetzen für j./e.	to stand up for a p./t.
sich einstellen auf j./e.	to adapt oneself to a p./t.
sich entscheiden für/ gegen j./e.	to decide in favour of/against a p./t.
sich entschließen für/ gegen j./e.	to make up one's mind for/ against a p./t.
sich entschuldigen bei j./ wegen e./j.	to apologize to a p. for a t.
sich erinnern an j./e.	to recollect/call to mind a p./t.
sich freuen über/an e.	to be pleased about/over a t.
sich freuen auf e.	to look forward to a t.
sich fürchten vor j./e.	to stand in fear of a p./t.
sich gewöhnen an j./e.	to get accustomed/used to a p./t.
sich interessieren für j./e.	to take an interest in a p./t.
sich konzentrieren auf j./e.	to concentrate on a p./t.
sich kümmern um j./e.	to care for/be worried about a p.t.
sich richten nach e./j.	to be governed/guided by a p./t.
sich schämen vor j. wegen e.	to be ashamed in a p.'s presence about a t.
sich täuschen über e./in j./e.	to be mistaken about a t./in a p./t.
sich verlassen auf j./e.	to rely on/depend upon a p./t.
sich wehren gegen j./e.	to defend oneself against/resist a p./t.
sich wenden an j./gegen j./e.	to turn to a p./ against a p./t.
sich wundern über j./e.	to be surprised at a p./t.

All the above verbs express personal attitudes and actions.

Special verbs

91 Verbs taking the dative

There are a number of verbs which take the dative; that is to say,
they are followed by an indirect object, which is in the dative case.
Examples are:

Er antwortete mir in einem schroffen Ton.
He answered me in a harsh tone.
Ich danke dir.   Es bleibt ihm nichts anderes übrig als . . .
I thank you.   There is nothing left to him but . . .
Die Vorstellung entsprach nicht meiner Erwartung.
The performance did not come up to my expectations.

92 A list of common verbs taking the dative

antworten	to answer	**mißlingen**	to miscarry
begegnen	to meet	**mißtrauen**	to distrust
bleiben	to remain	**nachlaufen**	to run after
danken	to thank	**schaden**	to harm
dienen	to serve	**trauen**	to trust
entsprechen	to accord with	**verzeihen**	to forgive
fehlen	to be missing	**widersprechen**	to contradict
folgen	to follow	**widerstehen**	to oppose
gefallen	to please	**zugeben**	to agree (to)
gehören	to belong to	**zuhören**	to listen (to)
gelingen	to succeed	**zusagen**	to assent
genügen	to be sufficient	**zustehen**	to belong to
helfen	to help	**zustimmen**	to consent

93 Verbs which may be followed by the dative

Some common verbs may be followed by the dative, if a person is
directly involved or affected as the object of the sentence. For
example:

Es gelang ihm.   Mir tut der Kopf weh.
He succeeded.   *My head hurts.*
Es tut mir leid.   Das liegt mir nicht.
I'm sorry.   *That doesn't suit me.*
Es sagt mir etwas.
It means something to me.

These are sentence structures with the dative, and are not to be
confused with sentences in which the verb (see para. 92) can only

take the dative. The verbs **tun**, **sagen**, and **liegen** in the above sentences only take the dative under special circumstances, namely when a person is directly involved or affected as the object of the sentence.

94 Verbs taking the dative plus the accusative

There are verbs which have both a direct object and an indirect object. The direct object is in the accusative, and the indirect object is in the dative. The order of words should be noted:

(a) **Sie gibt dem Mann das Buch.** (I.O. + D.O. two nouns)
(b) **Sie gibt das Buch dem Mann.** (D.O. + I.O. two nouns)
(c) **Sie gibt ihm das Buch.**   (I.O. + D.O. pronoun + noun)
(d) **Sie gibt es ihm.**   (D.O. + I.O. two pronouns)

(D.O. is the direct object, I.O. is the indirect object.)

Both (a) and (b) are possible, although it is preferable to put a person before a thing.
In (c) the pronoun comes before the noun.
If two pronouns (d) are used the accusative usually comes before the dative.
These are not rules of speech and writing, but observations of common usage.

95 A list of verbs taking the dative plus the accusative

The following list is given in order to show the kind of verbs which may be followed by both the dative and the accusative. The word order will depend on the factors mentioned in para. 94.

Er bringt mir etwas	He brings me something
Er erklärt mir etwas	He explains something to me
Er erzählt mir etwas	He tells me something
Er gibt mir etwas	He gives me something
Er kauft mir etwas	He buys something for me
Er leiht mir etwas	He lends me something
Er macht mir etwas klar	He explains something to me
Er teilt mir etwas mit	He informs me of something
Er schenkt mir etwas	He gives me something as a present
Er sendet mir etwas	He sends me something
Er überläßt mir etwas	He leaves me something
Er verspricht mir etwas	He promises me something
Er liest mir etwas vor	He reads something to me
Er ruft mir etwas zu	He calls something to me
Er traut mir etwas zu	He entrusts me with something

The verbs may be used in any tense, and of course are not limited to the third person singular.

96 Verbs taking the genitive

A very few reflexive verbs are followed by the pronoun or noun in the genitive. The examples show how these verbs are used in sentences. The few verbs with the genitive are not often encountered, and therefore no list is given.

Er bediente sich seiner Hände.
He used his hands.
Er enthielt sich der Stimme.
He withheld his vote. / He refrained from voting.
Er schämt sich seiner Untreue.
He is ashamed of his infidelity.

97 Verbs taking the accusative and an adverbial phrase

There are verbs which may be followed by the direct object (accusative) and an adverbial phrase. The problem usually lies in the use of the correct preposition at the beginning of the adverbial phrase. For example:

Er beschützte seine Schwester vor den betrunkenen Fans.
He protected his sister from the drunken fans.
Er wußte nichts von der Angelegenheit.
He knew nothing about the matter.

98 A list of verbs taking the accusative and an adverbial phrase

The list contains only examples of verbs in common use, and is given in an abbreviated form.
N.B.: **j. (jemand)** means a p. (person), and **e. (etwas)** means a t. (thing).

auffordern j. zu e.	to challenge a p. to a t.
befreien j. von e.	to free a p. from a t.
benutzen e. zu e.	to use a t. for a t.
beschäftigen j. mit e.	to occupy a p. with a t.
beschützen j. vor e.	to protect a p. from a t.
bitten j. um e.	to ask a p. for a t.
entlasten j. von e.	to exonerate a p. from a t.
erinnern j. an e.	to remind a p. of a t.
fragen j. nach j. oder e.	to ask a p. about a p. or t.
gewöhnen j. an e.	to familiarize a p. with a t.

haben Anspruch auf e.	to be entitled to a t.
hören e. über j. oder e.	to hear a t. about a p. or t.
interessieren j. an e.	to interest a p. in a t.
interessieren j. für e.	to interest a p. for a t.
nehmen Notiz von j. oder e.	to take notice of a p. or t.
nehmen Rücksicht auf j. oder e.	to take a p. or t. into consideration
sagen e. über j. oder e.	to say a t. about a p. or t.
schreiben e. an j.	to write a t. to a p.
schreiben e. über e.	to write a t. about a t.
überreden j. zu e.	to persuade a p. to do a t.
verkaufen e. an j.	to sell a t. to a p.
verwenden e. zu e.	to use a t. to do a t.
warnen j. vor j. oder e.	to warn a p. against a p. or t.
wissen e. von j.	to know a t. about a p.
wissen e. über e.	to know a t. about a t.

The imperative

99 Definition of the imperative

The imperative is the form of the verb used to give a command, an order or an instruction, or to make an earnest request.

The form of the verb is always connected with that of the second person, singular or plural, of the present tense.

100 Forms of the imperative in the singular

(**a**) The singular form is that of the stem of the second person singular, without **du**. The letter **e** may be added. Weak and irregular verbs are as follows:

2nd person singular, present	Imperative
du fragst	**frag** (stem) + **e** (optional)
du antwortest	**antwort** (stem) + **e**
du denkst	**denk** (stem) + **e** (optional)
du nennst	**nenn** (stem) + **e**

(**b**) The imperative of strong verbs is formed in exactly the same manner. The second person singular of strong verbs has the same stem as the third person singular, and these forms are to be found in the table in para. 17. For example:

2nd person singular, present	Imperative
du schreibst	**schreib** (stem) + **e** (optional)
du gibst	**gib** (stem)
du liest	**lies** (stem)
du ißt	**iß** (stem)

(**c**) Strong verbs with the letter **a** in the stem have an umlaut in the present tense, but not in the imperative:

du läßt (present)	**laß** (stem without umlaut)
du läufst (present)	**lauf** (stem without umlaut)

(**d**) The forms of **haben** and **sein** are:

habe (not often used)   **sei** (frequently used).

(**e**) With **e** or without **e**?

The decision to use, or not to use, an **e** after the stem of the imperative depends on the speaker or writer, and on the situation. It must be borne in mind that the situation must be within the family, amongst relatives, in the younger groups at school, or among close friends, since **du** is used. The atmosphere is likely to be informal.

Under these circumstances the short, sharp command or instruction is more likely in colloquial German; that is to say without the **e** after the stem. For example: **Frag deine Mutter!** is more likely than **Frage deine Mutter!** The elevated style of writing the singular imperative, that is, using the **e** where possible, may be used deliberately to create a stiff, formal atmosphere.

It is always necessary to add an **e** if the stem ends in a sound which seems to invite a continuation. The consonant combinations **ck**, **nn**, **rt**, **tt**, are examples. The imperatives are **backe**, **nenne**, **antworte**, and **bitte**, and the form without the letter **e** is not used.

Generally speaking, the short forms are preferred in everyday life. Certain verbs never take an **e**. Examples are given in (**b**) above.

101 Forms of the imperative in the plural

There are two forms of the imperative in the plural, the familiar and the polite form.

The familiar form is the same as the second person plural, without **ihr**. For example:

Eßt nicht so schnell!   Lest die Schlagzeilen!
Don't eat so quickly!   Read the headlines!

There are very few exceptions. For example: **seid! laßt! vergeßt!**

The polite form is the same as the third person plural of the present tense. The words are transposed, however, and the pronoun **Sie** begins with a capital letter. For example:

Geben Sie mir bitte das Buch.
Give me the book please.

The only irregular form is that of the verb **sein**: **seien**.

Seien Sie bitte geduldig.
Please be patient.

102 Uses of the imperative

The uses of the imperative are to give a command, an order or an instruction, or to make an earnest request. Since a command, an order, and an instruction can often only be distinguished by the tone of voice, or in a given situation, they are grouped together. The following distinction is therefore somewhat artificial:

(**a**) Melden Sie sich beim Feldwebel. (command)
Report to the sergeant-major.

Warten Sie draußen. (order)   Nehmen Sie bitte Platz. (instruction)
Wait outside.   *Take a seat.*

(b) The word **bitte** (*please*) is used to moderate a command, an order, or an instruction.

(c) The imperative is used for an earnest request:

Entschuldigen Sie bitte, können Sie mir sagen, wo . . .
Excuse me please, can you tell me where . . .
Geben Sie mir bitte Zeit zum Überlegen.
Please give me time to think.

103 Alternative forms and uses of the imperative

(a) The imperative can be expressed by the first person plural of the present tense, with the pronoun and verb in the reverse order, if a supposed situation is suggested. For example:

Nehmen wir an, daß eine Wahl im März stattfinden würde.
Let us suppose that an election were to take place in March.

(b) The supposition may be in parenthesis:

Es kamen höchstens, sagen wir mal, zwei Hundert zur Großkundgebung.
Two hundred at the most, let's say, came to the mass demonstration.

(c) The imperative of **lassen** is often used in connection with the first and third persons:

Laß mich etwas sagen.   Laß ihn ausreden.
Let me say something.   *Let him say what he wants to say.*

104 Other ways of expressing commands

Commands, order, and instructions may sometimes be expressed in other ways than by using the imperative. For example:

(a) By using the infinitive:

Aufhören!   Einsteigen!   Umsteigen!
Stop (playing)!   *In the train!*   *All change!*

(b) By making a statement in a commanding tone of voice:

Du machst deine Hausarbeit jetzt, sofort!
Do your homework now, at once.

(c) By the use of a single word of warning, whereby the imperative remains unspoken:

Achtung!   Vorsicht!   Fertig!   Los!   So nicht!
Attention!   *Look out!*   *Ready!*   *Go!*   *Not that way!*

Infinitives and participles

105 Definitions

The infinitive is the name of that form of a verb which simply
expresses the general concept or idea of that verb.
A participle is a verbal adjective, which retains some qualities of a
verb, and qualifies a noun.

106 Forms of the infinitive

The form of the infinitive which is commonly used (e.g. **fragen**,
sprechen, **tun**), and which is used in vocabularies and dictionaries
to express the general concept of the verb, is, in fact, only one of the
forms of the infinitive.

The infinitive may be active or passive, present or perfect:

	Active	*Passive*
Present:	fragen	gefragt werden
Perfect:	gefragt haben	gefragt worden sein
	gewesen sein	

The following sentences illustrate the various forms in use:

Ich muß ihn fragen.   (Present active)
I must ask him.
Ich möchte vorher gefragt werden.   (Present passive)
I like to be asked beforehand.
Er mußte gefragt haben, aber ich habe vergessen, was er
sagte.   (Perfect active)
He must have asked, but I've forgotten what he said.
Er mußte gefragt worden sein, bevor die Angelegenheit besprochen
wurde.   (Perfect passive)
He must have been asked before the matter was discussed.

The last sentence is contrived to show how the perfect passive
infinitive could be used, but the use of this form is restricted, as it is
an awkward grammatical structure, and there are simpler ways of
saying the same thing.

107 The infinitive with and without 'zu'

(**a**) The infinitive is used without **zu** after the modal verbs:

Er durfte es nicht erwähnen.   Er mußte gehen.
He was not allowed to mention it.   *He had to go.*

Sie sollte warten.
She should wait.
Er konnte gehen.
He could go.

Sie mochte nicht gehen.
She didn't like to go.
Sie wollte nicht mitgehen.
She did not want to go with (him).

(**b**) It is also used without **zu** after the following verbs: **lernen**, **lehren**, **helfen**, **heißen**.

Er hieß die Gäste willkommen.
He welcomed the guests.
Sie lernt Klavier spielen.
She is learning to play the piano.

(**c**) The infinitive is used with **zu** to form verbal expressions:

Die Frage ist schwer zu beantworten.
The question is hard to answer.
Die Waren sind noch zu kaufen.
The goods are still on sale.
Die Eltern wurden gezwungen, zu Hause zu bleiben.
The parents were forced to stay at home.

(**d**) In compound verbs the word **zu** in verbal expressions comes between the prefix and the basic verb:

Er versuchte mir entgegenzukommen.
He tried to meet me half-way.
Es ist notwendig, etwas Besseres anzubieten.
It is necessary to offer something better.
Die Bergsteiger wurden wegen der schlechten Wetterlage gezwungen, umzukehren.
The climbers were forced to turn back because of the bad weather conditions.

(**e**) The infinitive with **zu**, and the infinitive without **zu** can be used in nominal groups (noun expressions). See para. 109.

108 Um ... zu, ohne ... zu, (an)statt ... zu

Purpose (**um ... zu**), result (**ohne ... zu**), and manner (**(an)statt ... zu**) can be expressed by an infinitive construction.

(**a**) Purpose:
Sie ging in die Stadt, um Einkäufe zu machen.
She went to town (in order) to go shopping.
Um Erfolg zu haben, muß mehr Geld investiert werden.
In order to be successful more money must be invested.

(**b**) Result:
Sie suchte ihre Handtasche, ohne sie zu finden.
She looked for her handbag without finding it.

Ohne ein Wort zu sagen, ging er von ihr fort.
Without saying a word he left her.

(c) Manner:

Er drehte sich um und schwieg, anstatt sich zu entschuldigen.
He turned round and remained silent instead of offering his apologies.

109 Infinitives used as nouns

The infinitive may also be used either as a noun, or as part of a
group of words doing the work of a noun in a sentence.

(a) When the infinitive is used as a noun either with or without a
definite or indefinite article, it begins with a capital letter:

Können ist besser als Theoretisieren.
Practical ability is better than the ability to theorize.
Das ewige Hin- und Hergehen stört mich.
The continuous walking up and down disturbs me.

(b) The article before the infinitive-noun may be combined with a
preposition:

Sie hat ihn vom Schlafen abgehalten.   Sie ist beim Bügeln.
She kept him from sleeping.   *She is ironing.*

(c) When the infinitive is part of a group of words with **zu**, the
group may be used as a noun. This nominal group may be the
subject, the complement, or the object of the sentence, or serve as
an adjunct, as in the following examples:

(Ganz einfach zu schweigen) ist keine Antwort.   (Subject)
Simply keeping quiet is not an answer.
Die Antwort wäre (doch zu schweigen).   (Complement)
The answer would nevertheless be to keep quiet.
Sie entschieden, (einen neuen Verein zu gründen).   (Object)
They decided to form a new association.
Er hatte weiter nichts im Sinn, (als nur Geld auszugeben).
(Adjunct)
He had nothing more in mind than to spend money.

N.B.: The infinitive with **zu** is not written with a capital letter, even
though the infinitive group is doing the work of a noun.

110 The form of the present and the past participle

The present participle is formed by adding the ending **–d** to the
infinitive:

fragen + d = fragend   **zustimmen + d = zustimmend**
N.B.: The present participle of **sein** is **seiend**.

The past participle of strong verbs ends in **-en** or **-n**, and the past participle of weak verbs ends in **-t** or **-et**. For example:

Strong verbs		*Weak verbs*	
gehen	— **gegangen**	**fragen**	— **gefragt**
laufen	— **gelaufen**	**warten**	— **gewartet**
nehmen	— **genommen**	**atmen**	— **geatmet**
N.B.: **tun**	— **getan**		

The past participles of strong and irregular verbs (see paras. 17 and 18) have to be memorized, but the past participles of weak verbs are formed to a pattern by adding **ge-** as a prefix and **-t** or **-et** to the stem of the infinitive. The letters **-et** are added if the stem ends in **d** or **t**, and also with some verbs whose stem ends in **m**. (See above.)

The prefix **ge-** is omitted in strong and weak verbs if the stress comes after the first syllable of the infinitive form of the verb. This applies to compound verbs, especially those with the prefixes **be-, emp-, ent-, er-, ge-, ver-,** and **zer-**. (See para. 9 (a).) For example: **(hat) beendet, empfohlen, entschieden, erreicht, gestanden, vergessen, zerrissen**.

Other examples: **(hat) studiert, reflektiert, akzeptiert**. (Double prefixes (see para. 124) are exceptions.)

111 The past participle used to form tenses

The past participle is used to form such tenses as the perfect and the pluperfect. For example:

Er hat gefragt. Sie ist gegangen. Er hatte angerufen.
(See the notes on the various tenses.)

112 The past participle used as an adjective

When the past participle is used adjectivally, then it is declined like an adjective. (See paras. 161 et seq.) For example:

ein **erfahrener** Lehrer　　eine **ausgebildete** Lehrerin
an experienced teacher　*a trained teacher*
in **abgelaufenen** Schuhen herumgehen
to go around with worn out shoes
eine **eingebildete** Person
a conceited person

113 The past participle used as a noun

(**a**) A past participle used as a noun always begins with a capital letter.

Some of the past participles so used have been accepted into the language as nouns, and have almost lost their original verbal functions. For example: **der Beamte** (*the official, the civil servant*) or **der Abgeordnete** (*the member of the Bundestag, the delegate*).

(**b**) Past participles which are used as nouns retain the characteristics of the adjective, and must be declined like an adjective. (See paras. 161 ff.)

So, for example, the above two examples appear in the dictionary as follows:

Beamt-e(r), m. (-en, -en)
Abgeordnet-e(r), m. or f. (-en, -en)

These words are declined like adjectives. See para. 172.

(**c**) The past participle is used as a noun especially in abstract or neutral thinking:

Er ißt lieber Gebratenes als Gekochtes.
He prefers fried to boiled food.
Seine Auserwählte heißt Gerda.
His chosen one is called Gerda.
(This could imply that the speaker does not necessarily agree with 'his' choice.)

(**d**) the past participle may also be used to objectivize the feelings and the inner workings of the mind:

Das Gefürchtete traf ein.
That which was feared actually happened.
Er äußerte nie etwas Unüberlegtes.
He never uttered an unthinking word.
Die älteste Nachricht über die Erscheinungen des Auferstandenen liegt im ersten Korintherbrief des Apostels Paulus vor.
The oldest reference to the appearances of the Risen Christ appears in the Apostle Paul's First Letter to the Corinthians.

114 Further uses of the past participle

The past participle is also used to form participial phrases, which relate to a person, thing, or idea. The phrases give descriptive detail, and are usually separated by a comma or commas within the sentence. In detail:

(**a**) The participial phrase may describe the manner or way in which something is or was done:

Er saß still und regungslos, in Gedanken vertieft.
He sat still and motionless, deep in thought.

Abgeschlagen und erschöpft, gab der Langläufer auf.
Dejected and exhausted, the long-distance runner gave up.
Abgesehen von ein paar blauen Fleckchen, stieg er unverletzt aus dem völlig zertrümmerten Auto.
Apart from a few light bruises he climbed uninjured out of the completely demolished car.

(**b**) The participial phrase may describe a step in time:

Einmal gewarnt, wurde er vorsichtig.
Once having been warned, he became careful.

(**c**) A sequence may be expressed in concentrated form:

Gesagt, getan.
No sooner said than done.
Gedacht, getan.
No sooner said than done. (Literally '*No sooner thought of . . .*')

(**d**) The participial phrase has sometimes become a set phrase which is more revealing of the state of mind of the speaker or writer than of the topic on which he or she is speaking or writing. The remarks are often in parenthesis, and are usually indicated in writing by commas. For example:

Wir müssen, ganz allgemein gesprochen, so etwas erwarten.
We must, generally speaking, expect something like that.
Er ist, ehrlich gesagt, nicht immer in Topform.
He is, to tell the truth, not always in top form.
Sie ist, unter uns gesagt, nicht gerade die Schönste!
Between you and me she isn't exactly the most beautiful person.

(**e**) The following set phrases (and others) are in common use:

davon abgesehen (*apart from that*), offen gesagt, offen gestanden (*frankly speaking*), ehrlich gesagt (*to tell the truth*), im Grunde genommen (*basically*), streng genommen, genau genommen (*strictly speaking*), gut gemeint, aber . . . (*well meant, but . . .*), wie gesagt (*as stated, as has been said*), im großen und ganzen gesehen (*seen by and large*).

115 The present participle used as an adjective

The present participle, like the past participle, is a verbal adjective which retains some qualities of a verb and qualifies a noun.
The present participle can be used simply as an adjective:

steigende Preise
rising prices

laufende Kosten
current expenses

der abnehmende Mond   die aufgehende Sonne
the waning moon   *the rising sun*
aufregende Szenen   klingende Münzen
exciting scenes   *tinkling coins*
im laufenden Jahr   eine werdende Mutter
(during) this year   *an expectant mother*

116 The present participle used as a noun

If the present participle is used as a noun, it is nevertheless declined
like an adjective (see paras. 161 ff.), but begins with a capital letter.
For example:

Die Anwesenden gaben dem Plan ihre Zustimmung.
Those present gave their consent to the plan.
Er schickte einen Brief an alle Abwesenden.
He sent a letter to all those absent.
Der Leidende gab die Hoffnung nicht auf.
The person suffering did not give up hope.

117 Translating the English present participle phrase

An English present participle phrase, like 'looking sternly at him',
or 'resting his arms on the table', cannot be translated word for
word into German, as there is no similar sentence structure. There
are, however, several ways of translating such a participial phrase,
but by using a different sentence structure. These are illustrated by
the translation of the phrase '*Turning from his work*, he noticed her
standing in the doorway.'

Er wandte sich von seiner Arbeit ab, und sah sie im Türrahmen
stehen.
Als er sich von seiner Arbeit abwandte, sah er sie im Türrahmen
stehen.
Nachdem er sich von seiner Arbeit abgewandt hatte, sah er sie im
Türrahmen stehen.
Er sah sie, wie sie im Türrahmen stand, als er sich von seiner Arbeit
abwandte.
Er drehte sich um, und sah sie im Türeingang stehen.
Er drehte sich um, und sah die Frau, die im Türeingang stand.

The choice of translation is a matter of style.

The following conjunctions are useful in reconstructing such
sentences: **als**, **wenn**, **bevor**, **ehe**, **während**, **nachdem**, **da**, **weil**,
und. A relative clause might also be considered.

118 A participial structure peculiar to German

One particular participial structure in German is not to be found in
English, and sometimes causes problems in translation. The
structure is best explained by an example:

die aus der Schweiz eintreffende Gruppe   (1)
die   eintreffende Gruppe   (2)
die   Gruppe   (3)
the group arriving from Switzerland

(1) is the structure with a present participle,
(2) is the structure simplified to show that the participle is declined
  to agree with the noun, and
(3) is the simple structure of article and noun.

There is no limit to the number of structures which can be formed
in this way. Here are a few examples:

der am 2. Januar per Einschreiben abgeschickte Brief
the letter which was sent by registered post on the 2nd January
in meinem vorher erwähnten Brief
in my letter mentioned previously
mit allen ihm zur Verfügung stehenden Mitteln
with all the means available to him
durch einen aus Westfalen stammenden Vertreter
through a representative who comes from Westfalen

The construction with the relative clause is usually the most
satisfactory in English.

Compound verbs

119 Definitions

If a prefix is added to a simple verb the resulting word is a compound verb.

A separable verb is one in which the prefix can be separated from the verb in the present and past tenses.

An inseparable verb is one with a prefix which is never separated in the present and past tenses.

120 Separable verbs

Compound verbs with prefixes such as the following are separable:
ab-, an-, auf-, aus-, bei-, ein-, entgegen-, fort-, (gegen-), her-, herab-, heran-, herauf-, heraus-, herein-, herum-, hervor-, hin-, hinaus-, hinein-, hinunter-, hinzu-, mit-, nach-, vor-, weg-, zu-, zusammen-, (zwischen-).

Compound verbs formed by adding another verb, an adverb, an adjective, or a noun to the simple verb are also separable. That is to say, they are separated in the present and past tenses. For example:

Infinitive	*Past tense*		*Perfect tense* (showing participle)
		(but)	
sitzenbleiben	er blieb sitzen		er ist sitzengeblieben
festhalten	er hielt fest		er hat festgehalten
freilassen	er ließ ihn frei		er hat ihn freigelassen
teilnehmen	er nahm daran teil		er hat daran teilgenommen

121 Separable verbs and word order

A separable verb is only split up in the present and past tenses of a simple sentence (see para. 250), or a multiple sentence (see para. 261), or in the main clause of a complex sentence (see para. 265). The prefix is always placed at the very end of a simple sentence:

(**teilnehmen**):	Er **nahm** an der Diskussion **teil**.
(To take part):	*He took part in the discussion.*
(**fortfahren**):	Er **fuhr** in seiner Rede **fort**,
(**hinzufügen**):	und **fügte** ein paar weise Worte **hinzu**.
(to continue):	*He carried on with his speech,*
(to add to):	*and added a few words of wisdom.*

If the compound verb is used in a subordinate clause, then the verb is not split up in the present and past tenses:

Nachdem er mehrere Pfunde **abgenommen hatte**, fühlte er sich wie neugeboren.
When he took off a few pounds he felt as fit as a fiddle.
Sie lebt nach Diät, damit sie mehrere Pfunde **abnimmt**.
She is following a diet so that she takes off a few pounds.
The stress falls on the prefix of separable verbs. Thus: **'teilnehmen**, **'fortfahren**, **hin'zufügen**, **'abnehmen**, **'weitermachen**.

122 Inseparable verbs

The unstressed prefixes **be-**, **emp-**, **ent-**, **er-**, **ge-**, **ver-**, and **zer-** help to form inseparable compound verbs. The two parts, prefix and simple verb, are never separated under any circumstances.

Der Politiker beendete seine Rede mit einem Appell an die Jugend.
The politician ended his speech with an appeal to young people.
Der große Erdbagger zermahlte die Ziegelsteine.
The large bulldozer crushed the bricks to pieces.

123 Verbs which may be separable or inseparable

Certain verbs which have the prefixes: **durch-**, **(miß-)**, **über-**, **um-**, and **(unter-)**, may be either separable or inseparable, according to the meaning. If the stress occurs on the prefix, then the verb is separable, but if the stress is on the basic verb, then the compound verb is inseparable. Not every verb which has one of the above prefixes has both forms. Dictionaries indicate the forms by sep. (separable), insep. (inseparable), and sep. & insep. (separable and inseparable).

The following examples concern only those verbs which may be both separable and inseparable, according to stress and meaning:

'durchfahren, sep.:	Sie fuhren bloß durch.
(to go, pass through)	*They were only passing through.*
durch'fahren, insep.:	Sie durchfuhren die Lüneburger Heide.
(to traverse, go across)	*They drove across the Lüneburg Heath.*
'überlaufen, sep.:	Die Augen laufen ihr über.
(to run or flow over)	*The tears are running down her cheeks.*
über'laufen, insep.:	Es überläuft mich kalt, wenn ich daran denke.
(to overrun, run down)	*I shudder when I think of it.*
'umgehen, sep.:	Sie geht gerne mit schönen Dingen um.
(to have to do with)	*She likes nice things.*
um'gehen, insep.:	Sie umgingen das Gesetz.
(to get around, evade)	*They evaded the law.*

Verbs with the prefixes **miß–** and **unter–** are almost entirely either separable or inseparable, but not both. The same applies to many verbs with the prefixes **durch–**, **über–**, and **um–**.

124 Double prefixes

Double prefixes occur in German, such as:

herab–, heran–, herauf–, heraus–, herum–, hervor–, hinab–, hinauf–, hinaus–, hinein–, hinüber–, hinunter–, usw.

The negative prefix **un–** is often added to a particular form of a compound verb, such as the past participle, and only the one form is in common use. For example:

unangefochten *(undisputed)*, unangemessen *(unsuited)*, unbeachtet *(unnoticed)*, unbearbeitet *(in the raw state)*, unbefangen *(unprejudiced)*, unbegabt *(not gifted or clever)*, unbekannt *(unknown)*, unentschlossen *(undecided)*, unerfahren *(inexperienced)*, ununterbrochen *(uninterrupted)*, unverhofft *(unexpected)*.

The above forms are almost exclusively used as adjectives or adverbs.

125 Unusual prefixes to verbs

The term 'unusual' prefix is given to a type of prefix which can be thought up by any user of the German language, but which is unlikely to find any permanent place in a dictionary. For example:

das Ewig-Hin-und-Hergehen
the eternal going to and fro
das Auf-der-Straße-Stehen-und-Mädchen-Anstarren
the standing on the street and gaping at girls

The first word of the compound has a capital letter, as well as any noun, and also the infinitives used as nouns. The examples show the somewhat '**volkstümliche**' nature of these expressions.

There are, however, a number of such expressions – usually shorter – which have found a permanent place in the language, such as:

das Weiterkommen, das Weiterleiten, das Weitergeben, das Weiterbestehen, das Eislaufen, das Radfahren, das Maßhalten, das Maßregeln, das Wohlbefinden, das Wohlgefallen, das Wohltun, das Wohlwollen, das Wegschicken, das Wegwerfen, das Wegfallen, das Wegkommen, das Unwohlsein, das Leichtmachen, usw.

The forms which are given are the infinitives used as nouns. These are, in fact, declined like adjectives. The words may also be used in a verbal function. It is only the infinitives themselves, or the past participles, which are in common use.

Gender of nouns

126 Grammatical gender

There are three genders in German, masculine, feminine, and neuter. The gender of a German noun is a grammatical gender. Males are usually masculine, and females feminine, but there are exceptions, however, such as **das Mädchen**, **das Fräulein**, and **das Kind** which are all neuter. The gender of a noun is sometimes determined by its ending. All general statements about gender have to be qualified by calling attention to the exceptions.

127 Persons, animals, things, and abstract ideas

Male persons and animals are usually masculine, and female persons and animals are usually feminine. For example:

der Mann	die Frau	der Bulle	die Kuh
der Arzt	die Ärztin	der Gänserich	die Gans
der Sohn	die Tochter	der Kater	die Katze

There are some common exceptions. The endings **-chen** and **-lein** (diminutives) make any noun a neuter noun. For example: **das Mädchen** (the girl), **das Fräulein** (the young lady), **Männlein und Weiblein** (man, woman and child). Other exceptions are words such as **das Kind** (the child) and **das Mädel** (the girl). Young animals are also sometimes neuter, such as **das Lamm** (the lamb), **das Kalb** (the calf), **das Ferkel** (the piglet), **das Küken** (the chick). Note also: **das Pferd** (the horse).

There are no general rules which cover the genders of things and abstract ideas, but observations which cover certain groups of things, and also certain endings, may be helpful in the learning of genders. These are included in the following sections.

128 Masculine nouns

The following nouns are masculine:

(**a**) Male persons such as: **der Mann**, **der Vater**, **der Onkel**, **der Neffe** (the nephew), **der Schauspieler** (the actor), **der Professor**.

(**b**) Male animals such as: **der Bulle** (the bull), **der Kater** (the tomcat), **der Löwe** (the lion), **der Fuchs** (the fox). Note, however, **das Pferd** (the horse) and **das Nilpferd** (the hippopotamus). Note also that the young animals listed in paragraph 127 are neuter. Certain animals like **der Elefant** are grammatically masculine, and so the female is referred to as **die Elefantenkuh**, while the male is called **der Elefantenbulle**.

(**c**) Days of the week, months, and seasons. For example:
der Montag, **der Mittwoch**, **der Sonnabend**, **der Sonntag**, **der Januar**, **der März**, **der Juni**, **der August**, **der Dezember**, **der Frühling**, **der Sommer**, **der Herbst**, **der Winter**.
Note, however, **das Jahr** and **die Woche**.

(**d**) Points of the compass, such as: **der Norden**, **der Osten**, **der Süden**, **der Westen**, **der Nordost(en)**, **der Südwest(en)**, **der Nordnordwest(en)**, **der Ostnordost(en)**, usw.

(**e**) Weather features, such as: **der Wind**, **der Regen**, **der Schnee**, **der Frost**, **der Nebel** (the mist or fog), **der Taifun** (the typhoon), **der Monsun** (the monsoon), **der Föhn** (the warm wind), **der Hagel** (the hail), **der Reif** (the hoar-frost), **der Tau** (the dew).

(**f**) Types of rocks and soils, such as: **der Sand, der Granit**, **der Basalt**, **der Schiefer** (slate or schist), **der Kalkstein** (limestone), **der Lehm** (loam, clay), **der Boden** (soil), **der Sumpf** (the swamp). Note, however, **die Kreide** (chalk), **die Marsch** (alluvial soil, marsh, fen), **das Land** (land, soil), **das Ackerland** (arable soil).

(**g**) Nouns ending in **-ig**, **-ling**, **-ich**, **-s**, **-en** and **-er**:
der König (the king), **der Pfennig**, **der Honig** (honey), **der Lehrling** (the apprentice), **der Zwilling** (the twin), **der Teppich** (the carpet), **der Knirps** (the dwarf, little fellow), **der Schnaps** (spirits), **der Schwips** (the fuddled state after drink), **der Garten**, **der Boden** (the ground or soil), **der Fußballer, der Läufer** (the runner), **der Schwimmer**, **der Gauner** (the rogue).

(**h**) Foreign nouns ending in **-and**, **-ant**, **-är**, **-ast**, **-eur**, **-ent**, **-ier**, **-iker**, **-ismus**, **-ist**, and **-or**:
der Doktorand (candidate for a doctor's degree), **der Kommandant** (the commandant), **der Fabrikant** (the manufacturer), **der Legionär** (the legionary), **der Reaktionär** (the reactionary), **der Cineast** (the film-fan), **der Palast** (the palace), **der Friseur** (hair-stylist, hairdresser), **der Amateur, der Student**, **der Abiturient** (candidate for the Abitur), **der Bankier** (the banker), **der Croupier, der Offizier, der Techniker** (the technician), **der Konservatismus, der Kommunismus, der Sozialismus, der Liberalismus, der Sozialist, der Moderator** (the TV or radio moderator), **der Organisator** (the organizer).

129 Feminine nouns

The following nouns are feminine:

(a) Female persons such as: **die Frau**, **die Mutter**, **die Schwester**, **die Tante**, **die Nichte** (the niece), **die Schauspielerin** (the actress), **die Professorin**.

(b) Female animals such as: **die Kuh**, **die Katze**, **die Löwin** (the lioness), **die Wölfin** (the she-wolf), **die Sau** (the sow).

(c) Names of flowers: **die Rose, die Lilie** (the lily), **die Tulpe** (the tulip), **die Narzisse** (narcissus), **die gelbe Narzisse** (the daffodil), **die Primel** (the primrose).
Note: **das Vergißmeinnicht** (the forget-me-not), **das Veilchen** (the violet), **das Maiglöckchen** (the lily of the valley).

(d) Names of trees: **die Eiche** (the oak), **die Esche** (the ash), **die Birke** (the birch-tree), **die Buche** (the beech-tree), **die Weide** (the willow), **die Ulme** (the elm), **die Erle** (the alder).
Note also: **die Stechpalme** (holly), **die Mistel** (mistletoe), and **der Ahorn** (the maple).

(e) Specific whole numbers: **die Eins**, **die Zwei**, **die Neunundzwanzig**, **die Hunderteins**, **die Million**. (Numbers are normally numeral adjectives.) Note however: **das Hundert**, **das Tausend**.

(f) Nouns ending in **-ei**, **-heit**, **-keit**, **-schaft**, **-ung**, and also **-in**: **die Brauerei** (the brewery), **die Schlägerei** (the brawl, free-for-all), **die Bücherei** (the library), **die Einheit** (unity or the unit), **die Eitelkeit** (vanity, conceit), **die Gelegenheit** (the opportunity), **die Fähigkeit** (the ability), **die Gesellschaft** (society, company), **die Freundschaft** (friendship), **die Hoffnung** (hope), **die Erwartung** (the expectation). Also **die Freundin** (the girl-friend), **die Engländerin**, **die Schottin**, **die Waliserin**, **die Irin**.

(g) Foreign nouns ending in **-a**, **-ade**, **-age**, **-ance**, **-anz**, **-elle**, **-ette**, **-euse**, **-ie**, **-enz**, **-ik**, **-ine**, **-ion**, **-tät**, **-itis**, **-ose**, **-sis**, **-ur**, **-üre**:

Die Kamera, **die Marmelade** (the jam), **die Limonade**, **die Schokolade**, **die Garage**, **die Renaissance**, **die Toleranz**, **die Arroganz**, **die Bagatelle** (trifle, negligible amount), **die Toilette** (the toilet), **die Dompteuse** (female wild animal tamer), **die Philosophie**, **die Geographie**, **die Anthropologie**, **die Tendenz** (the tendency), **die Existenz** (the existence), **die Logik** (logic), **die Mathematik** (mathematics), **die Kusine** (the cousin), **die Margarine**, **die Reformation**, **die Universität** and the abbreviated form **die Uni** (the university), **die Realität** (reality), **die Bronchitis**, **die Arthritis**, **die Neurose** (the neurosis), **die Basis**, **die Natur**, **die Kultur**, **die Lektüre** (the reading matter).

130 Neuter nouns

The following nouns are neuter:

(**a**) Nouns with the endings **–chen**, **–lein**, and **–el** (regional): **das Mädchen**, **das Fräulein**, **das Mädel** (the girl) (regional and colloquial), **das Päckchen** (the packet, small parcel), **das Köfferchen** (the small suitcase), **das Nickerchen** (quick, short snooze), **das Brüderchen** (the little brother), **das Schwesterchen** (the little sister). Many of the diminutives, such as the last four, are used mainly in colloquial speech. For example, the translation of the words 'the little sister' is more likely to be **die kleine Schwester** or **die jüngere Schwester** than **Schwesterchen**.

(**b**) Nouns expressing a fraction:

das Drittel, **das Viertel**, **das Zwanzigstel**. N.B. **die Hälfte** (half).

(**c**) Infinitives used as nouns:

das Gehen, **das Schwimmen**, **das Denken**, **das Nichtstun**.

(**d**) Other parts of speech used as nouns:

das Geschriebene (the written material), **das Gesprochene** (spoken material), **das Erwünschte** (that which is desired), **das Unangenehme** (that which is unpleasant), **das Pro und Kontra** (the for and against), **das A und das O** (the first and the last, the beginning and the end), **das vertraute Du** (the confidential or confiding **du**), **das endgültige Nein** (the final no).

(**e**) Collective nouns beginning with the prefix **Ge–**:

das Gebirge (the mountain range), **das Gebüsch** (the undergrowth, bushes), **das Getreide** (grain, cereals), **das Geflügel** (poultry), **das Gelände** (the tract of country), **das Gespräch** (the conversation).

(**f**) Metals:

das Eisen, **das Zink**, **das Zinn**, **das Uran** (uranium), **das Gold**, **das Silber**, **das Platin** (platinum), **das Kupfer** (copper). N.B. **der Stahl** (steel, which is a metal alloy).

(**g**) Many chemical elements and compounds:

das Helium, **das Chlor**, **das Natrium** (sodium), **das Natriumhydrat** (caustic soda), **das Natriumnitrat** (sodium

nitrate), **das Natriumsulfat** (sodium sulphate), **das Sulfat** (the sulphate), **das Sulfid** (the sulphide), **das Kohlenoxyd** (carbon monoxide), **das Kohlendioxyd** (carbon dioxide).
Note: **der Stoff** (matter, stuff) is masculine and **die Säure** (the acid) is feminine, so compound words like **der Sauerstoff** (oxygen), **der Wasserstoff** (hydrogen), **der Stickstoff** (nitrogen), **der Kohlenstoff** (carbon), **die Kohlensäure** (carbonic acid), **die Salzsäure** or **der Chlorwasserstoff** (hydrochloric acid), **die Schwefelsäure** (sulphuric acid) take the gender of **Stoff** and **Säure**. Note also: **der Schwefel** (sulphur).

(**h**) Foreign nouns ending in **-ett, -ium, -ma, -ment, -um**:
das Ballett, das Quintett, das Stadium, das Studium (study, or attendance at a university), **das Komma, das Klima** (the climate), **das Thema** (the theme or topic), **das Dokument, das Experiment, das Apartment** (the apartment), **das Datum** (the date).

(**i**) The names of certain young animals, such as:
das Lamm (the lamb), **das Kalb** (the calf), **das Ferkel** (the piglet), **das Küken** (the chick), **das Fohlen** (the foal).

(**j**) Measurements of weight:
das Gramm, das Kilogramm

The German words **Hektar** (about 2.5 acres), **Meter** and **Liter**, and all the compounds like **Kilometer** and **Kubikliter** are both masculine and neuter. The choice of gender is personal and sometimes regional, so that no clear statement is possible. Both are customary. (See para. 136 (b).)

131 Names of particular persons

Persons who are known to the speaker or writer are given their natural gender. For example: **der Michael, der kleine Hans, die Liselotte, die junge Sabine.**

Sometimes the diminutive endings **-chen** and **-lein** are added to a name, mostly affectionately. In that case the grammatical neuter must be used: **das kleine Karlchen, das kleine Mariechen.** A letter might be signed **Dein Kätchen** (your (very own) Kate or Cathy).

132 Names of particular countries, regions, and places

General statements about the names of countries, regions, mountains, rivers, and places always have to be modified by referring to the exceptions. General observations and statements are helpful, though, as an aid in daily conversations, when reference books are seldom immediately available. The following notes should be read with this point in mind.

(**a**) Continents

Afrika, **Amerika**, **Asien**, **Australien**, and **Europa** are almost always written without reference to any grammatical gender. Expressions like **in Afrika**, **aus Australien**, **von Asien**, are common, as well as phrases like **die Olländer Asiens** (the oil countries of Asia), and **die Entwicklungsländer Afrikas** (the developing countries of Africa). An **s** is added to the words **Asien** and **Afrika** in the above phrases. Although no gender is normally given for continents, students are advised to consider continents as neuter, although the noun (**der Kontinent**) is masculine.

(**b**) Countries

Countries are usually neuter, although the use of the gender is mostly avoided. Examples: **(das) England**, **Schottland**, **Wales**, **Nordirland**, **Eire**, **Frankreich**, **Belgien**, **Luxemburg**, **Deutschland**, **Österreich**.

Note: **die Bundesrepublik Deutschland**, **die Schweiz**, **die Niederlande**, **die Vereinigten Staaten**, **die UdSSR (die Sowjetunion)**, **die Tschechoslowakei**, **die Türkei**, **der Iran**, **der Irak**, **der Sudan**.

(**c**) Regions

Regions are also sometimes neuter. Examples: **(das) Sauerland**, **Münsterland**, **Schleswig-Holstein**, **Nordrhein-Westfalen**, **Ostwestfalen**, **Hessen**, **Baden-Württemberg**.

There are exceptions such as: **der Harz**, **der Taunus**, **der Hunsrück**, **die Lüneburger Heide**, **die Eifel**, **die Rhön**, **die Normandie**, **die Bretagne**, **die Riviera**, **die Sahara**, **die Antarktis**, **die Pfalz**.

(**d**) Places

Places are usually neuter. Examples: **(das) alte London**, **Münster**, **Hildesheim**, **Nördlingen**, **Salzburg**.

(**e**) Rivers

Rivers are generally feminine. For example: **die Elbe**, **die Weser**, **die Donau**, **die Saar**, **die Themse** (the Thames), **die Ems**, **die Ruhr**, **die Mosel**, **die Rhone**, **die Seine**, **die Loire**.
The big rivers in Africa, Asia, and America are, however, masculine. For example: **der Kongo**, **der Niger**, **der Nil**, **der**

Sambesi, **der Ganges**, **der Indus**, **der Mississippi**, **der Missouri**.
In Europe a few rivers are masculine, such as: **der Rhein**, **der Main**, **der Neckar**, **der Inn**, **der Lech**.

(**f**) Mountains and mountain ranges

Mountains are generally masculine, but mountain ranges are often in the plural, so that the question of gender is not grammatically important. Example: (**der**) **Montblanc**, **Monte Rosa**, **Mount Everest**, **Eiger**, **Piz Palü**, **Kilimandscharo**. If the name of a mountain is a compound noun, then the gender of the noun is that of the last word. For example: **das Horn** and **die Spitze** lead to names like **das Matterhorn** and **die Zugspitze**.
Mountain ranges (**das Gebirge** = the mountain range) either end in **-gebirge**, in which case they are neuter, or are in the plural. Examples: **das Rothaargebirge**, **das Erzgebirge**, but **die Alpen**, **die Anden**, **die Rocky Mountains**, **die Pennines**, **die Cairngorms**, **die Karpaten** (the Carpathians), **die Vogesen** (the Vosges).
Note: **der Jura**, **der Fränkische Jura**, **der Schwäbische Jura**, **der Ural**.

133 Names of things

(**a**) Ships

Ships are feminine. For example: **die Bismarck**, **die Graf Spee**, **die Scharnhorst**, **die Gneisenau**. There are occasional exceptions such as **der Fliegende Holländer**.

(**b**) Cars

Cars are masculine. For example: **der VW** (Volkswagen), **der Mercedes**, **der Ford**, **der Porsche**, **der BMW** (Bayerische Motorenwerke AG).

(**c**) Aircraft and aircraft types

Aircraft are feminine. For example: **die Boeing**, **die Concorde**, **die Messerschmitt 109**, **die Heinkel 111**, **die Focke-Wulf**.
The aircraft types are masculine, and usually depend on the gender of the last section of a compound noun, such as: **der Airbus**, **der Starfighter**, **der Düsenjäger**, **der Hawker Harrier**, **der Senkrechtstarter** (vertical take-off plane), **der Hubschrauber** (the helicopter), **der Jäger** (the fighter), **der Jagdbomber** (the fighter-bomber).
Airlines are usually feminine. For example: **die Lufthansa**, **die Swissair**, **die Air France**, **die British Airways**.

134 Gender of compound words

The gender of a compound word is always that of the last word or section. For example:

die Stätte	die Auto bahn rast stätte
das Kreuz	das Auto bahn kreuz
der Gang	der Bahn über gang
das Schiff	das Flug zeug mutter schiff
die Kräfte (pl.)	die Unter wasser streit kräfte

135 Gender of abbreviations

The gender of an abbreviation is usually the gender of the last word. For example:

die EG (die Europäische Gemeinschaft), der WDR (der Westdeutsche Rundfunk), das ZDF (das Zweite Deutsche Fernsehen), die CDU (die Christlich-Demokratische Union), die CSU (die Christlich-Soziale Union), die FDP (die Freie Demokratische Partei), der DGB (der Deutsche Gewerkschaftsbund).

Note: die SPD (die Sozialdemokratische Partei Deutschlands), die ARD (die Arbeitsgemeinschaft der öffentlich-rechtlichen Rundfunkanstalten der Bundesrepublik Deutschland), die BBC. The words Partei, Arbeitsgemeinschaft, Corporation are feminine.

136 Nouns with two genders

There are a number of nouns which have two genders according to meaning, and there are also a number of nouns which have more than one gender. The reasons for the latter may be regional, etymological, or even personal.

(a) The nouns which vary in gender according to meaning are often two words of identical spelling, but with different word histories. Typical examples are:

der Band (volume (book))	das Band (ribbon, tape; bond)
der Bund (league, confederation)	das Schlüsselbund (bunch of keys)
der Flur (entrance hall)	die Flur (pasture or common land)
der Gehalt (contents, capacity)	das Gehalt (salary, wages)
der Kunde (customer, client)	die Kunde (information, tidings)
der Moment (moment, instant)	das Moment (impetus, motive, impulse)
der See (lake)	die See (sea, ocean)
die Steuer (tax, duty)	das Steuer (steering-wheel, rudder)

der Verdienst (gain, profit,   **das Verdienst** (deserts, merit)
  earnings)
der Weise (wise man)   **die Weise** (manner, way)

(**b**) There are nouns which vary in gender, without changing their
meaning. The decision on the gender may be a matter of regional
choice, or it may depend on the whim of the speaker. The student is
therefore left with a free choice, even though he may meet
individual resistance to his choice. Typical examples are:

der Keks/das Keks (biscuit)
der Bonbon/das Bonbon (sweet)
der Radar/das Radar (radar)
der Gummi/das Gummi (rubber)
but **der (Radier) gummi** (eraser)
der Pyjama/das Pyjama (pyjamas)
der Liter/das Liter (litre)
der Meter/das Meter (metre)
der Kilometer/das Kilometer
der Meteor/das Meteor (meteor)
der Dschungel/die Dschungel/das Dschungel (jungle)

The fact that the masculine gender is used first in the above
examples does not mean that this is the gender most widely used.
The regional variations are often the differences between German
and Swiss or Austrian usages. It can be seen from the above list that
the words are invariably of foreign origin.

The articles

137 Definitions

The definite article is used with specific reference to a particular noun, which is either masculine, feminine, or neuter. For example: **der Mann**, **die Maschine**, **das Recht**.

The indefinite article is used without any specific reference (but with generic reference) to a noun. For example: **ein Wagen**, **eine Frau**, **ein Buch**.

Both definite and indefinite articles are declined into four cases: nominative, accusative, genitive, and dative. A case is the form of the word which shows the function of the noun in a sentence.

The subject is always nominative.
The complement after the verbs **sein** and **werden** is nominative.
The direct object is always accusative.
Belonging to, or possession is shown by the genitive.
The indirect object is dative.

138 The forms of the definite and indefinite articles

The form of the definite or indefinite article depends on three factors: gender, singular or plural, and case. An article always agrees in gender, number, and case with the noun.

The definite article is declined as follows:

singular

	masculine	*feminine*	*neuter*
nom.	der Mann	die Frau	das Buch
acc.	den Mann	die Frau	das Buch
gen.	des Mannes	der Frau	des Buch(e)s
dat.	dem Mann	der Frau	dem Buch

plural

	masculine	*feminine*	*neuter*
nom.	die Männer,	Frauen,	Bücher
acc.	die Männer,	Frauen,	Bücher
gen.	der Männer,	Frauen,	Bücher
dat.	den Männern,	Frauen,	Büchern

The indefinite article is declined as follows:

singular

	masculine	feminine	neuter
nom.	ein Mann	eine Frau	ein Buch
acc.	einen Mann	eine Frau	ein Buch
gen.	eines Mannes	einer Frau	eines Buch(e)s
dat.	einem Mann	einer Frau	einem Buch

plural

	masculine	feminine	neuter
nom.	Männer,	Frauen,	Bücher
acc.	Männer,	Frauen,	Bücher
gen.	Männer,	Frauen,	Bücher
dat.	Männern,	Frauen,	Büchern

The definite article is the same for masculine, feminine, and neuter in the plural. There is no form of the indefinite article in the plural.

The articles are:

	singular			plural
	masculine	feminine	neuter	m. f. n.
nom.	der	die	das	die
acc.	den	die	das	die
gen.	des	der	des	der
dat.	dem	der	dem	den

	singular			plural	
	masculine	feminine	neuter	m. f. n.	
nom.	ein	eine	ein	–	(keine, meine,
acc.	einen	eine	ein	–	seine, etc. in
gen.	eines	einer	eines	–	plural – see paras.
dat.	einem	einer	einem	–	164/165)

139 Agreement of article and noun

The article always agrees with the noun in:

(a) Gender   (masculine, feminine, or neuter)
(b) Number (singular or plural)
(c) Case   (nominative, accusative, genitive, dative).

The form of the article shows the function of the noun in the clause or sentence.

140 Premodifying adjectives and articles

Certain adjectives like **dieser** and **jeder** are declined like **der**, and
have the same function as the definite article in premodifying the
noun. That is to say, they come before the noun and show the case,
thereby showing the function of the noun in the sentence. Similarly
there are adjectives like **kein** and **irgendein** which are declined like
ein, and also have the same function.

141 Article or no article?

The following notes are mainly concerned with the occasions on
which no article is used. German and English are related languages,
especially grammatically, and the use or non-use of an article is
mostly the same under similar circumstances.

There is no article:

(**a**) In the indefinite generic plural (which shows the type or kind of
thing): **Bücher**, **Stühle**, **Gläser**.

(**b**) In expressions such as: **eine Tasse Tee** (a cup of tea), **ein Glas
Bier** (a glass of beer), **ein Glas guten Weins** (a glass of good wine),
eine Einrichtung guten Geschmacks (furnishings in good taste).

(**c**) Before the names of the continents: **Sie kommt aus Asien**,
Afrika, **Südamerika**.

(**d**) Before the names of countries: **Österreich und Italien
unterzeichneten ein Handelsabkommen**. (Austria and Italy
signed a trade agreement.)
Note, however, that countries with the feminine article are referred
to as follows: **Die Bundesrepublik Deutschland und die Schweiz
unterzeichneten ein Handelsabkommen**. (The Federal Republic
of Germany and Switzerland signed a trade agreement.)

(**e**) Before the **Bundesländer**, and towns: **Soest in Westfalen war
früher eine Hansestadt**. (Soest in Westfalia was formerly a Hansa
town.)

(**f**) Before the names of particular buildings or places: **Schloß
Neuschwanstein; er wohnt Flensburger Straße 4**; **er wartete
auf Bahnsteig 2**.

(**g**) Before the names of specific persons: **Frau Brüggemann**,
Luise, **Markus**, **Wilhelm I**, **Vater**, **Mutter**, **Mutti**.
Note however: **die Brüggemeiers**, **Karl der Große**, **die kleine
Lotti**, **der Vater meines Freundes**.

(**h**) Before the names of specific religious festivals: **Weihnachten**, **Ostern**, **Pfingsten**.

(**i**) In a good number of fixed expressions which usually have a long traditional use: **an Bord** (on board), **bei Tageslicht** (in daylight), **nach Hause**, **auf Erden** (on earth), **mit Kind und Kegel** (with bag and baggage), **Fortschritte machen** (to progress), **Nachrichten hören** (to hear the news), **aus Eifersucht** (through/out of jealousy), **mit Absicht** (deliberately), **ohne Rücksicht** (regardless), **in aller Eile** (in haste, in a hurry).

142 Abbreviated forms of the article

Abbreviations of the article are used when certain prepositions are immediately followed by the article. The following abbreviations are in common use both in speech and in writing: **am (an dem)**, **ans (an das)**, **beim (bei dem)**, **im (in dem)**, **ins (in das)**, **vom (von dem)**, **zum (zu dem)**, and **zur (zu der)**.

The following abbreviations are most likely to occur in colloquial speech: **aufs (auf das)**, **durchs (durch das)**, **fürs (für das)**, **hinterm (hinter dem)**, **überm (über dem)**, **ums (um das)**, **unterm (unter dem)**, **vorm (vor dem)**. Students are advised to use words in the latter list sparingly.

The singular and plural of nouns

143 Agreement of noun and verb

The noun and the verb always agree in number; that is to say that if the noun is singular the verb is singular, and if the noun is plural then the verb is plural.

Confusion may arise in the case of collective nouns, as it is possible in English to say 'The team is going', and also 'The team are going', depending on whether the speaker or writer is thinking of one team or perhaps eleven or fifteen players. This is not possible in German. Since **die Mannschaft** (the team) is singular the verb must also be singular. Thus: **die Mannschaft geht** ... There is, of course, a plural of the word **Mannschaft**, but this refers to more than one team. Thus: **die Mannschaften gehen** ...

144 Feminine nouns – plural forms

(**a**) Almost all feminine nouns form the plural by adding **-n** or **-en** to the singular:

die Blume → die Blumen	die Frau → die Frauen
die Katze → die Katzen	die Person → die Personen
die Lampe → die Lampen	

die Glühbirne (light bulb) → **die Glühbirnen** (N.B. **die Birne** is often used as a short form of **die Glühbirne**.)

(**b**) Feminine words with the ending **-in** double the **n** before adding **-en**:

die Sängerin → die Sängerinnen
die Ärztin → die Ärztinnen
die Freundin → die Freundinnen
die Lehrerin → die Lehrerinnen

(**c**) A few feminine nouns with **a** in the stem change the **a** to **ä**, and add only **-e** in the plural:

die Hand → die Hände   die Kraft (strength) → die Kräfte
die Streitkräfte (pl.) (the armed forces)

(**d**) There are very few exceptions to the above observations among the feminine nouns in common use. Note, however:

die Mutter → die Mütter   die Tochter → die Töchter

145 Masculine nouns – plural forms

There are several forms of the plural endings of masculine nouns, but there is no way of knowing the correct ending in the plural from the singular form. The nearest things to general rules are in (a) and (b) below. A good dictionary gives not only the gender but also the genitive singular and the plural of every noun.

The following observations, however, are worth noting:

(a) Masculine nouns ending in **-en**, **-el**, **-er** remain the same in the plural. There may be an umlaut in the plural form. For example:

der Lehrer	→ die Lehrer
der Schwimmer	→ die Schwimmer
der Wagen	→ die Wagen
der Bügel (coat-hanger)	→ die Bügel
der Nagel (nail)	→ die Nägel
der Garten	→ die Gärten

(b) Masculine nouns which are formed from adjectives, and which, in fact, are declined like adjectives, end in **-n** in the plural, but only if they follow a premodifying adjective like **dieser**, **jener**, **jeder**, or **der**.
For example:

der Abgeordnete (member of Bundestag)	→ die Abgeordneten
dieser Beamte (official)	→ diese Beamten
der Vorsitzende (chairman)	→ die Vorsitzenden

(c) Some other masculine nouns also end in **-n** or **-en**, such as:

der Präsident	→ die Präsidenten
der Mensch	→ die Menschen
der Nachbar (neighbour)	→ die Nachbarn
der Fremde (foreigner)	→ die Fremden
der Assistent	→ die Assistenten
der Staat	→ die Staaten

(d) Some masculine nouns – often of one syllable – add an **-e** in the plural, and some of these have an umlaut in the plural form. Examples are:

der Tisch → die Tische		der Stuhl	→ die Stühle
der Fisch → die Fische		der Storch (stork) → die Störche	

(e) A few masculine nouns add **-er** in the plural, usually with an umlaut, such as:

der Mann → die Männer		der Wald → die Wälder

(**f**) Some masculine words of foreign origin add an **-s** in the plural, such as:

der Jet	→ **die Jets**	**der Jumbo**	→ **die Jumbos**
der Bikini	→ **die Bikinis**	**der Jeep**	→ **die Jeeps**
der Laser	→ **die Lasers**	**der Bob**	→ **die Bobs**

(**g**) In colloquial speech a family might be referred to as: **der Brinkmann**, **die Brinkmann**, **der Brinkmann Sohn**, or **die Brinkmanns**.

This could either mean that the speaker knows the family well, or that he puts on a superior air when he refers to the members in this way.

146 Neuter nouns – plural forms

As with the masculine nouns, there is no way of judging the correct ending in the plural from the singular form. A good dictionary gives the details of every noun.

The following observations, however, are worth noting:

(**a**) A few neuter nouns end in **-er**, **-el**, and **-en**, and do not change their form in the plural. For example:

das Messer → **die Messer**	**das Übel** (evil)	→ **die Übel**
das Fenster → **die Fenster**	**das Siegel** (seal)	→ **die Siegel**
das Wesen (being, creature; substance)	→ **die Wesen**	

Note however: **die Regel** (rule) → **die Regeln**

(**b**) There are very few neuter nouns which add **-n** or **-en** in the plural:

das Ohr → **die Ohren**   **das Ende** → **die Enden**

(**c**) Many neuter nouns add **-e** in the plural:

das Tor (gateway)	→ **die Tore**
das Paar (pair)	→ **die Paare**
das Maß (measure)	→ **die Maße**
das Stück (piece)	→ **die Stücke**
das Symbol	→ **die Symbole**
das Netz (net)	→ **die Netze**

(**d**) Some neuter nouns add **-er** in the plural, and some of these also take an umlaut:

das Buch	→ **die Bücher**
das Dach (roof)	→ **die Dächer**
das Bild (picture)	→ **die Bilder**
das Tal (valley)	→ **die Täler**

(**e**) A few nouns, particularly those of foreign origin, add **-s** in the plural:

das Radio → **die Radios**   **das Hotel**   → **die Hotels**
das Team → **die Teams**   **das Restaurant** → **die Restaurants**

147 Plurals of weights, measures, and distances

(**a**) When weights, measures, and distances are combined with a number (2 or above), then the singular form of the noun is used for the plural. See, however, para 147 (**d**). For example:

250 Gramm Butter (250 g)   **5 Kilo Kartoffeln** (5 kg)
2 Pfund Äpfel (2 Pfd.)   **2 Zentner Kartoffeln** (2 Ztr.)
2 Liter Bier (2 l)   **3 Meter lang, 2 Meter breit** (3/2 m)
der 42,2 Kilometer Marathonlauf (42,2 km)
20 Grad Kälte ($-20°$C)   **35 Grad Hitze** (35°C)

(**b**) In colloquial speech, if only the number and the name of the item are important, then the singular form of the item is often used in the plural. If, for example, one of a group of friends orders drinks, he or she might say: **4 Glas Bier, 4 Weißwein, 2 Kaffee, und 2 Tee, bitte.** In a shop a woman might purchase: **2 Paar Strümpfe** (stockings) or **zwei Paar Handschuhe** (two pairs of gloves). The noun **Paar** is the singular form, but **Strümpfe** and **Handschuhe** are obviously plural, as they are always sold in 'pairs' (plural).

(**c**) The singular form of certain nouns involving weights and measures is never used instead of the plural. For example: **die Dose** (tin), **die Flasche** (bottle), **die Tasse** (cup), **die Tonne** (ton), but **2 Dosen Milch, 2 Flaschen Wein, 2 Tassen Kaffee, 2 Tonnen Weizen** (wheat).

(**d**) If things are regarded item by item, then the plural is used, even if the number is specified. For example:

Er betrachtete mit Interesse die fünf alten römischen Gläser.
He looked with interest at the five old Roman glasses.
Sie aß vier große Stücke von der Sahnetorte.
She ate four large pieces of the cream cake.

Sections (**a**) and (**d**) above should be compared carefully.

148 Plurals of money units

(**a**) The use of the singular form for the plural is common, but only with reference to certain currencies, coins, or notes. For example:
ein 10-Pfennig-Stück (Germany)

ein 20–Mark–Schein (note) (Germany)
ein 10–Centime–Stück (Belgium, Luxemburg, France)
100 Schilling (Austria), **100 Franken** (Switzerland)

Note however: **100 dänische, isländische, norwegische,
schwedische Kronen (die Krone), 1000 Lire (die Lira), 100
Peseten (die Peseta).**

(**b**) The following examples should be compared the one with the
other, as they show two ways of expressing pounds sterling and
dollars:

ein 5–Pfund–Schein   ein 100–Dollar–Schein
Er tauschte seine Pfunde um.
He exchanged his pound notes.
Er zählte die Dollars, Schein für Schein.
He counted the dollars, note by note.
N.B.: Eine bessere Qualität kostet nur ein paar Pfennige mehr.
   A better quality only costs a few pfennigs more.

149 Plurals of words of foreign origin

(**a**) Words of Latin or Greek origin either retain their foreign plurals,
or have a German form of the plural. For example:

casus belli (cause or origin of war) → **casus belli** (pl.)
das Studium (study) → **die Studien**
das Axiom   → **die Axiome**
der Radius   → **die Radien**
das Dogma   → **die Dogmen**
das Stadion (Greek) → **die Stadien**
das Stadium (Latin) → **die Stadien**
das Paradox   → **die Paradoxe**
der Atlas   → **die Atlanten/Atlasse**

(**b**) Words of British English, American English, or French origin
usually have the English or French plural ending of **–s**. For example:

das Hotel   → **die Hotels**
das Apartment → **die Apartments**
der Shop   → **die Shops**
das Restaurant → **die Restaurants**
das Weekend   → **die Weekends**
der Cowboy   → **die Cowboys**

(**c**) The same ending **–s** is added in the plural to words taken from
other languages, but which still have foreign associations. For
example:

der Señor → die Señores (Spanish), also die Señoritas
der Senhor → die Senhores (Portuguese), also die Senhoritas
die Mango → die Mangos
der Gaucho → die Gauchos

(d) Most words of foreign origin, however, have already been
assimilated into the language, especially products like:

die Banane → die Bananen   die Orange → die Orangen
die Tomate → die Tomaten   die Zitrone → die Zitronen

150 Words occurring only in the plural

Certain words occur only in the plural. For example:

(die) Leute (people)   (die) (Blue) Jeans
Lebensmittel (food or foodstuffs)   (die) Shorts
(die) Hosenträger (braces)   (die) Eltern (parents)
(die) Ferien (holidays)   (die) Möbel (furniture)
(die) Trümmer (wreckage or ruins)
(die) Kosten (costs, or expenditure)
(die) Unkosten (expenses or charges)
(die) Zinsen (interest (on an investment))
(die) Einkünfte (income or ingoings)
(die) Mittel (wealth or means)
N.B. das Mittel (remedy, way or means)

Two family relationships are worth noting. **Die Geschwister**
(brother and sister, or brothers and sisters) can be expressed in the
singular as **das Geschwisterpaar**, if only a brother and a sister are
involved; also **die Zwillinge** (the twins) is plural, but **der
Zwillingsbruder** or **die Zwillingsschwester** refers to the brother
or the sister who is involved.

151 General terms and abstract ideas in the singular

(a) Certain general terms are only used in the singular. For example:

(die) Milch (milk)
(das) Vieh (cattle)
(das) Obst (fruit)   N.B. (die) Obstsorten (kinds of fruit)
(der) Käse (cheese)   N.B. (die) Käsesorten (sorts of cheese)
(die) Butter (butter)   N.B. (die) Buttersorten (sorts of butter)
(das) Fleisch (meat)   N.B. (die) Fleischarten (kinds of meat)
(das) Gepäck (luggage)
(der) Inhalt (contents)

(**b**) Abstractions and abstract ideas are almost invariably in the singular. For example:

'Also bleiben Glaube, Hoffnung, Liebe, diese drei; am größten unter ihnen ist die Liebe.' (1 Kor 13.13)
'In a word, there are three things that last for ever: faith, hope, and love; but the greatest of them all is love.' (1 Corinthians 13.13)

The abstractions (**der**) **Glaube**, (**die**) **Hoffnung**, (**die**) **Liebe**, like other abstractions, are always used in the singular, and the dictionaries indicate that there is no plural by only giving the singular form.

(**c**) Very occasionally, however, a plural form of an abstract noun is used under special circumstances. For example, **die Hoffnungen der Menschheit** (the hopes of mankind) would refer to the spiritual, political, social, economic, all the various hopes of mankind. The plural form, though, is a contrived construction.

The declension of nouns

152 Declension – a definition

The change in form which a noun undergoes is called its declension.
This may depend on:

(a) Number (singular or plural)

(b) Case   (nominative, accusative, genitive, or dative)

(c) Gender   (masculine, feminine, or neuter).

153 The nominative

(a) The nominative is the form of the noun which is given in the
dictionary. Since every complete sentence must have at least a
subject and a verb, it is the most frequently used case, for the subject
of a sentence is always in the nominative.

(b) The nominative is also used for the complement (noun
completing the sentence) when the verbs **sein** and **werden** are used
as main verbs, and not as auxiliaries. For example:

Der Vorsitzende (subject) ist Arzt (complement).
The chairman is a doctor.
Ihr Bruder (subject) wurde ein guter Schauspieler (complement).
Her brother became a good actor.

The nouns **Vorsitzende** and **Bruder** are nominative because they
are the subjects of the sentences, and **Arzt** and **Schauspieler** are
also nominative because they come after a form of the verbs **sein**
and **werden** which is used as a main verb.

154 The accusative

(a) The direct object of a sentence is in the accusative case. For
example:

Er (subject) sah den Film (direct object).
He saw the film.
Er (subject) sah den Präsidenten (direct object).
He saw the president.

(b) The accusative form of the noun (masculine, feminine, and
neuter) is almost always the same as the nominative, which is the
form given in the dictionary. The accusative plural form is always
the same as the nominative plural form.

(c) There are, however, some exceptions which have to be learned. For example:

der Präsident (nominative) → **den Präsidenten** (accusative)
der Vorsitzende → **den Vorsitzenden**
der Abgeordnete → **den Abgeordneten**
der Beamte → **den Beamten**
der Alte → **den Alten**
der Dirigent (conductor of an orchestra) → **den Dirigenten**

The acc., gen. and dat. sing. end in **-n** or **-en**, but see para. 157 (Types VI and VII) for the plurals.

(d) Some prepositions are always followed by the accusative case, such as **um** and **ohne**; other prepositions may be followed by the accusative (or the dative), such as **vor** and **zwischen**. (See para. 236.)

155 The genitive

(a) The genitive case shows that a word belongs to, or refers to, someone or something. For example:

Er (subject) regulierte die Drehzahl (direct object) des Motors (genitive).
He regulated the running speed of the motor.
Der Vorsitzende (subject) des Vereins (genitive) trat zurück.
The chairman of the association (or society) resigned.
Das Komitee (subject) diskutierte die Frage (direct object) der Mitgliedschaft (genitive).
The committee discussed the question of membership.

(b) The genitive singular form of feminine nouns is the same as the nominative, accusative, and dative forms.

(c) The genitive singular of masculine and neuter nouns is formed by adding **-s** or **-es** to the stem. The choice of ending is determined by the sound of the word. The firm choice for the ending of some words has long since been made, and present-day usage only accepts one or the other form, as in the following examples:

der Wagen	→ **des Wagens**	**der Sitz** → **des Sitzes**
der Motor	→ **des Motors**	**der Arzt** → **des Arztes**
das Motorrad	→ **des Motorrads**	**der Satz** → **des Satzes**
der Ski	→ **des Skis**	**der Fuß** → **des Fußes**

(d) Masculine and neuter nouns ending in **-el**, **-en**, and **-er** generally add only an **-s** in the genitive.

Masculine and neuter nouns ending in a sound like **-tz**, **-zt**, or **-ß** usually add **-es** in the genitive.

(e) The genitive of the large majority of masculine and neuter nouns is shown as **-(e)s** in the dictionary. This means that both endings are possible, **-s** which is part of the previous syllable, or **-es** which is a separate syllable. Generally speaking, the shorter form is more likely to occur in conversation, and the longer form in writing, especially if a stylistic effect is desired. Personal choice may also be the deciding factor. Examples are:

das Buch	→ **des Buch(e)s**	**der Stuhl**	→ **des Stuhl(e)s**
das Dach	→ **des Dach(e)s**	**der Tisch**	→ **des Tisch(e)s**

The use of **des Stuhls** or **des Stuhles**, for example, might also depend on the rhythm of the sentence, and whether or not the person has a feel for the sound of language.

(f) Some masculine and neuter nouns which end in **-ß** change the **-ß-** to **-ss-** in the genitive singular (and in all forms of the plural). For example:

der Fluß	→ **des Flusses**
der Prozeß	→ **des Prozesses**
der Kongreß	→ **des Kongresses**
der Haß (hate)	→ **des Hasses**
N.B. **der Bus**	→ **des Busses**
der Atlas	→ **des Atlas** or **des Atlasses**

(g) The genitive of certain nouns (para. 155c) ends in **-n** or **-en** in the singular. See para. 157 (Types VI and VII) for plurals.

(h) A few prepositions, such as **abseits** (off from), **angesichts** (in view of), and **außerhalb** (outside of) are followed by the genitive case. (See para. 237.)

(i) A few verbs are followed by the genitive case. For example: **sich einer Sache vergewissern** (to make sure of a thing).

156 The dative

(a) The indirect object of a sentence is in the dative case. For example:

Er (subject) gab dem Passanten (indirect object) ein Flugblatt (direct object).
He gave the passer-by a handbill.
Sie (subject) schickte der Firma (indirect object) eine Broschüre (direct object).
She sent the firm a brochure.

(b) A number of verbs are always followed by the dative case. (See para. 92.) For example: **zuhören** + dative.

Der Richter (subject) hörte dem Angeklagten (dative) aufmerksam zu.
The judge listened attentively to the accused.

(**c**) Certain prepositions (see para. 235) such as **mit** and **von** are always followed by the dative, and others (see para. 236) such as **in** or **vor** may be followed by the dative (or accusative).

(**d**) The dative singular of masculine and neuter nouns, especially words of one syllable, may be followed by an **-e**. This is an established custom in such expressions as **nach Hause**, **zu Hause**, and **auf dem Lande**. The choice usually lies with the speaker or writer though. A certain elegance, and rhythmic speech, may be achieved by adding an **-e** to the dative. For example:

Vor dem Tore stand der Herzog.
The duke was standing in front of the gateway.

On the other hand the indiscriminate use of the dative ending can create the opposite effect, and be ludicrous, a mere parody. This effect can, of course, be the desired one. For example:

Vor dem Tore stand der einsame Torwart.
In front of the goal stood the lonely goalkeeper.

(**e**) The dative plural of all nouns normally ends in **-n** or **-en**. Feminine plurals normally end in this way in all four cases, but the masculine and neuter nouns also require this ending. Examples of all genders are:

den Männern   **den Frauen**   **den Büchern**
den Stühlen   **den Müttern**   **den Ländern**
den Wagen   **den Töchtern**   **den Rädern**

(**f**) The only exceptions are the nouns of foreign origin which retain the foreign plural **-s** in all forms of the plural, including the dative plural. For example:

in den Hotels, **Restaurants**, **Büros**, **Jets**, **Jumbos** . . .

157 Types of declensions

The following tables show types of declensions. A good dictionary shows the genitive singular and the plural form of the noun, and these determine the classification of nouns. For example: **Buch, n. (-es, ¨er)**.
The umlaut over the hyphen indicates that the vowel of the stem takes the umlaut. **Buch** is declined as type II.

Type I Masculine and neuter plurals in **-e**

	singular	*plural*
nominative	der Film	die Filme
accusative	den Film	die Filme
genitive	des Film(e)s	der Filme
dative	dem Film	den Filmen

Neuter nouns with plurals in **-e** are similarly declined.

Type II Masculine and neuter plurals in **-er**

	singular	*plural*
nominative	das Buch	die Bücher
accusative	das Buch	die Bücher
genitive	des Buches	der Bücher
dative	dem Buch	den Büchern

Masculine nouns with plurals in **-er** are similarly declined. The stem vowels **a**, **o**, and **u** in many words take an umlaut in the plural.

Type III Masculine and neuter with unchanged plurals

	singular	*plural*
nominative	der Wagen	die Wagen
accusative	den Wagen	die Wagen
genitive	des Wagens	der Wagen
dative	dem Wagen	den Wagen

Neuter nouns with unchanged plurals are similarly declined. The stem vowels **a**, **o**, and **u** of a few nouns take an umlaut in the plural.

Type IV Feminine nouns

	singular	*plural*
nominative	die Frau	die Frauen
accusative	die Frau	die Frauen
genitive	der Frau	der Frauen
dative	der Frau	den Frauen

Type V Masculine and neuter plurals in **-n** or **-en** (see type VI)

	singular	*plural*
nominative	der Motor	die Motoren
accusative	den Motor	die Motoren
genitive	des Motors	der Motoren
dative	dem Motor	den Motoren

The dictionary shows this type of noun thus:
Motor, m. (-s, -en)
Ohr, n. (-(e)s, -en)

Type VI Masculine and neuter plurals in **-n** or **-en** (see type V)

	singular	*plural*
nominative	der Präsident	die Präsidenten
accusative	den Präsidenten	die Präsidenten
genitive	des Präsidenten	der Präsidenten
dative	dem Präsidenten	den Präsidenten

The dictionary shows this type of noun thus:
Präsident, m. (-en, -en). Type VI is tending to become type V.

Type VII Masculine nouns declined like adjectives

	singular	*plural*	*singular*	*plural*
nom.	der Beamte	die Beamten	ein Beamter	Beamte
acc.	den Beamten	die Beamten	einen Beamten	Beamte
gen.	des Beamten	der Beamten	eines Beamten	Beamter
dat.	dem Beamten	den Beamten	einem Beamten	Beamten

Type VIII Nouns of recent foreign origin

	singular	*plural*
nominative	das Radio	die Radios
accusative	das Radio	die Radios
genitive	des Radios	der Radios
dative	dem Radio	den Radios

There has been a large intake of foreign words into the German language since 1945.

158 Miscellaneous notes on declension

(a) The tables in para. 157 cover almost all the nouns in the German language. A good dictionary shows the key features of each noun, including those with irregular forms such as **Bus, m. (-ses, -se)**, **Fluß, m. (-sses, ̈sse)**, and **Name, m. (-ns, -n)**.

(b) Compound nouns are declined in the same way as the last word of the compound. For example: **der Feuerstuhl** (slang for motorcycle) is declined like **Stuhl**, **die Strohwitwe** (grass-widow) like **Witwe**, and **das Paukerpult** (school slang for teacher's desk) like **Pult**.

(c) Personal names are singular. The only form which requires an ending is the genitive singular, which is formed by adding **-s**, or **-es**. For example:
Schillers Wilhelm Tell, Peters Buch, Vaters Auto, Mutters Kochbuch (note the **-s** on the feminine noun), **Elisabeths Kleid, Staat und Kirche zur Zeit Elisabeths der Ersten**.
Note the Latin form: **Jesu Christi**.

(d) If the pronunciation of the genitive form of a personal name presents some difficulty, then it is avoided. For example: **Hans' Buch** is perhaps acceptable, but **Fritz' Fahrrad** is not. Both can be avoided by referring to **das Buch von Hans** and **das Fahrrad von Fritz**.

(e) Plurals of names are sometimes used in German, but the plurals are not declined. For example: **die Schmidts**, **mit den Schmidts**.

(f) Place names, like personal names, are usually singular. The only form which requires an ending is the genitive singular, which is formed by adding **-s** or **es**. For example:

die Länder Europas, **Deutschlands Geschichte**, **Schleswig-Holsteins Küsten** (coasts), **Stuttgarts Fernsehturm** (television tower), **Neudorfs Bürgermeister**.

(g) If the pronunciation of the genitive form of a place name is difficult, then it is avoided. For example: **die Schlösser in Sussex** and not **Sussex' Schlösser**.

(h) The genitive ending **-s** is usually omitted when abbreviations are used. For example: **das Programm des DGB**, **das Lernen des ABC**, **die Registrierung eines PKW** (the registration of a private car).

(i) Note the word to which the genitive ending **-s** or **-es** is added in the following expressions:

der Genuß eines Stück Brots mit Käse und eines Glas Biers nach einem langen Marsch
(the enjoyment of a piece of bread with cheese and a glass of beer after a long march);
die Gewalt des Wind und Regens (the force of the wind and rain).

(j) Nouns in apposition, that is in a position adjacent to another noun and relating to the same verb, take the case of the main noun. For example:

Karl der Große (subject), der fränkische König (noun in apposition to subject), wurde im Jahre 800 von Papst Leo III zum Kaiser gekrönt.
In 800 Charlemagne, King of the Franks, was crowned Emperor by Pope Leo III.
Das Stück ,,Die Physiker" ist von Friedrich Dürrenmatt (dative), dem Schweizer Schriftsteller (noun in apposition to the dative) geschrieben worden.
The play 'Die Physiker' was written by Friedrich Dürrenmatt, the Swiss writer.

The declension of adjectives

159 Use of the adjective to premodify or postmodify a noun

An adjective which comes (immediately) before a noun is a premodifying adjective. For example: *the old house*, or *such a house*. The adjectives *old* and *such* come before the noun *house*, and are premodifying adjectives.

An adjective which comes somewhere after the noun in a sentence, and relates to it, is a postmodifying adjective. For example: *The house was old.* Or: *The house in which we lived was old.* The adjective *old* comes after the noun *house* in both sentences, and is in both sentences a postmodifying adjective.

In English the position of the adjective does not make any difference to the spelling of the word, but in German it does, for premodifying adjectives are declined, and postmodifying adjectives are not. The details are given in the following paragraphs.

160 Postmodifying adjectives

Postmodifying adjectives are not declined; that is to say, they do not have endings according to number, case, and gender. For example:

Das Haus war alt und verfallen.
The house was old and going to ruin.
Ihr Gesichtsausdruck war frisch und lebendig.
Her (facial) expression was fresh and lively.

The adjectives **alt**, **verfallen**, **frisch**, and **lebendig** are postmodifying adjectives, and are therefore not declined. This applies to all postmodifying adjectives.

161 Declension of premodifying adjectives

Premodifying adjectives are always declined according to one of the following three types.

Type I **der**, **die**, **das** + adjective + noun

singular

	masculine	*feminine*	*neuter*
nom.	der junge Mann	die junge Frau	das junge Kind
acc.	den jungen Mann	die junge Frau	das junge Kind
gen.	des jungen Mann(e)s	der jungen Frau	des jungen Kind(e)s
dat.	dem jungen Mann	der jungen Frau	dem jungen Kind

plural

	masculine,	feminine,	neuter
nom.	die jungen Männer,	Frauen,	Kinder
acc.	die jungen Männer,	Frauen,	Kinder
gen.	der jungen Männer,	Frauen,	Kinder
dat.	den jungen Männern,	Frauen,	Kindern

Type II **ein, eine, ein** + adjective + noun

singular

	masculine	feminine	neuter
nom.	ein junger Mann	eine junge Frau	ein junges Kind
acc.	einen jungen Mann	eine junge Frau	ein junges Kind
gen.	eines jungen Mann(e)s	einer jungen Frau	eines jungen Kind(e)s
dat.	einem jungen Mann	einer jungen Frau	einem jungen Kind

plural

	masculine,	feminine,	neuter
nom.	(no article) junge Männer,	Frauen,	Kinder
acc.	junge Männer,	Frauen,	Kinder
gen.	junger Männer,	Frauen,	Kinder
dat.	jungen Männern,	Frauen,	Kindern

N.B. See also para. 165 for plural forms.

Type III Adjective only + noun

singular

	masculine	feminine	neuter
nom.	guter Wein	gute Milch	kaltes Bier
acc.	guten Wein	gute Milch	kaltes Bier
gen.	guten Weins	guter Milch	kalten Biers
dat.	gutem Wein	guter Milch	kaltem Bier

plural

	masculine,	feminine,	neuter
nom.	gute Weine,	Obstsorten,	Kleidungsstücke
acc.	gute Weine,	Obstsorten,	Kleidungsstücke
gen.	guter Weine,	Obstsorten,	Kleidungsstücke
dat.	guten Weinen,	Obstsorten,	Kleidungsstücken

The accusative, genitive, and dative mostly occur after prepositions which govern those cases. For example: **für guten Wein, statt guten Weins, bei gutem Wein**. The plural of Type III is used after a cardinal number of two or more, if it is used without an article. For example: **vier (4) gute Weinsorten**.

162 Endings of premodifying adjectives

The adjectival endings of types I, II, and III, as shown in para. 161 are as follows:

Type I	singular			plural
	masculine	*feminine*	*neuter*	*m. f. n.*
nominative	–e	–e	–e	–en
accusative	–en	–e	–e	–en
genitive	–en	–en	–en	–en
dative	–en	–en	–en	–en

Type II	singular			plural
	masculine	*feminine*	*neuter*	*m. f. n.*
nominative	–er	–e	–es	See paras. 161
accusative	–en	–e	–es	and 165 for plural
genitive	–en	–en	–en	forms.
dative	–en	–en	–en	

Type III	singular			plural
	masculine	*feminine*	*neuter*	*m. f. n.*
nominative	–er	–e	–es	–e
accusative	–en	–e	–es	–e
genitive	–en	–er	–en	–er
dative	–em	–er	–em	–en

163 Declension of two or more successive premodifying adjectives

Two or more premodifying adjectives which refer to the same noun are declined in parallel; that is to say, they have the same endings. There are some exceptions, though, which are considered in paras. 165, 167, 172, and 173.

die kahle, öde Landschaft   in jüngster oder neuester Zeit
the bare, bleak landscape   *alternative forms of 'quite recently'*
die junge, kecke Dame im Karnevalskostüm
the pert young lady in fancy dress (for Karneval)
nach mühsamer, langwieriger Arbeit·...
after painstaking, protracted work ...

The adjectives are separated by a comma if the one immediately follows the other.

164 Declension of possessive pronouns used as adjectives

The possessive pronouns used as adjectives: **mein** (my), **dein** (your), **sein** (his), **ihr** (her), **sein** (its), **unser** (our), **euer** (your), **Ihr** (your), and **ihr** (their), as well **kein** (not a, not one) are declined like **ein** in para. 138.

For example: **deine Liebe, seine Gleichgültigkeit** (indifference), **durch ihre Willenskraft** (through her strength of mind, or will-power), **mit eurer Hilfe**, or **mit Ihrer Hilfe** (with your help). The endings are the same as the endings of **ein**.

165 Declension of adjectives following possessive pronouns used as adjectives

The declension of an adjective which immediately follows a possessive pronoun used as an adjective is shown in the following tables.

singular

	masculine	*feminine*	*neuter*
nom.	sein neuer Film	ihre gute Idee	sein bestes Buch
acc.	seinen neuen Film	ihre gute Idee	sein bestes Buch
gen.	seines neuen Films	ihrer guten Idee	seines besten Buch(e)s
dat.	seinem neuen Film	ihrer guten Idee	seinem besten Buch

plural

	masculine,		*feminine,*	*neuter*
nom.	seine/ihre	neuen Filme,	guten Ideen,	besten Bücher
acc.	seine/ihre	neuen Filme,	guten Ideen,	besten Bücher
gen.	seiner/ihrer	neuen Filme,	guten Ideen,	besten Bücher
dat.	seinen/ihren	neuen Filmen,	guten Ideen,	besten Büchern

The descriptive adjective (**neu**, **gut**, **beste**) is declined in the same way in the singular as the adjective in type II (see para. 161), but in the plural the descriptive adjective has the same weak ending **-en** in all four cases.

166 Declension of demonstrative adjectives

Demonstrative adjectives such as **dieser und jener** (this and that), **jeder** (every), **jeglicher** (each, every), are declined like **der**, **die**, **das** (see para. 138). The nominative and accusative neuter singular forms, however, end in **-es (dieses)**. For example: **dieses Buch**, **jedes Buch**. The other forms have the endings of **der**, **die**, **das**, such as: **jeder Autofahrer, jegliche Möglichkeit** (each and every possibility).

N.B. The interrogative adjective **welche?** (which?) is also declined in the same way. For example:
Welchen Anzug wollen Sie anziehen? (Which suit do you want to put on?)

167 Declension of adjectives following demonstrative adjectives

An adjective following a demonstrative adjective is declined according to the following tables:

singular

	masculine	*feminine*	*neuter*
nom.	dieser neue Film	diese gute Idee	dieses neue Buch
acc.	diesen neuen Film	diese gute Idee	dieses neue Buch
gen.	dieses neuen Films	dieser guten Idee	dieses neuen Buch(e)s
dat.	diesem neuen Film	dieser guten Idee	diesem neuen Buch

plural

	masculine	*feminine*	*neuter*
nom.	diese neuen Filme	guten Ideen	neuen Bücher
acc.	diese neuen Filme	guten Ideen	neuen Bücher
gen.	dieser neuen Filme	guten Ideen	neuen Bücher
dat.	diesen neuen Filmen	guten Ideen	neuen Büchern

The second, descriptive adjective is declined in the same way in both singular and plural as the adjective in type I (see para. 161).

168 The declension of an adjective in an apposition

When two nouns are in apposition, that is to say in a position adjacent the one to the other, and both have the same function in the sentence, then the accompanying adjectives are also declined in the same case. For example:

Der junge Werner Glück (subject), unser neuer Spieler (noun in apposition), spielt morgen nachmittag zum erstenmal in unserer Mannschaft.

Young Werner Glück (nominative), our new player (nominative), is playing for the first time tomorrow afternoon in our team.

N.B. The forms of the adjectives **junge** and **neuer** are both nominative. (See paras. 161 and 165 for the explanation.)

Wir sprachen gestern abend mit Herrn Schnurbus (dative after **mit**), dem berühmten Rennfahrer (dative in apposition).

We spoke yesterday evening to Herrn Schnurbus, the famous racing driver.

The nouns are in the dative after the preposition **mit**, and are in apposition. The adjective **berühmten** as well as the article **dem** are therefore in the dative.

169 Declension of participles used as adjectives

Participles are declined like adjectives.
This also applies to participles used as nouns.
The fact that participles are formed from verbs is irrelevant for the purpose of declension.
The following examples illustrate the point that participles are declined as adjectives:

eine ausgezeichnete Vorstellung (an excellent performance), **ein ausgeprägter Stil** (a pronounced, distinct style), **laufende Nummern** (consecutive numbers), **am laufenden Band** (one after the other, on the assembly line), **ein verzerrtes Bild** (a distorted picture).

170 Declension of adjectives used as nouns

Adjectives used as nouns are declined in the manner shown in para. 161, types I and II. For example:

singular	*plural*
der Abgeordnete	die Abgeordneten
den Abgeordneten	die Abgeordneten
des Abgeordneten	der Abgeordneten
dem Abgeordneten	den Abgeordneten
ein Abgeordneter	Abgeordnete
einen Abgeordneten	Abgeordnete
eines Abgeordneten	Abgeordneter
einem Abgeordneten	Abgeordneten

An adjective used as a noun always begins with a capital letter.

Ein Abgeordneter is a male member of the Bundestag. A female member is **eine Abgeordnete**, and the word is declined in the feminine. There are also adjectives, mainly expressing abstract ideas, which are neuter, such as **das Gute** (the good), **das Beste** (the best).

171 Nouns with an adjectival function

(**a**) Nouns which have an adjectival function may add **–er** if the word is a name. They are not declined. For example:

der Teutoburger Wald, der Plöner See, der Hamburger Hafen, die Lübecker Bucht, das Paderborner Hochland.

(**b**) Names which have an adjectival function are often combined with another noun to form a compound word. For example:

der Schwarzwald, Bremerhaven, das Saarland.

(c) Adjectives which are combined in this way are not usually declined within the compound word. For example:

Neumünster, der Großglockner, Kleinasien, der Altmarkt.

(d) There is an increasing tendency to join the words of road and street names together with hyphens. For example:

die Konrad-Adenauer-Allee und die Friedrich-Ebert-Allee

172 Declension of adjectives following indefinite adjectives

(a) There is no overall standard method of declining the adjective which immediately follows an indefinite adjective (or pronoun) such as:

ähnlich- (similar), **all-** (all), **andere** (other), **beide** (both), **gewiß-** (certain), **irgendwelch-** (of any kind), **manch-** (many a), **mehrere** (several), **sämtlich-** (all, every), **solch-** (such), **sonstig-** (remaining), **übrig-** (left over), **verschieden-** (different, various), **viel-** (much), **weiter-** (further), **welch-** (what a), **wenig-** (few).

(b) There is, however, a standard method of declining all adjectives which come after the definite (**der**, **die**, **das**) and the indefinite (**ein**) article, for under those circumstances all adjectives are declined in parallel; that is to say that they have the same endings. This applies also to the indefinite adjectives listed in (a) above, if they follow the definite or indefinite article. For example:

die beiden letzten Tage (the previous two days), **von der ähnlichen, neuen Gruppe** (from the similar new group), **eine gewisse friedliche Ruhe** (a certain peaceful quiet), **aus einer ähnlichen unangenehmen Situation** (arising out of a similar unpleasant situation).

(c) The same method applies to possessive adjectives, like **mein**, **sein**, **ihr**, **unser**, which are declined like **ein**, and also to demonstrative adjectives like **dieser** and **jeder**, which are declined like **der**, **die**, **das**. All of the following adjectives are declined in parallel. For example:

jede einzelne gute Idee, sein anderer brauner Anzug (his other brown suit), **seine verschiedenen guten Schlipse** (his various good ties).

(d) There is no general rule if one of the indefinite adjectives listed in para. (a) is at the head of the noun phrase. The grammatical form of the adjective which follows one of these indefinite adjectives is sometimes a matter of choice by the individual writer, and can be indicative of the period in which he or she was writing.

In short, there are no longstanding norms which an educated writer would be expected to follow. The notes in the following sub-paragraphs are therefore confined to a simplified form of current procedure and general usage.

(e) Adjectives which follow the indefinite adjectives **ähnlich-**, **andere-**, **einzeln-**, **gewiß-**, **sonstig-**, **übrig-**, **verschieden-**, and **weiter-** are declined in parallel with one of those words; that is to say, they have the same endings. For example:

gewisse namhafte Persönlichkeiten (certain famous personalities), **von verschiedenen bekannten Autoren** (by various well-known authors), **mit ähnlicher besonderer Sorgfalt** (with similar laborious care).

(f) The indefinite adjectives, **einige** (some), **etliche** (some, a few), and **mehrere** (several) are almost always used in the plural only. The adjectives which follow them are also declined in parallel. For example:

einige berühmte Schauspieler (some famous actors), **Gerüchte über mehrere bekannte Filmstars** (rumours about several well-known film stars), **mit etlichen unangenehmen Überraschungen** (with several unpleasant surprises).

(g) The indefinite adjectives, **all-** (all), **beide** (both), and **sämtlich-** (all, every), are usually followed nowadays in the plural by an adjective in the weak form; that is to say that the adjective is declined as if it follows **der**, **die**, **das**. (See para. 161 type I.) For example: **beide jungen Männer, alle guten Bücher, sämtliche guten Bücher.**

(h) No clear guidance can be given about the form of the adjective following **irgendwelch-** (of any kind), as both forms of the succeeding adjective are possible. For example: **irgendwelche gute Ideen**, or **irgendwelche guten Ideen** (some good ideas or other).

(i) Four indefinite adjectives, **folgend-** (the following), **manch-** (many a), **solch-** (such a), and **viel-** (many) react differently on the following adjective in the singular and in the plural. The succeeding adjective is weak (declined like type I in para. 161) in the singular, and is declined in parallel (with the same endings) in the plural. For example:

manches neue Buch (many a new book), **bei solchem herrlichen Wetter** (in such wonderful weather), **mit vielem guten Willen** (with much good will), **manche neue Bücher** (many new books), **viele neue Ideen** (many new ideas), **solche geglückte Tage** (such successful days), **folgende neue Gesetze** (the following new laws).

(j) Should the undeclined forms **manch**, **solch**, **welch**, **wenig**, and **viel** be used in the singular, then the following adjective is declined like type III in para. 161. For example:

manch guter Rat (many a good piece of advice), **mit viel geduldiger Mühe** (with much patient effort), **solch guter Mann** (such a good man), **welch starker Mann** (what a strong man), **ein wenig gutes Essen** (not such a good meal). Note also the plural: **wenig gute Freunde** (only a few good friends).

(k) Students will come across exceptions to the above notes, especially in literature, but the above guidance has been given for their own writing. A decision has sometimes to be taken, this way or that, and it is not always possible to skirt round this confused field of grammar. The above notes reflect current practice. Exceptions are most likely to be met with in the masculine and neuter dative singular, and in the genitive plural.

(l) Two exceptions should be noted. (i) The dative singular, masculine and neuter only, of **ander-** and **wenig-** are followed by an adjective in the weak form. For example: **aus anderem besseren Anlaß** (arising from another better cause). (ii) The plural forms of **sämtlich-** and **solch-** are sometimes followed by an adjective declined in parallel. For example: **sämtliche gute Ideen** or **solche gute Ideen**, as well as **sämtliche guten Ideen** or **solche guten Ideen**.

173 Declension of an adjective or participle used as a noun, and following an indefinite adjective

The following tables show the declension of an adjective or participle used as a noun, when it follows an indefinite adjective. The tables also summarize parts of the previous paragraph. In order to simplify the tables the words **Gute/Gutes** and **Abgeordnete/Abgeordneten** have been used throughout. Note the alternative forms for **sämtlich-** and **solch-**, and the forms which differ in the singular and plural.

Weak forms	*Forms in parallel*
alles Gute/alle Abgeordneten	andere Abgeordnete
beide Abgeordneten	einige Abgeordnete
	etliche Abgeordnete
folgendes Gute	folgende Abgeordnete
irgendwelches Gute/	irgendwelche Abgeordnete
irgendwelche Abgeordneten	
	mehrere Abgeordnete
manches Gute (sing.)	manche Abgeordnete (pl.)

sämtliche Abgeordneten
solche Abgeordneten
vieles Gute (sing.)
wenig Gutes (sing.)

sämtliche Abgeordnete
solche Abgeordnete
viele Abgeordnete (pl.)
wenige Abgeordnete (pl.)

174 Miscellaneous points concerning adjectives

(**a**) The adjective **hoch** (high) has two forms, **hoch** and **hoh-**. The form **hoh-** is used if the adjective premodifies, and the form **hoch** is only used to postmodify. For example:

ein hohes Haus, **höhere Löhne** (higher wages), **der Fernsehturm ist hoch** (the television tower is high).

(**b**) Adjectives ending in **-el** drop the **e** if the word is declined. For example:

dunkel, **übel**, but **ein dunkles Geschäft** (a doubtful transaction), **ein übler Scherz** (a nasty prank).

(**c**) Colours are not always declined, especially the pastel shades or exotic colour combinations. For example:

ein schwarzes Kleid, ein blauer Rock, but **ein lila Kleid**.

A distinct preference is shown for using colours as postmodifying adjectives. They are therefore not declined. For example:

ein elegantes Abendkleid in weinrot (an elegant wine-red evening dress), **ein Plisseekleid in bordeaux-rot, Oberteil in uni weiß, mit separater Weste** (a pleated dress in bordeaux red, upper part in plain white, with a separate bolero).

(**d**) A number of adjectives such as **ähnlich**, **bekannt**, **bewußt**, **fremd**, **gleich**, and **leid** govern the dative case when they refer to a person. For example:

Das ist mir fremd.
That's strange to me.
Es tut mir leid.
I'm sorry (about that).

Das ist mir gleich.
It's all the same to me.
Mir ist bewußt, daß . . .
I'm aware that . . .

(**e**) The adjectives **viel** and **wenig** are often not declined. For example:

Sie hat wenig Geld.
She has little money.
Er gibt sich viel Mühe.
He takes a lot of trouble.

(**f**) The adjective **solch** can also be used without being declined, especially in everyday speech. For example:

Er fuhr mit solch einer Geschwindigkeit, daß . . .
He drove at such a speed that . . .

The comparison of adjectives

175 Definitions

The comparative form of the adjective is that used when two persons or things are compared with each other. In German, as in English, the comparative is formed by adding **-er** to the positive (simple) form.

The superlative form of the adjective is that used when three or more persons or things are compared with each other. In German the superlative is formed by adding **-ste** or **-este** to the positive (simple) form.

176 Comparative forms of the adjective

(a) The comparative is formed by adding **-er** to the positive (simple) form. For example:

breit (broad)	→ **breiter**	**fein** (fine, delicate)	→ **feiner**
eng (narrow)	→ **enger**	**klein** (small)	→ **kleiner**
hell (bright)	→ **heller**	**reif** (ripe)	→ **reifer**

(b) Most adjectives with the vowels **a**, **o**, or **u** in the stem, change the vowel to **ä**, **ö**, or **ü** in the comparative (and in the superlative). For example:

hart (hard)	→ **härter**	**groß** (large, tall)	→ **größer**
lang (long)	→ **länger**	**jung** (young)	→ **jünger**
grob (coarse)	→ **gröber**	**kurz** (short)	→ **kürzer**

(c) The few adjectives which end in **-el** omit the **e** in the comparative (but not in the superlative). For example:

dunkel (dark) → **dunkler**   **eitel** (vain) → **eitler**

(d) The few adjectives ending in **-en** or **-er** are somewhat similar, in that the **e** is usually omitted in speech, but usually included in formal writing. For example:

trocken (dry) → **trockner** or **trockener**
finster (gloomy, dark) → **finstrer** or **finsterer**

Adjectives of one syllable ending in **-er** always omit the **e** in the comparative (but not in the superlative). For example:

teuer (expensive) → **teurer**   **sauer** (sour) → **saurer**

(**e**) Irregular comparisons are:
gut (good) → **besser**
hoch (high) → **höher**
viel (many) → **mehr**

(**f**) There are adjectives which are never, in fact, used in the comparative (or in the superlative) for the simple reason that a comparison would not make sense, or there is rarely a situation in which a comparison could reasonably be drawn. The following words should illustrate this point:

absolut (absolute), **todkrank** (seriously ill), **hoffnungslos** (hopeless), **unübertrefflich** (unequalled), **ungeheuer** (monstrous, atrocious), **leer** (empty), **unhöflich** (impolite), **allein** (alone, lonely), **wörtlich** (word for word).

It might be thought that certain theoretical absolutes would be immune from comparison. Detergent firms, however, now advertise products which are '**weißer als weiß**', so that it is unwise to state that certain comparisons are impossible. They are, however, unusual.

(**g**) Two words (**leer** and **allein**) are included in the above list which appear not to admit of comparison, and yet under special circumstances such a comparison is nevertheless possible. For example:
Der Saal war leerer als ich erwartete.
The hall was emptier than I expected.
Heutzutage bin ich mehr allein als früher.
Nowadays I am more lonely than before.

The word **mehr** is sometimes used to form the comparative of words for which there is no acceptable form of the comparative available in the German language. It should, however, be used with discretion. There are occasions in English on which 'more' is used for a comparison whereas it is not used in German.
For example: *more beautiful* is **schöner**, *more comfortable* is **bequemer**.

(**h**) The appropriate conjunction for a comparison is **als**:
größer als ...   besser als ...   bequemer als ...

(**i**) If two persons or things are considered equal, then the comparison is made as follows:
so groß wie ...   so gut wie ...   so bequem wie ...

177 Superlative forms of the adjective

(a) The superlative is formed by adding **-ste** to the positive (simple) form. The definite article comes before the superlative form. Both article and superlative are declined as in para. 161 type I.
For example:

klein (small) → **der, die, das kleinste**
eng   (narrow) → **der, die, das engste**

(b) Some adjectives form the superlative by adding **-este** to the positive (simple) form. For example:

weit (far) → **der, die, das weiteste**
süß (sweet) → **der, die, das süßeste**

(c) The decision about the ending **-ste** or **-este** is taken according to the ease with which a particular form can be spoken. The decision is not difficult with words like **klein (kleinste)**, **weit (weiteste)**, **rasch (rascheste)**, but there are borderline cases in which both alternatives are reasonable, and for which, in fact, two forms exist.
For example: **frei** (free) → **der freieste** or **der freiste**.

(d) Most adjectives with the vowels **a**, **o**, or **u** in the stem, change the vowels to **ä**, **ö**, or **ü** in the superlative (as in the comparative).
For example:

hart → **der, die, das härteste**
lang → **der, die, das längste**
groß → **der, die, das größte**
jung → **der, die, das jüngste**

(e) The superlative is declined as in para. 161 type I. This is more realistically illustrated by examples rather than by tables:

der jüngste Spieler (the youngest player), **die berühmteste Sängerin** (the most famous singer), **das beste Ergebnis** (the best result), **das Datum des längsten Tages** (the date of the longest day), **die Länge des modernsten Kleides** (the length of the very latest (most modern) dress), **am kürzesten Tag** (on the shortest day), **mit der weichsten Wolle** (with the softest wool), **im ärgsten Falle** (if the worst comes to the worst; literally: in the utmost event), **die ältesten Bürger** (the oldest citizens), **die sorgfältigsten Vorbereitungen** (the most careful preparations), **die Ereignisse der jüngsten Jahre** (the happenings of the most recent years).

(f) The superlative forms such as **am größten**, **am wenigsten**, **am härtesten**, **am breitesten**, are considered in para. 195.

(**g**) The omission of the **e** in the comparative of certain adjectives which was noted in para. 176 (**c**) and (**d**) does not occur in the superlative. For example:

dunkel (dark)	→ **dunkler**	→ **das dunkelste**
finster (gloomy, dark)	→ **finst(e)rer**	→ **das finsterste**
teuer (dear, expensive)	→ **teurer**	→ **das teuerste**
sauer (sour)	→ **saurer**	→ **das sauerste**

(**h**) Irregular comparisons are:

gut (good)	→ **besser**	→ **das beste**
hoch (high)	→ **höher**	→ **das höchste**
viel (many, much)	→ **mehr**	→ **das meiste**
nahe (near)	→ **näher**	→ **das nächste**

(**i**) There are adjectives which are never, in fact, used in the comparative or the superlative. (See notes in para. 176 (**f**).)

178 Other variations of the positive, comparative, and superlative forms of the adjective

A speaker or a writer may wish to modify a comparison between persons or things. The reason might be the fear of making a clear value judgement, or the desire to show a personal feeling or attitude one way or the other, with the result that a simple statement or comparison is modified. The following notes deal with the various methods by which such modification is achieved.

(**a**) A restriction on a value judgement is made by the addition of **einigermaßen** (somewhat, to some extent) or **mäßig** (moderately) before the adjective. For example:

Sie ist einigermaßen (mäßig) gut im Fach Deutsch.
She is reasonably good in German.

(**b**) A more enthusiastic note is struck by the use of **recht** (quite) or **ziemlich** (fairly). For example:

Sie ist recht (ziemlich) gut im Fach Deutsch.
She is quite (fairly) good in German.

(**c**) A genuinely enthusiastic note is struck by using **sehr** (very), **wirklich** (really), **äußerst** (extremely), **besonders** (especially), **überaus** (exceedingly), **außerordentlich** (extraordinarily), **erstaunlich** (astoundingly). For example:

Sie ist sehr (besonders) (außerordentlich) gut im Fach Deutsch.
She is very (especially) (extraordinarily) good in German.

(**d**) Other modifying words, which could not be used in the above examples are: **ganz und gar** (totally, wholly), **vollkommen** (perfectly, fully), **reichlich** (amply, abundantly), **gänzlich** (completely), **beträchtlich** (considerably), **völlig** (fully), **weitaus** (by far), **bei weitem** (by far), **richtig** (genuinely).

(**e**) There is even a method of raising (or lowering) the superlative:
der klügste/dümmste Student
der allerklügste/allerdümmste Student
der allerallerklügste/allerallerdümmste Student

(**f**) Every language is subjected to fashionable misuse, and German is no exception. The following expressions have been heard, but are not put forward for imitation:
schrecklich gern (frightfully willingly or frightfully much), **enorm appetitlich** (enormously appetising), **furchtbar aufregend** (frightfully exciting), **phantastisch hübsch** (fantastically pretty), **greulich schlecht** (horribly bad), **scheußlich kalt** (abominably cold), **unerträglich heiß** (unbearably hot), **wahnsinnig dumm** (madly stupid).

(**g**) The superlative can be modified by the repetition of certain words:
Die Vorstellung war sehr, sehr gut.
The performance was very very good.
Sie brauchte unbedingt einen langen, langen Urlaub.
She undoubtedly needed a long long holiday.

(**h**) Note the following:
viel größer als ... noch größer als ... etwas größer als ...
much bigger than ... even bigger than ... somewhat bigger than ...

Numbers

179 Cardinal numbers

A cardinal number is a plain number such as 5 or 15.
The cardinal numbers are given below in groups.

(a) **null, eins, zwei, drei, vier, fünf, sechs, sieben, acht, neun, zehn, elf, zwölf,**

(b) **dreizehn, vierzehn, fünfzehn, sechzehn** (no **-s-**)**, siebzehn** (no **-en-**)**, achtzehn, neunzehn,**

(c) **zwanzig, einundzwanzig, zweiundzwanzig, dreiundzwanzig, vierundzwanzig, fünfundzwanzig, sechsundzwanzig, siebenundzwanzig, achtundzwanzig, neunundzwanzig,**

(d) **dreißig, vierzig, fünfzig, sechzig** (no **-s-**)**, siebzig** (no **-en-**)**, achtzig, neunzig,**
(the numbers in between are formed as in (c))

(e) **hundert** (or **einhundert**)**, hunderteins** (or **hundertundeins**)**, hundertzwei, hundertdrei,** . . . **hundertneunundneunzig, zweihundert,** . . . **neunhundert,**

(f) **tausend** (or **eintausend**)**, tausendeins** (or **tausendundeins**)**, zweitausend, zwanzigtausend, zweihunderttausend,**

(g) **eine Million** (1000 mal 1000)**, eine Milliarde** (1000 mal 1 000 000)**, eine Billion** (1000 mal 1 000 000 000). (Note the capital letters.)

180 Notes on the cardinal numbers

Several points arise in the use of a few of the cardinal numbers, and these points are given in the following notes:

(a) The word **null** is used for a simple description of the figure 0. A telephone number, for example, which includes this figure is always spoken with the word **null**.
The word **zero** is used very occasionally for instruments on which there is a scale, such as a thermometer. A temperature of −20° Celsius is referred to, however, as **20 Grad unter Null**.

(b) The word **eins** is used for a simple description of the figure 1. A telephone number, for example, which includes this figure is always spoken with the word **eins**.

When the number refers to a person or thing, it is declined.
For example: **ein Mann**, **von einem Mann**, **eine Frau**, **ein Kind**.
Note the following expressions:
Einmal eins ist eins. Es ist eins. Es ist ein Uhr. Es ist ein Uhr zwanzig. Er hat eine Uhr. Er bekam eine Eins in der Prüfung (he got a (grade) one in the test (examination)), **in ein bis zwei Wochen**, **einer muß gehen**.

(c) The word **beide** (both) is sometimes used instead of **zwei**, in referring to persons or things. For example: **die beiden Studenten**, **die beiden Bücher**. Students are advised to use the word **beide** with the definite article, as in the examples, or to avoid the word, as there is confusion as to some endings. For example, **wir beide gehen**, and **er sah uns beide** are spoken, but the identical endings of **beide** cannot be explained logically, and are not necessarily acceptable in all circles.
Note the following expressions:
Sie gingen zu zweit (the two of them walked together), **sie gingen zu dritt** (the three of them walked together), **sie gingen zu zweien** (they walked in pairs), **nach dem Karnevalsfest ging er auf allen vieren nach Hause** (after the carnival festivities he went home on all fours).
The word **zwo** is often used for **zwei** on the radio, on television, and on the telephone in order to distinguish the number quite clearly from **drei**.

(d) Note the following expressions:
ein Vierer (a (rowing) four), **ein Achter** (an eight), **ein Sechser** (a six out of six right in the pools (Lotto)), **in den sechziger, siebziger, achtziger, neunziger Jahren** (in the sixties, seventies, eighties, nineties), **er ist in den Vierzigern** (he is in the forties), 10% = **zehn von Hundert**.

(e) The word **Nummer** is feminine, and so all numbers except **das Hundert** and **das Tausend** are feminine. For example: **die drei** (Musikanten) or **die Drei**, **die einundzwanzig (Passagiere)** or **die Einundzwanzig**.

(f) A year is written **1990**, or **im Jahre 1990**. (The expression '**in 1990**' is an anglicism which is generally rejected.)

181 The use of capital letters for cardinal numbers

(a) Numbers have been given capital letters in some examples in paras. 179 (g), 180 (a) (b) (d) and (e). The explanation is simply that in every instance the number has been used as a noun.

(b) It is not easy, however, to decide instantly whether a number is used adjectivally, or as a noun, as most numbers can be used in both ways. Fortunately German and English are of the same language family, and so a rough test can be applied. If you intend to refer to a four, an eight, the nine, the twenty, using the article *a*, *an*, or *the* with the number but without adding a noun, then you are using the figure as a noun in both English and German. The capital letter is required in German. For example: **die Vier**, **ein Vierer**, **die Acht**, **ein Achter**, **die Neun**, **die Zwanzig**.

(c) The words **Million**, **Milliarde**, and **Billion** are feminine, and are always written with a capital letter. They are also declined. For example: **zwei Millionen**, **dreißig Milliarden**.

(d) The words **(das) Hundert** and **(das) Tausend** are mostly used as nouns, except when forming part of a mere number. They are declined. For example:

Es gibt Hunderte und Tausende von Menschen, die hungern.
There are hundreds and thousands of people who hunger.
Es gab mehrere Tausende, die anwesend waren.
There were several thousand present.
The plural ending **-e** is sometimes omitted from the words **Hundert(e)** and **Tausend(e)**.

182 Ordinal numbers

Ordinal numbers are used to place people or things in an arithmetical order, such as *the fifth* or *the ninety-ninth*.
The definite article usually comes directly before the ordinal number.
The ordinal numbers are given below in groups:

(a) **der erste**, **der zweite**, **der dritte**, **der vierte**, **der fünfte**, **der sechste**, **der siebente** (or **der siebte**), **der achte**, **der neunte**, **der zehnte**, **der elfte**, **der zwölfte** (note the words **erste**, **dritte**, **siebte**, **achte**, which are irregular, otherwise **-te** is added to the cardinal number)

(b) **der dreizehnte**, **der vierzehnte**, **der fünfzehnte**, **der sechzehnte**, **der siebzehnte**, **der achtzehnte**, **der neunzehnte** (**-te** is added to the cardinal number)

(c) **der zwanzigste**, **der einundzwanzigste**, **der zweiundzwanzigste**, **der dreiundzwanzigste**, usw. (**-ste** is added to the cardinal number)

(d) **der dreißigste**, **der vierzigste**, **der fünfzigste**, **der**

sechzigste, der siebzigste, der achtzigste, der neunzigste
(**-ste** is added to the cardinal number)

(**e**) **der hundertste, der hundertunderste, der
hundertzwanzigste, der neunhundertneunundneunzigste, der
tausendste, der millionste** (**-ste** is added to the cardinal number).

183 Declension of the ordinal numbers

The ordinal numbers are always declined. The definite article **der** is
used in the above lists for the sake of uniformity. The articles **die**
and **das** could equally well have been used.

The following sentences show the declension of the ordinal
numbers:

Sie ist die erste Verkäuferin in dieser Abteilung.
She is the first saleswoman in this department.
Sie saß in der ersten Reihe.   Er saß in der zwanzigsten Reihe.
She sat in the first row.   He was sitting in the twentieth row.
Er wurde zweihundertneunzigster im Volkslauf.
He was the 290th in the mass cross-country race.
Bei seinem achten Versuch war er erfolgreich.
He was successful at his eighth attempt.

184 The use of capital letters for ordinal numbers

Ordinal numbers begin with a capital letter if they are used as
nouns. A method of deciding whether an ordinal number is used as
an adjective or a noun is described in para. 181 (**b**). Briefly, the
ordinal number is a noun if the number is important and is not
immediately followed by a person or thing. For example:

Wilhelm der Erste (or **Wilhelm I**), **Heinrich der Achte** (or
Heinrich VIII), **Elizabeth die Erste** (**Elizabeth I**), **Jakob der
Erste** (James I in English), **Karl der Zweite** (Charles II in English),
Papst Johann der Dreiundzwanzigste (Pope John XXIII).

Er war der Erste in der Klasse.
He was top of the class.
Sie stand als Neunte in der Schlange.
She was standing ninth in the queue.

185 Fractions

Fractions are formed by adding **-tel** or **-stel** to the stem of the
ordinal number. For example:

(**a**) **das Drittel, das Viertel, das Sechstel, das Siebentel, das
Achtel, das Zehntel, das Zwölftel**

(**b**) Note **die Hälfte** (half), which begins with a capital letter, and is declined. Also **halb** (half) which is declined.

(**c**) **das Vierzehntel**, **das Neunzehntel**

(**d**) **das Zwanzigstel**, **das Einundzwanzigstel**, **das Siebenundzwanzigstel**

(**e**) **das Dreißigstel**, **das Sechzigstel**, **das Neunzigstel**

(**f**) **das Hundertstel**, **das Tausendstel**, **das Millionstel**

Fractions are normally written in figures, but are spoken in the following manner:

ein drittel, **zwei drittel**, **sieben achtel**, **neunzehn zwanzigstel**.

186 Declension of fractions

If a fraction is used as a noun, then it is a neuter noun.
For example: **ein Drittel**, **ein Viertel**, **ein Zehntel**. It is therefore declined like a neuter noun.

187 The use of capital letters for fractions

(**a**) **Die Hälfte** (half) is always used as a noun, and is declined.

(**b**) If a fraction is used as a noun, then the fraction begins with a capital letter. For example:

ein Drittel der Arbeit (one-third of the work), **nur ein Hundertstel des nötigen Geldes** (only a hundredth of the necessary money), **im letzten Viertel des Jahrhunderts** (in the last quarter of the century).

(**c**) Fractions are usually used as nouns, except for the purpose of reading off figures. Fractions therefore usually begin with a capital letter.

188 Notes on fractions

(**a**) When a fraction is combined with a noun, it forms a compound noun, which is declined like the last section of the compound. For example:

ein Viertelpfund, **eine Viertelstunde**, **ein Viertel Wein** (a quarter of a litre of wine), **ein Viertelliter**, **im Dreivierteltakt** (music in waltz time).

(**b**) Note the expressions:

ein halbes Jahr, **eine halbe Stunde**, **in einer halben Stunde**, **in ein (und) einhalb Stunden** (in one and a half hours' time), **in**

anderthalb Stunden (in one and a half hours' time) (spoken German), **in zwei(und)einhalb Stunden** (in two and a half hours' time), **in drei(und)einhalb Stunden** (in three and a half hours' time), **ein viertel Kilo** (a quarter of a kilo, the measure), **ein Viertelkilo** (a quarter kilo, the amount).

(**c**) Note the method of increasing a quantity:

zweifach (double), **dreifach** (treble), **fünffach** (five times as much), **zehnfach** (ten times as much), **hundertfach** (a hundred times as much), **ein zweifacher Sprung** (a double jump, a jump with two complete turns in the air), **ein dreifacher Salto** (a triple somersault), **eine zehnfache Vervielfältigung** (a tenfold reproduction), **eine zwanzigfache Steigerung** (a twentyfold increase), **ein doppelter Betrag** (double the amount), **vielfach** (manifold), **das Vielfache verdienen** (to earn many times as much).

(**d**) Note the method of describing the way in which items are arranged in order:

erstens, **zweitens**, **drittens**, **viertens**, **fünftens**, **sechstens**, **siebtens or siebentens**, **achtens**, **neuntens**, **zehntens . . .** (firstly, secondly, thirdly, fourthly, fifthly . . .)

These words are adverbs, and are only used adverbially. They are not declined.

(**e**) The word for the Church tenth, or tithe, is masculine: **der Zehnte**. The word is of historical interest.

189 The date on letters and teleprints

The date on a letter in German is normally written as **1. Januar 1985** or **1. Januar 85**. The full stop after the number of the day is in place of the old-fashioned **-ten**. Further examples are: **22. Mai 85** or **29. Februar 84**.

Teleprints or computer documents usually express the date in six figures. The first two represent the day, the second two the month, and the last two the year. For example:
010185, or 220585, or 290284, or 111186, or 251286.

Countries, peoples, languages

190 Notes on the grammar concerning countries

(a) Countries are mostly neuter and singular. They are declined in the genitive singular, in which an -s is added. For example: **die Exporte Großbritanniens**, **die Völkergruppen Jugoslawiens**, **Dänemarks Agrarprodukte** (agricultural products), **die Geschichte Frankreichs**, **das Öl Saudiarabiens**.

(b) A few countries are feminine and singular. They are therefore not declined in the genitive singular, but the case is deduced from the accompanying definite article. The main countries are:

die Bundesrepublik Deutschland (genitive and dative – **der Bundesrepublik Deutschland**), **die Schweiz**, **die Tschechoslowakei**, **die Türkei**, **die Mongolei**, **die Vatikanstadt**, **die Sowjetunion** which is officially **die UdSSR (die Union der Sozialistischen Sowjetrepubliken)**.

(c) A very few countries are plural, and are declined. For example: **die Niederlande (in den Niederlanden)**, **die Vereinigten Staaten** (also **die USA** which is plural and declined), **die Vereinigten Arabischen Emirate**, **die Seychellen (auf den Seychellen)**.

191 Notes on the grammar concerning people

(a) The male citizen of a country is often indicated by the ending **-er**, and the female by the ending **-erin**. For example: **der Engländer**, **die Engländerin**, **der Waliser** (Welshman), **die Waliserin**, **der Schweizer**, **die Schweizerin**, **der Österreicher**, **die Österreicherin**, **der Amerikaner** (which is often erroneously applied to a citizen of the USA only), **die Amerikanerin**, **der Kanadier**, **die Kanadierin**, **der Australier**, **die Australierin**, **der Neuseeländer**, **die Neuseeländerin**.
N.B.: **der Landsmann** (the fellow-countryman), **die Landsmännin** (the fellow-countrywoman), **Landsleute** (fellow-countrymen).

(b) The plural of the feminine form is made by adding **-nen**. For example: **die Waliserinnen**.

173

(c) The words for the male citizen of some countries end in **-e**, and they are declined like type VI in para. 157. For example: **der Schotte (den Schotten, des Schotten, dem Schotten, die Schotten, von den Schotten)**, **der Ire** (sometimes applied to the citizen of Eire only) (**der Irländer** is also used), **der Franzose**, **der Russe** or **der Sowjetrusse** (which is often erroneously applied to the citizens of all the republics of the UdSSR) (more correctly perhaps **der Sowjetbürger**), **der Däne**, **der Schwede**, **der Brite**.

(d) The words for the females are: **die Schottin**, **die Irin**, **die Britin**, **die Französin** (note the umlaut), **die Russin**, **die Dänin**, **die Schwedin**. The plurals are formed by adding **-nen**.

(e) The word **Deutsche** is an adjective used as a noun, and is therefore declined like type VII in para. 157. For example: **der Deutsche, den Deutschen, die Deutschen**, but **ein Deutscher**, **einen Deutschen, Deutsche**, and the feminine **die Deutsche** or **eine Deutsche**.

192 Notes on the grammar concerning languages

(a) The adjective is used as a noun to denote the European languages. A capital letter is always used for a language, and the word is not declined if it refers simply to the name of the language. For example: **Deutsch, Englisch, Französisch, Spanisch, Italienisch, Portugiesisch, Russisch, Dänisch, Norwegisch, Schwedisch, Griechisch, Tschechisch, Ungarisch**.

(b) Non-European languages occasionally end in **-sch** such as **Arabisch** or **Chinesisch**, but mostly have their own form such as: **Suaheli** (Swahili), **Hausa, Yoruba, Ibo, Hindi, Pandschabi** (Punjabi), **Urdu, Bengali, Marathi**.

(c) A few occasions arise when the name of the language is used adjectivally or adverbially, in which case the word begins with a small letter. The following expressions should be noted:
die deutsche Sprache (adjectival use of **deutsch**), **wie sagt man das Wort auf deutsch?** (adverbial use), **auf gut deutsch** (adverbial use), **er schreibt in deutsch** (adverbial use describing the manner in which he is writing), **wir müssen deutsch mit ihm sprechen** (we must speak to him boldly, clearly, and in plain, unmistakable language).

(d) The word **deutsch** has been used for the expressions in (c), and (e) and (f) below, but the same rules apply to any other language.

(e) The following expressions should be noted, in which the word

Deutsch is used as a noun, and therefore begins with a capital letter: **ich lerne Deutsch, wir haben (das Fach) Deutsch in der Schule, im heutigen Deutsch, er spricht Deutsch**.

(**f**) The expressions **das Deutsche, das Althochdeutsche, das Mittelhochdeutsche** are used as overall terms for the language itself, or for its branches. Note the expression: **er übersetzt aus dem Englischen ins Deutsche, und aus dem Deutschen ins Englische**.

Adjectives used as adverbs

193 A difference between German and English grammar

German grammar differs from English grammar on one essential point, namely on the exact nature of an adverb. Words like **schön** and **schwer** in German are adjectives which can be used as adverbs without a change of form. For example:

Es ist schön (adverb) warm (adjective) heute.
It is very warm today.
Ihre Aussprache ist schwer (adverb) verständlich (adjective).
Her pronunciation is very difficult to understand.

Not all German adjectives, though, can be used as adverbs, and there are German adverbs which are never used adjectivally. This section deals only with those German adjectives which can be used as adverbs.

194 Adjectives used as adverbs

As mentioned in the previous paragraph, not all German adjectives can be used as adverbs, as the use depends on the sense of the word, and not all adjectives can sensibly be used as adverbs. There is no grammatical reason why this should not be so, but the reasons are semantic.

A rough test for adjectives which can be used as adverbs is whether or not there is an adverbial superlative form of a word, whether there is a reasonable translation with the form 'most + the word + -ly'.

195 Comparison of adjectives used as adverbs

(**a**) The positive (simple) form, like **schön** or **schwer**, is never declined as an adverb, that is to say that the form never has an ending added.

(**b**) The comparative form, like **schöner** or **schwerer**, is also never declined when an adverb. The comparative is formed in exactly the same way as the comparative of the adjective. (See para. 176.)

(**c**) The superlative form of the 'adverb' differs, however, from the superlative form of the adjective.

(**d**) The superlative adverb is formed of two words, **am** and the word with an ending **–sten** or **–esten**. The question of the exact ending, **–sten** or **–esten**, is dealt with in paragraph 177. Examples of adverbial superlatives are:

am schönsten, am schwersten, am kleinsten, am weitesten, am härtesten, am längsten, am kürzesten, am meisten.

(e) It is not always easy to decide whether a postmodifying adjective is used adjectivally or adverbially. Briefly, the adverbial comparatives in the following examples modify the verb and not the nouns, and so are ad–verbs.

Am schönsten fand sie die weißen und nicht die roten Rosen.
She liked the white roses best of all, and not the red ones.
Seine Rede gefiel mir am besten.
I liked his speech best. (His speech pleased me most.)

(f) In the above sentences the adverbial comparative is coupled to the verb: **fand am schönsten, gefiel am besten**.

(g) There are a few irregular comparisons:

gut	→ **besser**	→ **am besten**
viel	→ **mehr**	→ **am meisten**
gern(e)	→ **lieber**	→ **am liebsten**
hoch	→ **höher**	→ **am höchsten**
nah(e)	→ **näher**	→ **am nächsten**

196 Further uses of the adjective as an adverb

(a) The close connection of the adverb to the verb has been shown in para. 195 (e). The function of an adverb may also be to modify an adjective. In English, for example, *very* (adverb) *good* (adjective), *beautifully* (adverb) *designed* (past participle used as an adjective), *well* (adverb) *known* (past participle used adjectivally).

(b) Adjectives, usually in the positive (simple) form, are also used in German to modify other adjectives. For example: **schnell** (adverb) **fertig** (adjective) **sein** (*to be ready quickly*), **hoch** (adverb) **interessant** (adjective) (*highly interesting*), **weit** (adverb) **entfernt** (past participle used adjectivally) (*far distant*), **recht** (adverb) **gut** (adjective) (*really good*).

(c) Certain expressions which are composed by linking two adjectives are used adverbially: **kurz und bündig** (in short and to the point), **kurz und gut** (in short), **einzig und allein** (only, purely and simply), **weit und breit** (far and wide), **nah und fern** (far and wide), **kurz und klein schlagen** (to smash to pieces), **ganz und gar** (totally, wholly), **ganz und gar nicht** (by no means, not at all).

177

Adverbs

197 The function of an adverb

The adverb has the greatest range of functions of any part of speech. It extends or modifies the meaning of another word or phrase. It can modify or extend (a) a verb (see para. 195 (**e**)), (b) an adjective (see para. 196 (**b**)), (c) another adverb (see para. 206 (**c**)), (d) a prepositional phrase (see para. 206 (**d**)), (e) an adverbial phrase (see para. 206 (**e**)), and (f) a conjunction (see para. 206 (**f**)).

198 Indeclinable adverbs

There are many adverbs such as those expressing time, place, order, manner, cause or reason, which are not declined. They have neither extra endings according to case, nor can they be expressed in the comparative or superlative.

Particular care should be taken to note certain words which can be used as a noun or as an adverb, since the adverbial form is always written with a small letter, and the noun with a capital letter. For example: **der Morgen** but **morgen** (tomorrow), **der Vormittag** but **heute vormittag** (this morning).

199 Adverbs and adverbial expressions of time

There are many indeclinable adverbs and adverbial expressions of time, of which the following are examples:

morgens, vormittags, nachmittags, abends, nachts, heute, heute morgen, heute vormittag, heute nachmittag, heute abend, heute nacht, morgen (tomorrow), **morgen früh, morgen vormittag, morgen nachmittag, morgen abend, übermorgen, übermorgen früh, gestern, vorgestern, vorher, nachher, vor 2 Jahren** (dative), **vor einer Woche** (a week ago) (dative), **vor einem Jahr** (a year ago) (dative), **letzte Woche** (accusative), **vorige Woche** (accusative), **voriges Jahr** (accusative), **vorigen Monat** (accusative), **nächste Woche** (accusative), **nächstes Jahr** (accusative), **nächsten Monat** (accusative), **übernächste Woche** (accusative), **montags, dienstags, mittwochs, donnerstags, freitags, samstags, sonnabends, sonntags, Dienstag morgen, Mittwoch abend, außer sonntags** (except Sundays), **werktags** (weekdays), **wochenlang, monatelang, jahrelang, am 4. Februar, am 1. Mai, am 24. Dezember, in diesem Jahrhundert, im vorigen**

Jahrhundert, im 18. Jahrhundert, vor Chr. (vor Christus)
(B.C.), **nach Christus** (A.D.), **anno dazumal** (in olden times),
heutzutage (nowadays), **damals** (then, in those days), **bisher**
(hitherto), **einst** (once, some day), **derzeit** (at the moment),
vorerst (for the time being), **zunächst** (first of all), **zuerst** (in the
first place), **nochmals** (once again), **jedesmal** (each time), **kürzlich**
(lately, recently), **bald** (soon), **oft** (often), **schon** (already), **soeben**
(just now), **dann** (then), **inzwischen** (meanwhile), **zuletzt**
(finally), **endlich** (at last, finally), **wiederum** (again, afresh),
jederzeit (at any time), **sofort** (at once), **jetzt** (now), **nun** (now),
gerade (just), **eben** (just), **danach** (afterwards), **daraufhin**
(thereupon), **schließlich** (finally), **stets** (always), **immer** (always),
neulich (recently).

200 Adverbs and adverbial expressions of place

There are many indeclinable adverbs and adverbial expressions of
place, of which the following are examples:
hin und her (to and fro, (walking) up and down), **da** (there), **wo**
(where).
(The compounds formed with the above adverbs are considered in
para. 203.)

Further adverbs of place are:
hier, dort, vorne, hinten, abseits (aside, apart), **diesseits** (on this
side), **jenseits** (on that side), **and(e)rerseits** (on the other side),
oben (on top) (N.B. **über** is a preposition), **unten** (down below)
(N.B. **unter** is a preposition), **unterwegs** (on the way), **halbwegs**
(half-way), **auswärts** (outwards), **nach außen** (outwards),
einwärts (inwards), **nach innen** (inwards), **stromauf** (up-stream),
stromab (down-stream), **überall** (everywhere), **nirgends**
(nowhere), **nirgendwo** (nowhere), **irgendwo** (somewhere),
bergauf (up-hill), **bergab** (down-hill), **da herum** (thereabouts),
seitwärts (sideways), **vorwärts** (forwards), **rückwärts**
(backwards).

The adverbs listed above indicate a place, but are not precise details
as to an exact spot or place. More accurate descriptions of place are
usually given in adverbial phrases such as the following:
an Ort und Stelle sein (to be on the spot), **auf der Stelle treten** (to
mark time), **an Ihrer Stelle** (in your place), **an meiner Stelle** (in
my place, in place of me), **am angegebenen Ort** (loc. cit., as
mentioned above), **am falschen Ort** (in the wrong place, out of
place), **am Markt, auf der Hamburger Chaussee, am Hafen, bei
Herrn Vonderheide, zu Tante Emma, in Tante Emmas**

Laden, auf dem Flughafen, an Bord (on board), **an der See** (by the sea), **auf See** (at sea), **zur See** (to sea), **in der Luft** (airborne), **auf dem (festen) Boden** (on the ground), **in der Stadt, auf dem Lande** (in the country), **im Zug, im Bus, im Wagen, auf dem Fahrrad, auf dem Motorrad.**

201 Adverbs and adverbial expressions of order, or place

(a) The following indeclinable adverbs are formed from the ordinal adjectives (see para. 182). In practice the adverbs are limited to a few numbers, as the words are usually used to express ideas, facts, details in an orderly way. The adverbs are:

erstens (firstly), **zweitens** (secondly), **drittens, viertens, fünftens, sechstens, siebtens, achtens, neuntens, zehntens, elftens** ...

(b) Adverbial expressions are also formed with the aid of ordinal adjectives (see para. 182). For example:

zum erstenmal (for the first time), **zum zweitenmal, zum drittenmal, zum viertenmal, zum fünftenmal** ...

202 Adverbs and adverbial expressions of manner

There are many indeclinable adverbs and adverbial expressions of manner, of which the following are examples. They are divided into groups for greater clarity:

(a) Limitation: **beinahe** or **beinah** (nearly, almost), **fast** (almost), **nahezu** (almost, nearly), **bereits** (already), **praktisch** (practically), **so gut wie** (as good as), **kaum** (hardly), **einigermaßen** (to some extent), **annähernd** (approximately), **ungefähr** (roughly), **rund** (round about), **ca.** or **zirka** (about, approximately), **an die 500** (getting on for five hundred), **um die 500** (round about five hundred), **fast 500** (almost five hundred), **bis zu 500** (up to five hundred), **etwa 500** (roughly five hundred), **gerade** (just), **nur eben** (only just).

(b) Extension: **ferner** (further), **außerdem** (besides, moreover), **überdies, zudem** (in addition), **weiter** (furthermore), **im übrigen** (moreover), **übrigens** (besides), **sonst** (otherwise), **dazu** (in addition), **auch** (also), **ebenfalls** (also, likewise), **gleichermaßen** (equally), **in gleichem Maße** (equally), **in gleicher Weise** (in the same way), **gleichfalls** (likewise, also), **genauso** (just as ...), **ebenso** (just as ...), **sogar** (even), **ziemlich** (fairly, rather), **einigermaßen** (somewhat, rather), **eigentlich** (rather, really), **vielmehr** (rather, much more).

(c) Exaggeration: **sehr** (very), **recht** (really), **überaus** (extremely, exceedingly), **äußerst** (extremely, exceedingly), **höchst** (extremely, most), **besonders** (especially), **ungeheuer** (colossally), **riesig** (immensely), **mächtig** (mightily), **kräftig** (strongly, powerfully), **beträchtlich** (considerably), **beachtlich** (notably), **unendlich** (infinitely), **zutiefst** (deeply), **maßlos** (boundlessly), **über alle Maßen** (beyond measure), **in höchstem Grad** (to the highest degree), **furchtbar** (frightfully), **schrecklich** (terribly, frightfully), **entsetzlich** (terribly, frightfully), **bitter** (bitterly), **herzlich** (heartily), **erheblich** (considerably), **ungemein** (uncommonly, greatly), **außergewöhnlich** (unusually).

Exaggeration is a feature of daily speech rather than scholarly appraisal. The adverbs in the above list are therefore more likely to be heard in daily conversations rather than seen in the written form. There are also words of exaggeration which seem over-exaggerated even in daily speech, such as **wahnsinnig** (madly, crazily), **irrsinnig** (insanely, madly), **verflucht** (confoundedly), and **mordsmäßig** (murderously). Such words enjoy a certain vogue, and then fade into obscurity.

(d) Caution: **vielleicht** (perhaps), **möglicherweise** (as far as possible), **womöglich** (if possible, perhaps), **eventuell** (possibly, perhaps), **unter Umständen** (under certain circumstances), **gegebenenfalls** (if the occasion arises), **allenfalls** (in any event), **notfalls** (if necessary), **anscheinend** (apparently), **vermutlich** (presumably), **möglich** (possibly), **wahrscheinlich** (probably, likely), **höchst wahrscheinlich** (very probably), **voraussichtlich** (probably, presumably), **angeblich** (allegedly), **offenbar** (obviously, manifestly), **scheinbar** (seemingly, apparently), **sichtbar** (visibly, perceptibly), **augenscheinlich** (evidently), **nachweislich** (evidently, demonstrably), **vernünftigerweise** (rationally, reasonably).

(e) Extent: **allemal** (always, still), **allenfalls** (at all events), **allesamt** (altogether), **allezeit** (at all times), **überall** (everywhere), **an allen Orten** (everywhere), **an allen Ecken und Enden** (everywhere), **vielerorts** (at many places), **ringsum, ringsherum, ringsumher** (round about), **nirgends, nirgendwo** (nowhere), **irgendwo** (somewhere or other), **zu** (too), **oft** (often), **oftmals** (often), **häufig** (frequently), **immer wieder** (again and again), **meistens** (mostly), **zum größten Teil** (mostly), **überwiegend** (mainly, chiefly), **vorwiegend** (predominantly), **mehrmals** (again and again, repeatedly), **vielfach** (often, frequently), **x-mal** or **zigmal** (countless times), **selten** (seldom), **vereinzelt** (singly, sporadically), **nicht oft** (not often), **fern** (far), **bei weitem** (by far),

181

in nächster Nähe (very close), **dicht dabei** (very close), **ganz in der Nähe** (very near), **genug** (enough), **ausreichend** (sufficiently), **bald** (soon), **höchstens** (at the most), **wenigstens** (at the least), **gerade** (just, quite), **jetzt** (now), **nun** (now), **nur** (only), **bloß** (only, merely), **nach und nach** (little by little, gradually).

(**f**) Manner: **gern** (willingly, gladly, readily), **ungern** (reluctantly, grudgingly), **links** (to the left), **rechts** (to the right), **geradeaus** (straight on), **rückwärts** (backwards), **umsonst** (for nothing), **so** (so, thus), **genauso** (just so, in the same way), **vorsichtshalber**, **aus Vorsicht** (as a precaution), **sicherheitshalber** (for safety's sake).

The majority of adverbs expressing manner are, however, adjectives used adverbially.

(**g**) Adverbs of 'convenience': **aber** (though, but), **doch** (yet, though, nevertheless, after all, for all that), **dennoch** (yet, still, however, nevertheless), **dann** (then, thereupon), **jedoch** (notwithstanding, yet), **wohl** (indeed), **denn** (then, in that case).

The adverbs of 'convenience' are words which are not essential to the meaning of a sentence, but are used to fill a temporary gap in the flow of thought, or to mark a pause, or for emphasis, or even to aid the rhythm of a sentence. They are convenient, but non-essential words. They are used, or misused, as follows:

Das ist aber gut.   Er ist doch gekommen.
That's good though.   He came after all.
Das kann ich mir wohl denken.
I can well imagine that indeed.

(**h**) Cause or reason: **daher** (thence, therefore), **darum** (therefore), **folglich** (accordingly, therefore), **demnach** (consequently), **somit** (consequently), **deshalb** (for that reason), **dadurch** (in that way, thereby), **dabei** (thereby), **demgemäß** (accordingly), **demnächst** (thereupon), **dementsprechend** (accordingly, correspondingly), **wobei** (whereby), **wonach** (whereupon).

203 Pronominal adverbs

(**a**) The adverbs **hier** (here), **da** (there), and **wo** (where) combine with most prepositions to form pronominal adverbs, that is to say adverbs which have a meaning which is partly adverb and partly pronoun. The pronominal aspect becomes clear in the examples in sub-paragraph (**c**) below.

(**b**) The adverbs **da** and **wo** end in a vowel. If a preposition begins with a vowel, then an **r** is inserted before the two words are joined. This is for the sake of the sound of the word, and ease of speech.

For example:

da-r-aus = **daraus**   wo-r-aus = **woraus**
da-r-ein = **darein**   wo-r-ein = **worein**
da-r-in = **darin**   wo-r-in = **worin**

N.B.: **damit**, **dabei**, **dafür**, **dazwischen**, **womit**, **wobei**.

(**c**) The translation of a pronominal adverb brings out the
pronominal aspect of the compound word. For example:

hierin, **darin**   (in it, in them)
hierzu, **dazu**   (to it, to them)
hiervon, **davon**   (from it, from them)
worin   (in which)
wozu   (in addition to which)
wovon   (from or about which)

It is clear from the above examples that the listener or the reader
must know the context or situation in which the words are used.
The pronouns 'it', 'them', and 'which' have no precise meaning
until we know to what they refer, but this applies to all pronouns.

(**d**) The pronominal adverbs are often used in speech, and usually
avoided in written German. They serve to keep the flow of thought
going in speech, but often appear vague and imprecise in writing.

(**e**) The compounds with **wo-** such as **worin**, **wozu**, and **wovon**
can either be used as interrogative or as relative adverbs in German
grammar.

(**f**) A characteristic of a pronominal adverb is that it can always be
exchanged for an adverbial phrase which includes a noun. For
example: **damit = mit dem Wagen**, **darüber = über das Thema**,
worauf er saß = auf dem Stuhl, **auf dem er saß**.

(**g**) Pronominal adverbs are used to form relative clauses in the
following way:

Wodurch die Epidemie ausgelöst wurde, ist noch nicht bekannt.
What really started the epidemic is not known.
Das worüber er gesprochen hat, ist mir neu.
That of which he spoke is new to me.
Ich weiß nicht, wo er war. (**Wo** is also a pronominal adverb.)
I don't know where he was.

Generally speaking, if it is possible to use a preposition and the
pronominal adverb **der**, **die**, **das**, then the structure with **wo-** or
wor- is avoided nowadays. For example:

Das Hotel, von dem (wovon) wir sprachen, ist ausgebucht.
The hotel we were talking about is booked up.

(**h**) Certain word combinations are used to link a relative clause to the main clause. Such combinations are:

der, der ...	allerhand, was ...	allerhand, was ...
derjenige, der ...	alles, was ...	einiges, was ...
derjenige, welcher ...	das, was ...	folgendes, was ...
derselbe, der ...	dasjenige, was ...	nichts, was ...
derselbe, welcher ...	dasselbe, was ...	vieles, was ...
etwas, das ...	etwas, was ...	weniges, was ...

These word combinations are often used in compact statements such as:

Der, der das sagt, lügt.
He who says that lies.
Es ist genau das, was ich sagen wollte.
It's just what I wanted to say.
Vieles, was gemacht wurde, war gut gemeint.
Much that was done was well-intended.
Es ist das gleiche, was ich schon x-mal gehört habe.
It's the same as I've heard many many times before.

204 Compound adverbs

The adverbs **da**, **dort**, **hier**, **hin**, **her**, **so** and **wo** combine readily with each other, or with other adverbs, or with prepositions to form compound adverbs such as:

dabei (thereby), **dafür** (instead of it), **dagegen** (on the contrary), **daher** (thence), **dahin** (thither), **dahinten** (behind, way back there), **dahinter** (at the back of it, down behind), **damit** (with it, therewith), **danach** (afterwards), **daneben** (close by, aside), **daran** (thereon, thereby), **darauf** (thereon, thereupon), **daraus** (therefrom), **darein** (thereto, therein), **darin** (therein), **darüber** (over it, thereon), **darum** (therefore), **darunter** (under it), **davon** (therefrom), **davor** (beforehand, before it), **dazu** (in addition, thereto), **dazwischen** (in between),

dorther (from there), **dortherum** (thereabouts), **dorthin** (to that place),

herab (down from), **heran** (near, up to, towards), **herauf** (up to, up towards), **heraus** (out from within), **herbei** (hither, this way), **herein** (in here), **hernach** (after this, afterwards), **herüber** (across to this side), **herum** (round about), **herunter** (downward, off),

hieran (at this, by this), **hierauf** (upon this, after that), **hieraus** (from here, arising out of this), **hierbei** (herewith, with this, enclosed), **hierdurch** (by this means, through here), **hierein** (into this place), **hierfür** (for this, instead of this), **hiergegen** (against this), **hierher** (this way, to this place), **hierherum** (hereabouts), **hierhin** (in this direction), **hicrin** (herein), **hiermit** (herewith), **hiernach** (after this, according to this), **hierneben** (close by, besides), **hierüber** (over here, concerning this (point)), **hierum** (about this place, concerning this), **hierunter** (under this, amongst these), **hiervon** (from this), **hierzu** (in addition to this), **hierzwischen** (between these things),

hinab (down, downwards), **hinauf** (up, upwards), **hinaus** (out, forth), **hinein** (inside, into), **hinüber** (over there), **hinunter** (down, downwards), **hinzu** (in addition, towards, besides),

soeben (just now), **sofort** (immediately, at once), **sogar** (even), **sogleich** (instantly), **somit** (consequently, then), **soso** (tolerably well), **soundso** (so-and-so, such-and-such), **soweit** (so far), **sowieso** (in any case, anyhow), **sozusagen** (so to speak),

wobei (whereby), **wodurch** (by means of which), **wofür** (for which), **wogegen** (against which), **woher** (whence), **wohin** (whither), **womit** (by which), **wonach** (whereupon), **worauf** (whereupon), **woraus** (whence), **worin** (wherein), **worüber** (whereat, over which), **worum** (about which), **worunter** (under which, among which), **wovon** (from which), **wovor** (before which), **wozu** (to what purpose, why).

A literal translation can be given to many of the above words. For example: **damit** (with it), **dazu** (to it), **hinzu** (towards it), **herauf** (up on this thing here), **wonach** (after which).

The prefix **hin** denotes a movement away from the speaker, and the prefix **her** denotes a movement towards the speaker

205 Abbreviated forms of compound adverbs

Some compound adverbs are abbreviated in speech and occasionally in writing. Such abbreviations are mostly regional, and are part of the Umgangssprache. Students are advised always to use the full form in writing, and preferably in speech. These abbreviations include:

drauf for **darauf**, **draus** for **daraus**, **drin** for **darin**, **dran** for **daran**, **drüber** for **darüber**, **drum** for **darum**, **'rein** for **herein**, **'ran** for **heran**, **'raus** for **heraus**, **'rum** for **herum**, **'runter** for **herunter**.

206 The use of adverbs

(**a**) Adverbs may be used to extend or modify a verb (see para. 195 (**e**)). Adverbs are also used to form compound verbs (see paras. 120 and 122).

(**b**) Adverbs may be used to extend or modify an adjective (see para. 196 (**b**)).

(**c**) Adverbs may be used to extend or modify another adverb. For example:

Er fuhr sehr (adverb) langsam (adverb).
He drove very slowly.
Er geht besonders (adverb) gern (adverb) ins Theater.
He very much likes going to the theatre.

The adverb **sehr** extends the adverb **langsam** and **besonders** extends **gern**.

(**d**) A few adverbs may be used to extend or modify a preposition. The compound adverbs in para. 204 are examples of the combination of an adverb and a preposition. The word **dazwischen**, for example, consists of two parts: **da** (there) and **zwischen** (between). The word **da** is an adverb, and **zwischen** a preposition, but the compound word is always an adverb.

(**e**) Adverbs may extend or modify an adverbial phrase. For example:

Sie fuhr langsam (adverb) nach Hause (adverbial phrase).
She drove slowly home.
Genau (adverb) um vier Uhr (adverbial phrase) morgens (adverb) kam sie nach Hause.
She came home at exactly four o'clock in the morning.

The adverb **langsam** modifies the adverbial phrase **nach Hause**, **genau** modifies the adverbial phrase **um vier Uhr**, and both together modify the adverb **morgens**.

(**f**) A few adverbs may be used to modify a conjunction. The combination functions as if it were a single conjunction.

Examples are: **wenn auch** (although, even if), **selbst wenn** (even though), **so daß** (so that), **um zu** (in order to), **wenn nur** (if only), **insofern als** (in that), **außer wenn** (except when), **wenn möglich** (if possible), **wenn nicht** (if not, unless). (See paras. 241–247 for the use of conjunctions.)

(**g**) Adverbs are also used to ask questions:

warum? (why?), **wann?** (when?), **wie?** (how?), **wo?** (where?), **womit?** (what?), **wozu?** (for what purpose?).

(See para. 204 for more such adverbs formed with **wo-**.)

207 Word order: position of an adverb in a sentence

Word order is considered in a separate section, and the question of
the position of an adverb in a sentence is considered there in detail.
Briefly, the principle is that the adverb is kept in close proximity to
the word it extends or modifies.

Pronouns

208 Types of pronouns

German pronouns are usually classified into six types: personal, reflexive, possessive, relative, interrogative, and indefinite pronouns.

A pronoun is a short word which stands for, or takes the place of, a noun.

209 Personal pronouns

In German, personal pronouns not only stand for persons but also for things. German grammar is different to English grammar, in that in English the word 'it' stands for an inanimate thing or an abstract idea. If the noun in German is masculine, then the personal pronoun is masculine; if the noun is feminine or neuter, then the personal pronoun is feminine or neuter. This applies to things as well as persons. For example: **er** stands for **der Löffel** (spoon), **sie** for **die Gabel** (fork), and **es** for **das Messer** (knife), even though all three are items of cutlery.

A personal pronoun, like the definite or the indefinite article, has several functions in a sentence:

(**a**) it indicates the gender of the noun which it represents.
(**b**) it shows the number: singular or plural.
(**c**) it shows the case: nominative, accusative, genitive, or dative, and thereby the function of the word in the sentence.
(**d**) it shows the person. The first person is used by a speaker or a writer about himself or herself (**ich**, **wir**); the second person is the person to whom he or she speaks or writes (**du**, **ihr**, **Sie**); the third 'person' is the person or thing about which the first person is speaking or writing (**er**, **sie**, **es**; **sie**). Things or ideas are only referred to in the third person.

210 Declension of personal pronouns

The following tables give the forms of the personal pronouns:

	singular					
	first	*second*		*third person*		
nominative	ich	du	Sie	er	sie	es
accusative	mich	dich	Sie	ihn	sie	es
genitive	meiner	deiner	Ihrer	seiner	ihrer	seiner
dative	mir	dir	Ihnen	ihm	ihr	ihm

	plural			
	first	*second*		*third person*
nominative	wir	ihr	Sie	sie
accusative	uns	euch	Sie	sie
genitive	unser	euer	Ihrer	ihrer
dative	uns	euch	Ihnen	ihnen

211 Use of the personal pronouns

(a) The German personal pronouns always have a grammatical gender. For example:

Der Wagen ist neu. Er steht in der Garage.
The car is new. It is in the garage.
Die Wäsche hängt auf dem Boden. Sie ist trocken.
The washing is in the loft (attic). It is dry.

(*N.B.*: **auf dem Boden** usually means 'on thc ground', but it can mean 'in the loft or attic'. In winter or wet weather the washing is often hung up in the loft or attic.)

(b) The nominative case is used for the subject, and the accusative case for the object. For example:

Ich (subject) **sah ihn** (object). **Er** (subject) **sah mich** (object).

(c) The genitive of the personal pronoun is used to indicate possession: **meiner** (mine), **deiner** (yours), **seiner** (his), **ihrer** (hers), **seiner** (its), **unser** (ours), **euer**, **Ihrer** (yours), **ihrer** (theirs).

The personal pronoun should not be confused with the possessive pronoun which is followed by a noun (**mein Wagen**, **sein Auto**). The genitive of the personal pronoun stands alone, without a noun, as in the following examples which are taken from the Umgangssprache:

Dieser Wagen ist meiner, der andere ihrer.
This car is mine, the other one hers.
Dieser Bus ist unser; Ihrer fährt von der anderen Haltestelle.
This bus is ours; yours goes from the other stop.

The personal pronouns **meiner**, **ihrer**, **unser**, and **Ihrer** obviously refer to specific things, namely the car and the bus, but these nouns are not expressed.

212 Use of 'du', 'ihr', and 'Sie'

(a) The singular **du** and the plural form **ihr** are used to speak to children, to pets, to close members of the family, and to close friends.

(**b**) The more formal **Sie** (always written with a capital letter) is used to speak to all persons who are neither close friends, nor members of the family, nor very young.

(**c**) There is a grey zone in which a speaker may not know whether to use **du** or **Sie**, and in that case it is always safer to use **Sie**. A young girl, very tall for her age, would probably feel flattered to be addressed as **Sie**, whereas a short, undersized young woman would be embarrassed at being addressed with **du**.

There are usually clear guide lines for teachers in a school, such as using **Sie** to all pupils from the **Obersekunda** (**Oberstufe**) upwards. This is roughly from the age of 16 onwards. The pupils continue to use **du** amongst themselves. If a pupil leaves school at 16, and begins an apprenticeship, he or she is automatically addressed with **Sie**.

There is a growing tendency among students at the university to use **du** to each other, especially if they are in the same seminar, or are studying the same subject. There are political undertones in the use of **du**, and not all students like, or follow, this custom.

When adults get to know each other later in life, and decide that the time has come to use the familiar **du**, then they normally drink to **Brüderschaft**. Men link their drinking arms, and then drink each other's health. Women do the same. A man usually seals the **Brüderschaft** to a woman with a kiss. From that time on only Christian names and **du** are used. A reversion to **Sie** gives offence, or can symbolize the end of a friendship. The speed of courting may still be judged by the speed at which **du** is first used.

213 Reflexive pronouns

If a reflex action takes place, whereby an action comes back on the persons concerned, then a pronoun is referred to as a reflexive pronoun. If I cut myself, then the word 'I' is a personal pronoun, but 'myself' is a reflexive pronoun.

In German there are many reflexive verbs (see paras. 86–90) which must always be used with a reflexive pronoun, even though the English translation does not require such a reflexive pronoun. For example:

Er rasiert sich.   Ich beuge mich Ihrer (genitive) Entscheidung.
He is shaving.   *I accept your decision.*

214 The forms of the reflexive pronoun

(**a**) The normal form of the reflexive pronoun is the accusative form.

The following table shows the personal pronoun with the appropriate reflexive pronoun:

ich (personal)	→	**mich** (reflexive)	**man** (one)	→	**sich**
du	→	**dich**	**wir**	→	**uns**
er	→	**sich**	**ihr**	→	**euch**
sie	→	**sich**	**Sie**	→	**sich**
es	→	**sich**	**sie**	→	**sich**

(**b**) A few verbs are always followed by the dative case, therefore the dative form of the reflexive pronoun is used. The dative forms are: **mir**, **dir**, **sich**, **sich**, **sich**, **uns**, **euch**, **sich**, and **sich**. For example:
Ich helfe mir selbst(I'll help myself, or I go in for self-help).
In fact the situations involving verbs which take the dative seldom occur.

(**c**) Pseudoreflexive verbs, however, which take the dative, are in common use in everyday speech. For example:
Ich kaufe mir ein neues Radio.
I am going to buy (myself) a new radio.
Sie kaufte sich ein neues Kleid.
She bought (herself) a new dress.

The dative pronouns **mir** and **sich** in the above examples mean 'for myself' and 'for herself', and in both sentences the speaker is emphasizing that the purchases are for personal use or the use of the individual concerned, and not for another person. The verb **kaufen** in this instance is called a pseudoreflexive verb, as it is apparently made to have a reflexive element.

(**d**) Another use of the reflexive pronoun occurs after the verb **lassen** (to let, allow):
Ich lasse mich überraschen.
I'll wait for the surprise. (Literally: *I'll let myself be surprised.*)

(**e**) Mutual actions can sometimes be expressed with the aid of the reflexive pronoun **sich**:

Sie grüßen sich.	Sie schütteln sich die Hände.	Sie küssen sich.
They greet each other.	*They shake hands.*	*They kiss.*

(**f**) There are no emphatic pronouns in German as there are in English. 'I myself' is translated by **ich selbst**, 'for me myself' by **für mich selbst**, 'by me myself' by **von mir selbst**, and so on. Whereas in English the emphatic pronoun has the same form as the reflexive pronoun, in German the emphasis is given by the indeclinable word **selbst**. The indeclinable pronoun **selber** is also used instead of **selbst** in the Umgangssprache.

215 Possessive pronouns

As the name implies, a possessive pronoun indicates a belonging, a belonging to, or a possessive function.

The German possessive pronouns are: **mein** (my), **dein** (your), **sein** (his), **ihr** (her), **sein** (its) **unser** (our), **euer** (your), **Ihr** (your), and **ihr** (their).

German possessive pronouns function as adjectives. They are declined like adjectives, and are sometimes classified as possessive adjectives.

216 Declension of possessive pronouns

(a) The German possessive pronouns, **mein**, **dein**, **ihr**, **sein**, etc. are declined like **ein** (or **kein** in the plural). The declension of the possessive pronoun (which has the function of an adjective) is as follows:

	singular		
	masculine	*feminine*	*neuter*
nominative	sein Anzug	seine Uhr	sein Buch
accusative	seinen Anzug	seine Uhr	sein Buch
genitive	seines Anzugs	seiner Uhr	seines Buch(e)s
dative	seinem Anzug	seiner Uhr	seinem Buch

	plural		
	masculine	*feminine*	*neuter*
nominative	seine Anzüge,	Uhren,	Bücher
accusative	seine Anzüge,	Uhren,	Bücher
genitive	seiner Anzüge,	Uhren,	Bücher
dative	seinen Anzügen,	Uhren,	Büchern

(b) Should an adjective come in between the possessive pronoun and the noun, then the adjective is declined as in para. 165. For example: **sein neuer Anzug**, **ihr neues Kleid**, **aus seinem neuen Buch**.

(c) The gender, number, and case of the following noun is shown by the form of the possessive pronoun which functions as an adjective.

(d) Note the forms of the possessive pronouns as they sometimes occur in the Umgangssprache: **der Wagen ist seiner**, **die Uhr ist seine**, **das Buch ist sein(e)s**.

(e) Sometimes in speech and in letter writing the **e** is omitted from **unser** and **euer**, as follows: **unsre (unsere) Pläne** (our plans), **Eure**

Marga, mit unsrem (unserem) Wagen, in eurem (euerem) Haus.

217 Demonstrative pronouns

A demonstrative pronoun points out or indicates a particular person or thing. The German words **dieser** (this here) and **jener** (that there) are typical demonstrative pronouns.

218 Declension of a demonstrative pronoun

The demonstrative pronoun is declined like **der**, **die**, **das**:

	singular			plural
	masculine	*feminine*	*neuter*	*m.f.n.*
nominative	dieser	diese	dieses	diese
accusative	diesen	diese	dieses	diese
genitive	dieses	dieser	dieses	dieser
dative	diesem	dieser	diesem	diesen

219 Function of a demonstrative pronoun

A demonstrative pronoun either functions as an adjective (together with a noun) or as a pronoun (instead of a noun). The following examples show the difference in the two functions:

Er kaufte dieses Buch.　　Er kaufte dieses (or dies).
He bought this book.　　*He bought this one.*
Dieser Wagen ist der beste.　Dieser ist der beste.
This car is the best.　　*This (one) is the best*

The first sentence shows the adjectival, and the second the pronominal use.

220 The words 'der', 'die', and 'das' used as demonstrative pronouns

(**a**) The words **der**, **die**, and **das** (meaning *this one* or *that one*) are sometimes used instead of **dieser** and **jener**, especially in everyday speech.

(**b**) The pronouns are declined as follows:

	singular			plural
	masculine	*feminine*	*neuter*	*m.f.n.*
nominative	der	die	das	die
accusative	den	die	das	die
genitive	dessen	deren	dessen	deren (*or* derer)
dative	dem	der	dem	denen

The genitive forms, and the dative plural differ from the forms of the same words used as a definite article, and the words **dessen**, **deren**, and **derer** are dealt with in para. 221.

(**c**) The words are used as follows:

Der ist gut. Die ist gut. Das ist gut.
He (that one) is good. She (that one) is good. That's good.
(Der Wagen ist neu.) Der ist neu. *(This or that one is new.)*
(Die Uhr is teuer.) Die ist teuer. *(This or that one is expensive.)*
Mit dem können Sie nichts erreichen.
With him you won't be able to achieve anything.
Den kann ich nicht leiden. Die ist garstig zu mir.
I can't bear him (that man). She's nasty to me.

Note that the demonstrative pronoun **der**, **die**, or **das** comes at the beginning, or very near the beginning of the sentence, for emphasis. The exact meaning of the demonstrative pronoun can only be understood in context, as the speaker is referring to a particular person or thing that must previously be known to the listener.

(**d**) There are a few vague expressions such as:

Ich habe den und den getroffen. *(I met this and that man.)*
Ich habe das und das gesehen. *(I saw this and that.)*
Die da ist hübsch. *(that girl there is pretty.)*
Die hier ist besser. *(this one is better.)*
Der, der am meisten redet, ist nicht immer der klügste.
(He who talks the most is not always the cleverest.)

221 The use of 'dessen', 'deren' and 'derer' as demonstrative pronouns

(**a**) The pronouns **dessen** and **deren** are mainly used as relative pronouns (see para. 227).

(**b**) The use of **dessen** (of him, his), **deren** (of her, her), **dessen** (of it, its), and **derer** (or **deren**) (of them, their) as demonstrative pronouns is as follows:

Ich sah den Mann und dessen Sohn.
Ich sah die Frau und deren Tochter.
Ich sah das Mädchen und dessen Freund.
Ich sah die Eltern (parents) **und deren (derer) Kinder.**

The demonstrative pronouns may well be used in the above manner for stylistic effect, and to display erudition, but there are simpler ways of expressing the same thoughts. In the above examples **und seinen Sohn**, **und ihre Tochter**, **und seinen Freund**, **und ihre Kinder** would be the usual way of saying the same thing. The use of the words **dessen** and **deren** imply a sure touch in the use of the grammar; so the words are not often heard in spoken German. They are also used to denote special possessiveness.

(**c**) The word **derer** (of those) is only used in the genitive plural. For example:

Er war nicht einer derer, die alles besser wissen.
He was not one of those who always know better.

(**d**) There is a tendency to avoid the genitive plural because 'it sounds too academic'. The sentence in (**c**) would therefore most likely to be spoken and written as follows:

Er war nicht einer von denen, die alles besser wissen.

222 Derjenige, diejenige, dasjenige

(**a**) The words mean 'the particular one', or in the plural form 'the particular ones'.

(**b**) The forms are declinable as follows:

	singular			plural
	masculine	*feminine*	*neuter*	*m.f.n.*
nominative	derjenige	diejenige	dasjenige	diejenigen
accusative	denjenigen	diejenige	dasjenige	diejenigen
genitive	desjenigen	derjenigen	desjenigen	derjenigen
dative	demjenigen	derjenigen	demjenigen	denjenigen

(**c**) The particular form of the word is always followed by a relative pronoun. For example: **derjenige, der ...** (the one who ...), **diejenigen, die ...** (those who ...), **mit demjenigen, der ...** (with the one who ...).
The appropriate form of the relative pronoun usually refers to persons, but it can be used for a thing if a specific thing is especially picked out for special mention, as in the third example in (**d**).

(**d**) The following examples show the words in use.

Er suchte die Spieler aus, die in Topform waren.
Er suchte diejenigen (Spieler) aus, die in Topform waren.
He picked those (players) who were in top form.
Er wollte mit denjenigen sprechen, die etwas von der Taktik verstanden.
He wanted to talk to the very ones who understood something about tactics.
Dieses Spiel war gerade dasjenige, das sie gewinnen mußten.
This match was the very one which they had to win.

223 The pronouns 'selbst' and 'selber'

(**a**) The emphatic pronouns **selbst** and **selber** are indeclinable.
Selbst is the word which is preferred.

(**b**) The use of the words is as follows:
Ich selbst werde die Arbeit ausführen.
I myself (and nobody else) will carry out the work.
Geschicklichkeit kommt nicht von selbst.
Skill doesn't come (from itself alone) naturally.
Sie ist mit sich selbst zufrieden.
She's contented. / She's self-satisfied.

224 Derselbe, dieselbe, dasselbe; der gleiche, die gleiche, das gleiche

(**a**) The words mean 'the same', and may be used as pronouns
without a noun, or as adjectives with a noun.

(**b**) The words are declined in exactly the same way as **derjenige**,
etc. in para. 222, except that the appropriate form of **der gleiche** is
always written as two words.

(**c**) The following examples show the words in use:
Ihr Kleid ist von derselben Schneiderin genäht wie das (Kleid) ihrer
Nachbarin.
Her dress is made by the same dressmaker as that of her neighbour.
Er trinkt immer aus derselben Tasse.   Er ist immer derselbe.
He always drinks out of the same cup.   *He's always the same.*

(**d**) **Der gleiche**, **die gleiche**, **das gleiche**, and the other forms of
the same words are written as two words. The difference in
meaning between **dasselbe** and **das gleiche** is shown in the
following examples:
Er trug tagtäglich denselben Anzug.
He wore the same suit day after day.
Er trug den gleichen Anzug wie sein Nachbar.
He wore the same suit as his neighbour. (Spoken English)

(**e**) **Der gleiche**, etc. can almost always be used instead of **derselbe**,
etc., but the reverse is not always possible, as **derselbe**, etc. means
'the very one' or 'the actual one'. The examples in (**d**) bring out this
difference.

225 Relative pronouns

Relative pronouns link or relate a subordinate clause grammatically
to a main clause. The most common relative pronouns are the

various forms of **der**, **die**, and **das**, as given below. These are then translated by 'who'; 'whom', 'whose' and occasionally 'that' for persons, and by 'which' and 'that' for things and abstract ideas.

226 The relative pronouns 'der', 'die', and 'das'

(a) The words **der**, **die**, and **das** when used as relative pronouns are declined in the following manner:

	singular			plural
	masculine	*feminine*	*neuter*	*m.f.n.*
nominative	der	die	das	die
accusative	den	die	das	die
genitive	dessen	deren	dessen	deren
dative	dem	der	dem	denen

The genitive forms and the dative plural differ from the forms of the definite article.

(b) The relative pronoun takes the gender and number of the noun to which it refers, but takes its case from its grammatical function in the subordinate clause.

(c) The use of the relative pronoun is shown in the following examples:

Der Nord-Ostsee-Kanal, der durch Schleswig-Holstein fließt, wird jährlich von fast 100.000 Schiffen passiert.
The Kiel Canal, which flows through Schleswig-Holstein, is traversed by almost 100,000 ships per year.
Der Nord-Ostsee-Kanal, den man früher den Kaiser-Wilhelm-Kanal nannte, ist 98 km lang.
The Kiel Canal, which was formerly called the Kaiser Wilhelm Canal, is 98 km long.
Die Nebenflüsse, die in den Rhein fließen, bestimmen den Pegelstand des Flusses.
The tributaries which flow into the Rhine determine the water level of the river.
Der Rhein, dessen Quellflüsse der Vorderrhein und der Hinterrhein sind, ist 1320 km lang.
The Rhine, which springs from the Vorderrhein and the Hinterrhein, is 1320 km long.

The gender and number of the relative pronoun is determined by the gender and number of the noun to which it refers. In the above sentences **der Nord-Ostsee-Kanal, der . . ., der Nord-Ostsee-Kanal, den . . ., die Nebenflüsse, die . . .,** and **der Rhein, dessen . . .** are the structures which show the relationship between the noun and the relative pronoun.

The case depends on the function of the relative pronoun within the relative clause. In the above sentences the functions of the relative pronouns are: subject, object, subject, possessive, in that order.

227 Use of 'dessen', 'deren', and 'denen'

(a) The use of **dessen** and **deren** as relative pronouns denotes possession. The translation is 'whose', 'of whom', or 'of which', according to circumstances.

The following sentences show the use of the words:

Der Mann, dessen Frau einen Autounfall hatte, ist selbst verunglückt.
The man whose wife had a car accident has himself met with an accident.
Die Frau, deren Mann ein berühmter Architekt ist, ist Ärztin.
The woman whose husband is a famous architect is a doctor.
Die Eltern, deren Sohn und Tochter an derselben Universität studieren, haben finanzielle Probleme.
The parents whose son and daughter are studying at the same university have financial problems.

The relative pronouns **dessen** and **deren** take the gender and number of the nouns to which they refer. The case is, of course, genitive.

(b) The word **denen** is the dative plural (masculine, feminine, and neuter) of the relative pronoun. The form **denen** should not be confused with **den**, which is the dative plural of the definite article. The following examples illustrate the difference:

Der Industrielle machte zusammen mit den Technikern Gebrauch von den Forschungsergebnissen. (the articles **den** and **den**)
The industrialist, together with the technical experts, made use of the results of research work.
Die Industriellen, mit denen die Theoretiker zusammenarbeiteten, verwirklichten die Ergebnisse der Grundlagenforschung. (the relative pronoun **denen**)
The industrialists, with whom the theoreticians collaborated, turned the results of basic research into reality.

228 Use of 'welcher', 'welche', 'welches' as relative pronouns

(a) The word **welcher** used as a relative pronoun is declined like **dieser** (see para. 218), except that there is no form of the genitive case. The genitive forms **dessen** and **deren** are used instead.

(b) The appropriate form of **welcher** is sometimes used as a substitute relative pronoun, in place of the appropriate form of **der**.

Welcher is a word which is dated when used as a relative pronoun, and its use as a relative pronoun is not recommended in modern German. Students are advised always to use the appropriate form of **der**.

(c) The word **welcher** is used frequently as an interrogative pronoun (see para. 231). It is only its use as a relative pronoun which should be avoided.

229 Interrogative pronouns

Interrogative pronouns are used to ask questions. There are very few of them: **wer?** (who?), **was?** (what?), **was für ein . . .?** (what kind of a . . .?), and **welcher?** (which one?).

230 'Wer?' and 'was?'

(a) **Wer?** (who?) is used for persons.
   Was? (what?) is used for things.

(b) **Wer** is declinable: **wer** (nominative), **wen** (accusative), **wessen** (genitive, and very seldom used), **wem** (dative).
The word is used as follows:

Wer ist das?	Wen trafen Sie?	Mit wem sprachen Sie?
Who is that?	*Whom did you meet?*	*With whom were you speaking?*

(c) **Was** also has a genitive form (**wessen**) which is very seldom used.

(d) **Wer** and **was** can also be used very occasionally as relative pronouns:

wer es auch sei, sollte . . .	*(whoever it may be should . . .)*
das, was ich haben wollte . . .	*(that which I wanted . . .)*

231 'Was für ein?' and 'welcher?'

(a) **Was für ein . . .?** (what kind of a . . .?) and **welcher?** (which) are both declinable and both usually refer to things, although both can also refer to persons as shown in the examples in sub-paragraph (c).

(b) **Was für ein** is declined as follows:

	singular			plural
	masculine	*feminine*	*neuter*	*m.f.n.*
nom.	was für ein	was für eine	was für ein	was für
acc.	was für einen	was für eine	was für ein	was für
gen.	—	—	—	—
dat. (mit)	was für einem	was für einer	was für einem	was für

(c) Examples of the pronoun in use are:

Was für ein (subject) **Mann ist er? Was für eine** (subject) **Frau ist sie? Was für ein** (subject) **Buch ist es? Was für einen** (object) **Film sahen Sie? Aus was für einer** (dative) **Familie kommt sie? Was für Bücher** (object, plural) **lesen Sie? Was haben Sie für Bücher** (object, plural) **gelesen?**

(d) The interrogative pronoun **welcher** is declined as follows:

	singular			plural
	masculine	*feminine*	*neuter*	*m.f.n.*
nominative	welcher	welche	welches	welche
accusative	welchen	welche	welches	welche
genitive	(welches)	(welcher)	(welches)	(welcher)
dative	welchem	welcher	welchem	welchen

The genitive form is seldom used.

(e) The word **welcher** and its various forms can be used as a pronoun without a following noun, or as an adjective with a noun:

Sehen Sie die beiden Fernsehgeräte an. Welches möchten Sie haben?
Look at both television sets. Which one would you like to have?
Welches Fernsehgerät möchten Sie haben?
Which (used adjectivally) television set would you like to have?

232 Indefinite pronouns

There are a number of pronouns which are indefinite in meaning, in that they do not refer to any particular person or thing, and are therefore called indefinite pronouns. The main ones are as follows:

(a) **man** (one): Das kann man nicht sagen.   Man erwartet mehr.
     One can't say that.   *More is expected.*

(b) **jemand** (someone, somebody, anyone, anybody), **irgend jemand** (anyone, anybody, someone or other), **niemand** (no-one, nobody), and occasionally the accusative and dative forms **jemanden/niemanden** and **jemandem/niemandem**:

Jemand hat mein Fahrrad gestohlen.
Someone has stolen my bicycle.
Niemand will etwas davon wissen.
Nobody wants to know a thing about it.
Ich möchte niemanden beschuldigen.
I don't want to accuse anybody.
Vielleicht ist das Fahrrad versehentlich von irgend jemand(em) mitgenommen worden.
Perhaps the bicycle has been taken by someone or other in error.

(c) **einer** (a one, one of a group): this pronoun is used mainly of persons, and seems to occur mainly in fixed expressions in everyday speech, such as:

Einer muß es tun.   Das ist einer!   Das tut einem gut!
One of us must do it.   That's a one!   That does one good.
Eins (instead of eines) möchte ich doch sagen . . .
I would like to say one thing though . . .
Sollen wir einen/eins trinken?
Shall we have a drink? (einen Schnaps/ein(s) Glas Wein)

The word **einer** is declined, and singular only of course.

(d) **keiner** (no-one, nobody): this pronoun is used in the same way as **einer**. It is also declinable:

Keiner möchte etwas tun.   Ich möchte keins (keines) davon.
Nobody wants to do a thing.   I don't want any of those.

(e) **etwas** (something, anything): this pronoun is indeclinable, and used for things or ideas:

Möchten Sie etwas essen?   Mir fällt etwas ein.
Would you like something to eat?   I've just thought of something.

(f) **nichts** (nothing): is indeclinable:

Ich möchte nichts darüber sagen.   Aus nichts, wird nichts.
I don't want to say anything on that point.   Nothing comes from nothing.

(g) **alle** (all), **andere** (others), **einige** (some, any), **etliche** (some, several, a few), **mehrere** (several): these are words expressing vague quantities which can be used as adjectives with a noun, or as pronouns without the nouns, as in the following examples:

Einige wollten mitmachen, andere nicht.
Some wanted to take part, others did not.
Mehrere haben schon zugesagt.
Some have already agreed to do so.

(h) **alle** (all) and **manche** (many) can be used as pronouns in the singular:

Vor allem.   Alles oder nichts.   Er ist mit allem zufrieden.
Before all.   All or nothing.   He's satisfied with everything.
Heutzutage verstehe ich manches nicht.
Nowadays I don't understand a lot (of what goes on).

All pronouns like **einige**, **mehrere**, **alle** and **manche** depend on both speaker and listener knowing the situation, and the group of people or things to which reference is made.

(i) ein bißchen (a little), **ein wenig** (a little), **ein paar** (a few): are indeclinable:

Mit ein bißchen (ein wenig) Glück hätte ich mehr erreicht.
With a little luck I would have achieved more.
Mit ein paar Freunden machte er eine Wandertour.
With a few friends he went on a walking tour.

(j) welcher (some, some of it): as an indefinitive pronoun it is declinable. It is only commonly used in everyday speech:

Ich möchte welche.   Ich möchte welches.
I'd like some. (plural)   *I'd like some of it.*

(k) jeder (each, every, everyone) is declinable. It is in common use both in speech and in writing:

Jeder muß wissen, wofür er steht.
Everyone must know what he stands for.
Aus jedem kann etwas werden.
Everyone can achieve something.

(l) einander (one another): is indeclinable:

Sie grüßten einander.   (Sie grüßten sich.)
They greeted one another.   (They (two) greeted each other.)
Sie plauderten miteinander.   Sie gingen auseinander.
They talked with one another.   They went their separate ways.
Note that **miteinander** and **auseinander** are compound words.

(m) meinesgleichen (people like me, my equals), **seinesgleichen**, **ihresgleichen**, etc.: are indeclinable:

Er bleibt in der Politik nur mit seinesgleichen sachlich.
He remains objective in politics only with people like himself (people of the same opinion as himself).
Sie verkehrte nur mit ihresgleichen.
She only went about with people of her own kind.

Prepositions

233 German prepositions

A preposition is a word which normally links a noun or pronoun to the rest of the sentence. It is generally in a pre-position, that is a position before the noun or pronoun. A preposition is occasionally used with an adjective or adverb.

The German prepositions are indeclinable, and always govern a particular case, either accusative, genitive, or dative; that is to say that they are normally followed by a noun or pronoun in a particular case.

Most of the words which function as prepositions in German are also used as prefixes to verbs, whereby they give a more specific meaning to those verbs. Under certain conditions the prepositional prefix is separated from the verb, and is not to be confused with the same word functioning as a preposition. This point is considered under separable verbs (see para. 121), and not in this section.

234 Prepositions with the accusative case

(a) The following prepositions are always followed by a noun or pronoun in the accusative case:

bis (till, until, up to), **durch** (through, by means of), **für** (for, instead of), **gegen** (against, contrary to, towards), **ohne** (without), **um** (about, near, around), **wider** (against) (a word of limited uses).

(b) The prepositions are used to form phrases such as:

bis nächsten Montag (until next Monday), **bis nächstes Jahr** (till next year), **durch den Wald** (through the wood), **durch guten Rat** (by means of (through) good advice), **für mich** (for me), **für den Klub** (for the club), **gegen den Wind** (against the wind), **gen (gegen) Norden** (towards the north), **ohne mich** (without me), **ohne Pause** (without a break), **um mich** (around me), **um die Erde** (round the world), **um diese Tatsache** (about (concerning) this fact), **wider Willen** (against one's will), **wider seinen Willen** (against his will).

(c) The words **bis** and **um** are found in word combinations such as:

bis zur Grenze (up to the limit), **bis an die Grenze** (up to the boundary), **bis vor kurzem** (up until recently), **bis zur Post** (as far as the post), **um 5 Mark herum** (round about 5 marks). It is necessary to decide which word governs the noun, as the preposition determines the case of the following noun or pronoun. In the above examples **bis** is used adverbially, and the determining prepositions are **an**, **vor**, **zur (zu der)**, and **um**.

235 Prepositions with the dative case

(a) The following prepositions are always followed by a noun or pronoun in the dative case:

aus (out of, from), **bei** (at, near), **binnen** (within), **entgegen** (against, contrary to, opposed to), **fern** (far off, far from), **gegenüber** (opposite, facing), **gemäß** (according to), **mit** (with), **nach** (after, behind, following), **nächst** (next to), **seit** (since), **von** (from, of, by, concerning), **zu** (to, towards, up to, at, in order to).

(b) The prepositions are used to form phrases such as:

aus der Stadt (from town), **aus der Bibel** (out of the Bible), **bei seiner Tante** (at his aunt's place), **bei der Kirche** (near the church), **binnen einer Woche** (within a week), **entgegen seinem Rat** (against his advice), **fern der Hauptstadt** (far from the capital), **gegenüber der Kirche**, or **der Kirche gegenüber** (opposite the church), **gemäß den Vorschriften** (according to the rules), **mit ihm** (with him), **mit dem Zug** (by train), **nach den Osterferien** (after the Easter holidays), **nach ihm** (after him), **nächst dem Rathaus** (next to the town hall), **seit einer Woche** (for the last week), **von der Stelle** (from the spot), **das Fernsehgerät von meinem Bruder** (the television set belonging to my brother), **von Goethe geschrieben** (written by Goethe), **zu mir** (to me), **zur See** (to sea), **zur Hälfte** (by half), **zu Hause** (at home).

(c) The prepositions **entgegen**, **gegenüber**, and **gemäß** may either be placed before the noun or after it. For example: **meinem Rat entgegen** or **entgegen meinem Rat** (against my advice), **gegenüber dem Hotel** or **dem Hotel gegenüber**, **dem Programm gemäß** or **gemäß dem Programm**. The choice may depend on the flow of words, on the order in which the words occur to the mind, or on the sound of the words. Both versions are, however, grammatically correct.

(d) If the prepositions **entgegen** and **gegenüber** are used with a pronoun, then the pronoun must be placed before the preposition, as in the following examples:

Er kam mir entgegen.
He came towards me. / He compromised with me.
Mir gegenüber ist sie freundlich, sonst wirkt sie abstoßend.
Towards me she is friendly, otherwise she tends to repel people.

(e) The word **gemäß** has a touch of *Amtsdeutsch* (official German), and is not used with personal pronouns.

236 Prepositions with the dative or accusative case

(a) The following prepositions are followed by the dative or the accusative case, according to circumstances:

an (at, by; towards), **auf** (on; on to), **hinter** (behind, at the back of; behind, to the back of), **in** (in; into), **neben** (beside, near, next to; near to, close to), **über** (over, above; across, beyond, on the other side of, concerning), **unter** (under, beneath; below), **vor** (before, in front of; ahead of), **zwischen** (between; amongst).

The meanings are given in brackets: those before the semi-colon refer to the use of the word with the dative; those after the semi-colon to the use with the accusative.

(b) The dative is used to denote a position or stable situation. Where? For example:

an der See (at the seaside), **auf der Straße** (on the road or street), **hinter den Bergen** (behind the mountains), **in der Bibliothek** (in the library), **neben der Post** (near the post-office), **über dem Gefrierpunkt** (above freezing-point), **unter der Brücke** (beneath the bridge), **vor dem Haus** (in front of the house), **zwischen den Bäumen** (between the trees).

(c) The accusative is used to express the movement or change from one place or situation to another. Whither? Where to? For example:

Er fährt oft an die See.
He often goes to the seaside.

Er ging hinter die Kulissen.
He went behind the scenes.

Das Kind läuft auf die Straße
The child runs on to the road.

Sie ging in die Bibliothek.
She went into the library.

Stellen Sie es neben mich.
Put it down near me.

Fahren Sie vor das Haus.
Drive in front of the house.

Er fuhr über die Brücke.
He drove over the bridge.

Sie fuhr unter die Brücke.
She drove under the bridge.

Er legte den Brief zwischen die Bücher.
He placed the letter between the books.

(d) There are situations in which it is not possible to say with absolute certainty whether the dative or the accusative should be used. Both forms are then possible, with fine shades of meaning:

Er befestigte ein Bild an der (*or* an die) Wand.
He hung a picture on the wall.

Sie verpackte Bücher in den (*or* in dem) Koffer.
She packed books in the suitcase.

(e) The fact that a verb implies motion is not always a good guide to the use of the accusative rather than the dative case. For example:

Die jungen Leute tanzen im Klub.
The young people are dancing at (in) the club.
Diese Fische schwimmen im verseuchten Wasser.
These fish are swimming about in the contaminated water.

237 Prepositions with the genitive

(a) The following prepositions are followed by the genitive case:

abseits (off from), **angesichts** (in view of, considering), **anhand** (by means of), **anläßlich** (on the occasion of), **anstatt** (instead of), **anstelle** (in the place of), **aufgrund** (by reason of, because of), **außerhalb** (outside of), **beiderseits** (on both sides of), **bezüglich** (with reference to), **diesseits** (on this side of), **hinsichtlich** (with regard to), **infolge** (as a result of, as a consequence of), **inmitten** (in the midst of), **innerhalb** (within), **jenseits** (on that other side of), **laut** (according to), **mangels** (for want of), **oberhalb** (at the upper part of), **seitens** (on the part of, from the side of), **trotz** (in spite of), **um ... willen** (for the sake of), **unterhalb** (at the lower part of), **unweit** (not far from), **während** (during), **wegen** (because of), **zwecks** (for the purpose of).

Some of the above words which are listed as prepositions may also be used as adverbs. The meanings of the adverbs are often slightly different to those of the words given in the list.

(b) The prepositions are used as follows:

abseits der Hauptstraße (way off the main road), **angesichts der ernsten Lage** (in view of the serious situation), **anstatt des Friedens, Krieg** (instead of peace, war), **aufgrund einer Verletzung** (because of an injury), **außerhalb der Stadtgrenze** (outside the town limits), **beiderseits des Rheins** (on both sides of the Rhine), **bezüglich Ihres Schreibens vom ...** (with reference to your letter of the ...), **infolge eines Unfalls** (as the result of an accident), **innerhalb der nächsten vierzehn Tage** (within the next fortnight), **mangels fester Beweise** (in the absence of firm proof), **oberhalb der Stadt** (above the town), **trotz einer guten Leistung** (in spite of a good performance), **um Himmels willen** (for heaven's sake), **während der Mittagspause** (during the midday break), **wegen einer Erkältung** (because of a cold).

238 Prepositions followed by the dative, accusative, or genitive

(a) There are a few prepositions which are followed by the one case or other, according to circumstances:

außer, dank, entlang, längs, zufolge, zugunsten.

(b) The preposition **außer** (out of, outside, besides, except) can be followed by the dative, accusative (not often), or genitive (rarely):

außer mir, niemand (apart from me, nobody), **außer aller Gefahr** (completely out of danger), **eine Maschine außer Betrieb setzen** (to put a machine out of action), **die Entscheidung wurde außer Kurs gesetzt** (the decision was invalidated), **außer Landes leben** (to live abroad).

It should be noted, however, that **außer** is usually followed by the dative, and that the other uses involve specialized expressions.

(c) The preposition **dank** (thanks to, owing to) is now used with the dative for preference, although the genitive is also still used. For example:

dank seinem Einsatz / dank seines Einsatzes (thanks to his all-out effort).

(d) The preposition **entlang** (along) is peculiar, in that the case which it takes depends on its position before or after the noun. The examples illustrate this:

den Rhein entlang (accusative), and occasionally **dem Rhein entlang** (dative); but **entlang dem Rhein** (dative), and occasionally **entlang des Rheins** (genitive) (along the Rhine).

The student is advised to use either **den Rhein entlang** (accusative), or **entlang dem Rhein** (dative). The position of **entlang** is then decisive.

(e) The preposition **längs** (alongside, along) is followed by the genitive case, and occasionally by the dative. The student is advised to use the genitive, as follows:

die Straße längs des Rheins (the road alongside the Rhine), **die Beleuchtung längs der Hauptstraße** (the lighting along the main road).

(f) The prepositions **zufolge** (by virtue of, according to) and **zugunsten** (in favour of, for the benefit of) take either the dative or the genitive, depending on whether the particular word comes after the noun or before the noun. With **zufolge** the use of the dative is to be preferred. For example:

dem Gesetz zufolge (according to the law), **seinem Wunsche**

zufolge (according to his wish), **zufolge seines Wunsches** (by virtue of his wish), **ihrem Konto zugunsten** (to the credit of her account), **zugunsten unserer Partei** (for the benefit of our party), **zugunsten meines Kontos** (to the credit of my account).

(g) The preposition **laut** is normally followed by the genitive: **laut des neuen Gesetzes** (according to the recent law), **laut letzter Information** (according to the most up-to-date information). The dative is also used: **laut Ihrem Schreiben vom . . .** (according to your letter of . . .), **laut dem Bericht unseres Reporters** (according to the account of our reporter). The preposition **laut** is also used with a noun, which follows immediately and which has no case ending: **laut Gesetz** (according to the law), **laut ZDF** (according to the ZDF), **laut Anordnung** (according to the order).

239 Prepositions with adjectives and adverbs

(a) Prepositions combine with adjectives and adverbs in fixed phrases. The adjectives are declined, but not the adverbs.

(b) Prepositions combine with adjectives in such phrases as:

auf deutsch (in German), **aufs beste** (in the best way possible), **seit kurzem** (lately, of late), **zu allerletzt** (last of all), **zum besten** (for the best), **in kurzem** (shortly), **seit langem** (for a long time), **bis bald** (see you shortly), **weit ab** (far off), **auf einmal** (suddenly).

Although such a phrase is formed by a combination of a preposition and an adjective, the phrase itself may well be used only adverbially.

(c) Prepositions combine with adverbs in such phrases as:

nach unten (downwards), **von oben** (from above), **von außerhalb** (from outside), **von außen** (from the outside), **nach außen** (outwards), **nach oben** (upwards), **vorne durch** (through from the front), **von fern** (from afar), **von drüben** (from over there, from the other side), **ab gestern** (from yesterday onwards), **ab heute** (from today onwards), **ab morgen** (from tomorrow onwards), **von nun an** (from now on).

The phrases are used adverbially.

240 Problems in choosing the right preposition

(a) The prepositions **in**, **nach**, **zu** have very similar meanings in such phrases as: **in die Schule gehen** (to go to school, or into the school), **nach Hause gehen** (to go home), **zur Schule gehen** (to go to school). The correct choice of preposition is not to be made by logical grammatical reasoning, but by following the accustomed language usage. This may, indeed, vary between North and South Germany, or between region and region. The following notes concerning **in**, **nach**, **zu** as well as other prepositions are observations on usage.

(b) The preposition **in** is used with an article in the accusative case to express direction 'into': **in die Schule**, **ins Theater** (to the theatre), **ins Zimmer** (into the room), **in den Hörsaal gehen** (to go into the university lecture-theatre), **in die Zukunft blicken** (to peer into the future), **in die Niederlande fahren** (to drive to the Netherlands).

(c) The preposition **nach** is also used to express direction 'to' or 'into', but always without any article. It is therefore used for place names, and for all countries except those preceded by an article: **nach London fliegen** (to fly to London), **nach München fahren** (to drive to Munich), **mit dem Zug nach Hamburg fahren** (to go by train to Hamburg), **nach Frankreich reisen** (to travel to France), **nach Österreich fahren** (to drive to Austria).

(d) The preposition **zu** is also used to express a somewhat vague direction 'to', but to definite people, who may either be mentioned by name or merely described: **zu Marianne** (to Marianne), **zu Tante Elisabeth** (to Aunt Elizabeth), **zu den Schmidts** (to the Smiths), **zu meiner Cousine**, **zu meinem Vetter** (to my cousin), **zum Bäcker** (to the baker's), **zum Arzt** (to the doctor's).
The preposition **zu** is also used in certain fixed expressions which only involve people indirectly: **zur Schule** (to school), **zum Bahnhof** (to the station), **zum Fußballspiel** (to the football match), **zur See** (to sea).

(e) The preposition **nach** is sometimes heard instead of **zu** in North Germany, but students are advised to keep to the usages demonstrated in (b), (c), and (d).

(f) The prepositions **an**, **auf**, and **in**, followed by the dative case, are used to express place or location. Problems arise in town life, especially when an exact description is required.

(g) The preposition **an** means 'very close by, touching or adjoining', as in the following expressions:
Er wohnt am Markt (he lives at the market-place), **die Tauben am Domplatz** (the pigeons on the cathedral square), **die neuen Häuserblocks an der Hamburger Chaussee** (the new blocks of houses along the Hamburger Chaussee), **Frankfurt am Main**, **Lauenburg an der Elbe**, **Cochem an der Mosel**.

(**h**) The preposition **auf** with the dative case means 'on' (actually on) something or somewhere: **auf der Straße** (on the road), **auf dem Boden** (on the ground), **auf der Autobahn** (on the autobahn), **auf dem Flughafen** (at the airport), **auf dem Flugplatz** (on the airfield), **auf der Brücke** (on the bridge), **auf dem Lande** (in the country), **auf der Post** ((on the premises) at the post-office), **auf der Universität** (at the university).

(**i**) The preposition **in** with the dative case normally means 'in', but also 'in the area of': **Sie wohnen in der Frankfurter Straße** (they live in the Frankfurter Straße). **Die Fabrik liegt in einem Vorort** (the factory is situated in a suburb). **Man sieht ein Programm im Fernsehen** (one watches a programme on television). **Seine Freundin wohnt in dieser Gegend** (his girl-friend lives in this neighbourhood).

(**j**) The prepositions **seit** (since, for) and **während** (during, for) are only confused if one is trying to translate the word 'for' without keeping in mind the other basic meaning. The examples should make the distinction clear: **seit vier Wochen** (for the last four weeks, since a time beginning four weeks ago), **seit Ostern** (since Easter), **seit 1. Januar** (since the first of January), **er wohnt hier seit August** (he has been living here since August), **während der Vorlesung** (during the lecture), **während der letzten vier Wochen** (during the last four weeks).

(**k**) The prepositions **ab** (from) and **von . . . an** (from then on) are almost identical in meaning and usage: **Ab Montag beginne ich eine neue Arbeit** (from Monday onwards I am starting a new job). **Ab 1. Januar werde ich nicht soviel Geld ausgeben** (from the first of January I won't spend so much money). **Von Montag an werde ich das Rauchen aufgeben** (from Monday onwards I'll give up smoking).

(**l**) The meaning of the prepositions **auf Grund** (on the basis of, on account of), **infolge** (as a consequence of, as a result of) and **wegen** (because of) need close attention, as the prepositions are sometimes confused. The following examples should differentiate the meanings:

Infolge neuer Überlegungen haben wir unsere Pläne geändert.
As a consequence of fresh deliberations we have changed our plans.
Auf Grund eines milden Winters vermehrte sich das Ungeziefer.
As a result of the mild winter (the number of) parasitic insects increased.
Wegen einer Verletzung konnte er nicht spielen.
Because of an injury he was not able to play.

Conjunctions

241 Definitions

A conjunction is a word (or words) used to link words, clauses, and sentences. Conjunctions in German are indeclinable.

A coordinating conjunction links words, clauses, and sentences. A subordinating conjuction, however, links clauses and sentences in such a way that one (or more) of the clauses depend(s) on the main clause for its (or their) meaning. Considered on its own, a subordinate clause does not make complete sense, but a main clause does.

In German grammar, but not in English grammar, there is a third type of conjunction, namely the infinitive conjunction which links an infinitive to the rest of the sentence.

Adverbs are sometimes used to restrict or extend the meaning of conjunctions, such as in the word combinations **wenn auch**, **wenngleich** (even if), **sobald** (as soon as), **sowohl . . . als auch** (not only . . . but also). The basic conjunction and the adverb are not necessarily kept together as in English.

242 Coordinating conjunctions

(**a**) The following conjunctions merely link words, clauses, or sentences: **und** (and), **aber** (but), **sondern** (but, after a negative statement), **oder** (or), **denn** (for, because, then). The conjunction **denn** only links clauses.

(**b**) The order of words is not changed when the above coordinating conjunctions are used:

Er sammelt Briefmarken und Münzen.   Sie ist klug aber faul.
He collects stamps and coins.   *She is clever but lazy.*
Er kommt heute nicht, sondern er kommt wahrscheinlich übermorgen.
He is not coming today, but he is probably coming the day after tomorrow

(**c**) If an adverb is added to the conjunctions **aber**, **denn**, **oder** and **und**, then the adverb becomes the first word of the following clause, so that the verb comes second, and the subject third, as in the following examples:

Die Wirtschaftslage ist ernst, aber trotzdem wird viel gekauft.
The economic situation is serious, but nevertheless a lot is being bought.

Die Wirtschaftskrise ist weltweit, und deshalb ist eine Preisstabilität vorläufig nicht zu erwarten.
The economic crisis is world-wide, and therefore a stabilization of prices is not to be expected for the time being.

The adverbs **trotzdem** and **deshalb** are the first words of the second clause (or sentence), and are followed immediately by the verb. The subject follows the verb.

(**d**) The following coordinating conjunctions can either be used with or without a change in the order of the other words: **jedoch** (yet), **doch** (yet, however, but), **nur** (but, though), **entweder** (either, followed by or). For example:

Sie geht gerne tanzen, nur hat sie keinen richtigen Partner.
Sie geht gerne tanzen, nur sie hat keinen richtigen Partner.
She likes to go dancing, only she hasn't got a suitable partner.
Entweder geht sie ohne Partner, oder sie hört Tanzmusik zu Hause.
Entweder sie geht ohne Partner, oder sie hört Tanzmusik zu Hause.
Either she goes without a partner or she listens to dance music at home.

Both German versions are grammatically acceptable. The choice depends on factors such as the sound and flow of the sentence, or on the intentions and speech habits of the individual speaker or writer. There is a slight difference in meaning between the two German versions.

(**e**) The conjunctions **weder ... noch** (neither ... nor), **sowohl ... als auch** (not only ... but also, both ... and also) join words and phrases, and the conjunctions **nicht nur ... sondern auch** (not only ... but also) join words, phrases, and clauses. For example:

Weder er noch seine Schwester ist intelligent.
Neither he nor his sister is (are) intelligent.
Sie ist sowohl hübsch als auch intelligent.
She is not only pretty but also intelligent.
Sie kommt nicht nur aus guter Familie, sondern sie ist auch reich.
She not only comes from a good family but she is also rich.

Note the position of **auch** in the third example.

(**f**) Similar combinations of conjunction and adverb are: **aber auch**, **aber doch**, **denn auch**, **denn doch**, **oder aber** (or on the other hand), **oder auch**, **oder vielmehr** (or rather), **und auch**, **und dann**, **und darum** (and therefore), **und dennoch** (and yet), **und deshalb** (and therefore), **und deswegen** (and because of that), **und zwar** (that is). After such combinations the verb is in the second position in the clause, and the subject follows the verb (see (**e**)).

243 'Als' and 'wie'

(a) There is considerable confusion in the use of **als** and **wie**. The following observations are concerned with the *Hochsprache*, and not with regional variations.

(b) The word **als** is used in the simple comparative:

Er ist größer als ich.   Lieber heute als morgen.
He is taller than I.   *Better today than tomorrow.*

(c) The word **als** is used after certain words such as: **niemand als** (no one else than), **kein anderer als, keiner als** (none other than), **anders als** (other than), **nichts als** (nothing but).

Kein anderer als der Präsident kommt.
None other than the president is coming.
Er sieht jung aus, anders als erwartet.
He looks young for his years, other than expected.

(d) The word **wie** is used to make an exact or favourable comparison in word groups such as: **so groß wie**, **so gut wie**, **so oft wie**. For example:

Er ist so groß wie ich.   Die Lage ist so, wie ich sie beschrieben habe.
He is as tall as I.   *The situation is just as I have described it.*

(e) The word **wie** is used in comparisons when a noun phrase follows the conjunction:

Er sieht aus wie sein Vater.
He looks like (his father) (noun phrase).
Er lief weg wie ein Besessener.
He ran away like one possessed (noun phrase).

Note: The word **wie** can also mean 'how', as in the sentence: **Ich sah wie er es machte**. (I saw how he did it.)

(f) The word **als** is also used as a subordinating conjunction of time (see para. 245 (a)). For example:

Als sie ihn sah, kehrte sie eiligst um.
When she saw him, she retreated hastily.

244 Infinitive conjunctions

In German there are five infinitive conjunctions: **zu** (to), **um . . . zu** (in order to), **ohne . . . zu** (without), **statt . . . zu** (instead of), **anstatt . . . zu** (instead of). As the name implies, they are used to link the infinitive to the rest of the sentence. Examples are:

Es ist schwer zu sagen.   Es war zu erwarten.
It is difficult to say.   *It was to be expected.*

Die beiden Staatsmänner hielten eine Konferenz, um eine gemeinsame Lösung ihrer Probleme zu finden.
The two statesmen held a conference in order to find a common solution to their problems.
Sie verhandelten, ohne eine Lösung zu finden.
They negotiated without finding a solution.

245 Subordinating conjunctions

A subordinating conjunction is used to link an adverbial clause to a main clause. There are eight types of adverbial clause in German, and the type can almost always be judged from the meaning of the subordinate conjunction. The word **daß** has several shades of meaning though.

The verb in a subordinate clause is always placed at the end of the clause, and the subordinate clause itself may cause a further change of word order. The examples in the following sub–paragraphs illustrate the position of the verb. The question of word order is also summarized separately in para. 246.

The subordinate conjunctions in German are those:

(a) Of time: **bis** (until), **bevor** (before), **ehe** (before, until), **wenn** (when, whenever, if), **als** (as, at the same time as), **sobald** (as soon as), **sooft** (as often as), **seit** (since), **seitdem** (since), **nachdem** (after). The conjunctions are used as follows:

Bevor er überhaupt ein Wort sagen konnte, wurde er angegriffen.
Before he could say a single word he was attacked.
Nachdem er zurückgeschlagen hatte, liefen seine Angreifer weg.
After he had hit back his assailants ran away.

(b) Of purpose: **daß** (that), **so daß** (so that), **damit** (so that):

Sie ging früh schlafen, damit (*or* daß) sie erholt aufstehen konnte.
She went to bed early so that she could get up refreshed.
Sie begnügte sich nur mit alkoholfreien Getränken, so daß sie später die 200 Kilometer ohne Pause zurücklegen konnte.
She was satisfied with only soft drinks so that she could later drive the 200 kilometres in one spell.

(c) Of result: **so daß** (with the result that, so that), **so ... daß** (that):

Sie fuhr so langsam, daß sie eine Verkehrsstauung verursachte.
She drove so slowly that she caused a traffic jam.
Er fuhr äußerst unvorsichtig, so daß er einen Verkehrsunfall verursachte.
He drove extremely carelessly, with the result that he caused a traffic accident.

(**d**) Of reason: **weil** (because, since, as), **da** (because, since, as):

Augenblicklich fährt er kein Auto, weil ihm sein Führerschein entzogen worden ist.

He is not driving a car at the moment as (because) his driving licence has been taken away.

Da sie erst 16 Jahre alt ist, darf sie kein Auto fahren.

Since she is only 16 years old she is not allowed to drive a car.

(**e**) Of condition: **wenn** (if), **falls** (if, in case), **sofern** (in so far as), **soweit** (as far as), **unter der Bedingung daß** (on the condition that). They are used as follows:

Rufen Sie mich an, falls Sie Ihre Meinung ändern.

Give me a ring in case you change your mind.

Wir unterschreiben den Vertrag unter der Bedingung, daß er sofort in Kraft tritt.

We are signing the contract on condition that it comes into force at once.

(**f**) Of concession: **obwohl** (although, though), **obgleich** (although, though), **obschon** (although, though), **wenngleich** (even though), **wennschon** (even though), **wenn auch** (even if). The conjunctions are used as follows:

Die Firma erweitert sich international obwohl (obgleich) (obschon) die weltweite Wirtschaftslage ungünstig ist.

The firm is expanding at international level although the world-wide economic situation is unfavourable.

Durch Rationalisierung in der Produktion bleiben die Preise stabil, wenn auch die Lohnkosten steigen.

The prices are keeping steady through rationalisation in production even though the wages bill is rising.

(**g**) Of manner: **als wenn** (as if), **als ob** (as if), (**in**)**sofern** (in so far as), (**in**)**soweit** (in so far as), **während** (whilst), **indem** (in that), **ohne daß** (but that, without), **anstatt daß** (instead of). They are used as follows:

Sofern (soweit) ich mich erinnern kann, wurde das Haus vor dem Zweiten Weltkrieg gebaut.

As far as I can remember, the house was built before the Second World War.

Er sprach, als wenn (als ob) er es wirklich wüßte.

He spoke as if he really knew.

Er erteilte die Information, ohne daß ihm die Tatsachen wirklich bekannt waren.

He gave the information without really knowing the facts.

(**h**) Of comparison: **als** (as) (see para. 243), **wie** (as, how) (see para. 243), **je … desto** and **je … um so** (see below for translation). Examples are:

Er ist älter als sein Bruder (ist).   Er sieht so aus wie sein Bruder.
He is older than his brother.   *He looks like his brother.*
Je höher die Nachfrage, desto höher die Preise.
The greater the demand, the higher the prices.

246 Conjunctions and word order

(**a**) Specific simple coordinating conjunctions, namely **und**, **aber**, **sondern**, **oder**, and **denn**, do not cause any change in the order of the following words. For example:

Er möchte zur See fahren, denn er möchte andere Länder sehen.
He would like to go to sea, as he would like to see other countries.

(**b**) The specific coordinating conjunctions **und**, **aber**, **sondern**, and **oder** are sometimes followed by an adverb, as follows: **und trotzdem**, **aber doch**, **sondern auch**, **oder vielmehr**. The adverb then takes the first place in the following clause, so that the verb comes immediately afterwards, in second place. The subject then follows the verb. For example:

Er ist sehr beschäftigt, und trotzdem findet er Zeit für die Familie.
He is very busy, but nevertheless he finds time for the family.

(**c**) The coordinating conjunctions **jedoch**, **doch**, **nur**, and **entweder** admit of both a change or no change in the word order of the following clause. Both versions are grammatically acceptable. For example:

Entweder kommt er heute abend mit dem Wagen, oder (er kommt) morgen früh mit dem Zug.
Entweder er kommt heute abend mit dem Wagen, oder (er kommt) morgen früh mit dem Zug.
He is either coming by car this evening, or he is coming by train tomorrow morning.

(**d**) The use of subordinate conjunctions always causes a change in word order. The complete subordinate clause is considered as one grammatical unit for the purpose of word order, and if it comes first in a sentence, then it is followed immediately by a verb in second place. For example:

Als er nach Hause fuhr, sah er einen Unfall.
As he was driving home, he saw an accident.

Within the subordinate clause, the verb is always placed at the end of the sentence: (**Als**) **er nach Hause fuhr, …**

(e) If an auxiliary verb is used to form a tense in the subordinate clause, the auxiliary is placed at the very end of the clause:

Nachdem er gefrühstückt hatte, fuhr er nach Köln.
After he had finished his breakfast he drove to Cologne.

The past participle (**gefrühstückt**) comes at the end of a simple sentence, but in a subordinate clause the auxiliary (**hatte**) comes at the end.

(f) If an auxiliary, and a modal verb, and another verb all come together in a clause or a sentence then the word order is as follows:

Er hätte es nicht sagen sollen. (simple sentence)
He ought not to have said it.

The order in a subordinate clause, however, can be seen from the following examples:

Sie glaubte, daß er es nicht hätte sagen sollen.
She believed that he ought not to have said it.
Sie meinte, daß er es früher hätte sagen müssen.
She was of the opinion that he ought to have said it earlier.

In the examples a main clause is followed by a subordinate clause, in which three verbs are grouped together. The auxiliary verb **hätte** might be expected to come at the end of the group, but that position is already taken by a modal verb. So under these circumstances the auxiliary remains the first word of the verb-group.

247 Translating English conjunctions into German

Problems of translation from English into German may arise because certain words have two or more meanings, and these require different words in German. The translator has to find out which meaning he or she intends to use. The following notes deal with the main problems.

(a) *as:* is an adverb (**so, ebenso**), and a conjunction. If used with a comparative 'as' is translated by **als** (**größer als ich**); if a precise comparison is made it is translated by **so . . . wie** (**so groß wie ich**); if the meaning is 'as a' then **als** is used (**als Klavierspieler ist er eine Null**); if the meaning is 'just as' then **wie** is the correct word (**wie ich sagte**); if the meaning is 'like a person or thing' **wie** is also used (**wie ich, wie eine Rakete**).

The word 'as' may also be used as a subordinating conjugation: of time (**als, während**), of manner (**wie**), of condition (**wenn**), of reason (**weil, da**).

(**b**) *before:* is an adverb (**vorher**, **voraus**), a preposition (**vor**), or a conjunction. There are two possible ways of thinking of the conjunction 'before', namely by thinking of something before something else in the past (**bevor**, **ehe**), or by thinking of something before something else in the future (**bis**).

(**c**) *but:* is translated by **aber** after a positive statement, and **sondern** after a negative (**warm aber regnerisch**), (**nicht warm sondern kühl**).

(**d**) *or:* is normally translated by **oder**, and by **noch** after a negative.

(**e**) *since:* is a preposition (**seit langem**, **seit einer Woche**) and a conjunction which either means 'from a given time or occasion' (**seitdem**, **seit**) or 'because' (**weil**, **da**).

(**f**) *that:* is an adjective (**dieses**, **jenes Buch**), a demonstrative pronoun (**gib mir das**), a relative pronoun (**das Buch**, **das . . .**), an adverb (**so dumm**), and also a conjunction. It is prudent to make sure firstly that the particular word 'that' really is a conjunction. If it is, then it can have the following meanings:

so that, for the purpose of (**so daß, damit**), in order that (**damit**), with the result that, so that (**so daß**), on the condition that (**unter der Bedingung daß**), he (said) that . . . (**er (sagte), daß . . .**).

(**g**) *then:* is an adverb (**dann**, **damals**), an adjective (**der damalige Präsident**), and a conjunction. It can either mean 'in that case' (**dann**, **folglich**), or 'in addition' (**ferner**, **außerdem**).

(**h**) *therefore:* is an adverb (**darum**, **deshalb**) and a conjunction. It either means 'for that reason' (**deswegen**, **deshalb**, **darum**) or 'with the result that' (**daher**, **also**, **folglich**).

(**i**) *when:* is translated by **wann?** if it is an interrogative adverb, and **wenn** if it is a conjunction. If *when* refers to a single event in the past, then it is translated by **als**. For example: **Als er nach München fuhr, sah er einen furchtbaren Unfall**. When (as) he was driving to Munich he saw a frightful accident.

Interjections

248 The nature of interjections

Interjections in German as in English are mostly emotional sounds which result directly from such feelings as anger, annoyance, approval, disapproval, fear, anxiety, joy, or surprise. They may also be imitations of sounds such as those made by birds or animals.

An interjection is not an integral part of a sentence, and it is therefore usually separated grammatically, so that it stands on its own, usually beginning with a capital letter and followed by an exclamation mark. It is indeclinable.

249 German injections

The emotional and the animal sounds made in German are usually quite distinct from similar sounds made in English. The following are sample sounds in German:

Emotional: **ha**, **oho** (anger), **ach** (annoyance), **aha**, **prima**, **bravo** (approval), **bah**, **pfui**, **puh** (disapproval), **uh**, **oje** (fear), **nanu** (anxiety), **ah**, **oh**, **juhu**, **juchhe** (joy), **oho**, **hoppla** (surprise).

Animal and bird sounds: **muh**(cow), **wauwau** (dog), **mäh** (sheep), **kikeriki** (cockerel), **toktoktoook** or **gackgackgaaack** (hen), **pieppiep** (a bird), **kuckuck** (cuckoo).

Other sounds are the **schnipp schnapp schnipp** of a pair of scissors, the **ritsch ratsch** of tearing cloth, the **knack** of nuts, the **trapp trapp** of a running person, the **ticktack** of a clock, and the **hopphopphopp** to speed on competitors, particularly in skiing.

Word order

250 Division of a sentence according to grammar

A simple sentence always has a subject and a verb. The activity implied in the verb may also require an object, either direct or indirect, or even both, and the simple sentence may be completed by one or more adverbs or adverbial phrases.

251 Division of a sentence according to meaning

A simple sentence can also be divided into parts according to meaning, but the terminology used to explain this division appears at first sight to be imprecise. A simple sentence can normally be said to have a beginning, a middle, and an end. The beginning is usually the most important place from the point of view of meaning; the end is the second most important place; the middle is the least important. There are a number of reasons for this, such as the degree of attention and concentration which the listener or the reader brings to bear on the opening word or words, and the fact that a sentence usually revolves round the key person, thing, or idea, which is often the subject. The reasons, however, are outside the scope of this reference grammar.

German is more flexible in some respects than English as far as word order is concerned, especially in the matter of the key position in a sentence – the beginning. For example:

Ich kenne den Inhalt.
Den Inhalt kenne ich.
I know the contents.
Wir wissen nicht, was wir zu tun haben.
Was wir zu tun haben, wissen wir nicht.
We don't know what we have to do.

252 Position of the verb in simple statements

The following points are equally true of verbs in main clauses and in simple sentences.

(a) The verb is the second idea in a simple statement. For example:

Es	steht	eine Kirche	unten im Tal.
Eine Kirche	steht	unten im Tal.	
Unten im Tal	steht	eine Kirche.	
There	*is*	*a church*	*down in the valley.*

The first idea is not often just the first word. It may be the subject of a sentence (such as **eine Kirche**), or it may be an extended subject (such as **die Kirche, die wir vor ein paar Tagen besichtigten**), or it may be an adverbial phrase (such as **unten im Tal**).

(**b**) The auxiliary verb is the second idea in a simple statement when the future tense is used. For example:

Er   wird   seinen Urlaub in Österreich verbringen.
Seinen Urlaub wird   er   in Österreich verbringen.
He   will be spending his holiday in Austria.

The auxiliary verb is the second idea, and the infinitive verb occupies the final position.

(**c**) The auxiliary verb is also the second idea in a simple statement when the perfect or pluperfect tense is used. For example:

Sie   hat   ihren Urlaub in Spanien verbracht.
Ihren Urlaub hat   sie   in Spanien verbracht.
She   spent her holiday   in Spain.

Sie   hatte vorher   viel Geld gespart.
Vorher hatte sie   viel Geld gespart.
She   had   previously saved   a lot of money.

253 Position of the verb in simple questions

(**a**) The subject and verb are normally inverted (turned round) in asking a simple question. The verb is therefore first. For example:

Gehen Sie in die Stadt?   Fahren Sie mit dem Auto?
Are you going to town?   Are you going by car?

(**b**) The use of a coordinating conjunction does not alter the inverted word order. For example:

Gehen Sie in die Stadt oder bleiben Sie zu Hause?
Are you going to town or are you staying at home?

(**c**) The subject and the auxiliary verb are inverted when the future tense is used in asking a simple question. The auxiliary verb comes first, and the infinitive last. For example:

Werden wir bald eine Antwort bekommen?
Will we get an answer soon?

(**d**) The subject and the auxiliary verb are also inverted when the perfect or the pluperfect tense is used in asking a simple question. The auxiliary verb comes first, and the past participle last. For example:

Haben Sie ihn schon angerufen? *Have you rung him up already?*

Hatten Sie ihn schon vorher angerufen?
Had you rung him up previously?

(e) Interrogative adverbs such as **wann? wie? wieso? wo? wohin? woher? warum? weshalb? womit? wodurch?** take precedence at the beginning of the sentence, but inversion of the subject and the verb (or auxiliary verb) still takes place. For example:

Wann fährt sie?   Wohin wird sie fahren?
When is she going?   Where will she be going?
Warum ist sie so früh abgefahren?
Why did she drive off so early?

254 Position of the verb in commands

(a) The verb usually comes first in a command.

(b) The familiar **du** is omitted in the singular:

Nimm dieses Taschentuch!   Hör(e) auf zu weinen!
Take this handkerchief.   Stop crying.

(c) The verb is the first word when the plural is used:

Fahren Sie zunächst geradeaus, und biegen dann in die zweite Straße rechts.
First drive straight on, and then take the second road to your right.

(d) Occasionally there is an adverb before the verb in a command. For example:

Nun hör auf!   Aber sag etwas!
Now shut up!   But say something!

(e) Commands are often in the form of a request. Notice the position of the word **bitte** (please):

Nehmen Sie bitte Platz! Bitte, nehmen Sie Platz!
Please take a seat.

255 Position of verbs used in the subjunctive

(a) Basically, the word order in a simple sentence does not change whether verbs are used in the subjunctive or in the indicative. For example:

Das wäre eine gute Idee.   Wäre das nicht eine gute Idee?
That would be a good idea.   Wouldn't that be a good idea?

(b) The verb comes first in exclamatory sentences, which are partly self-questioning, or expressing a fanciful wish. For example:

Hätte ich ihm nur nichts gesagt!   Hätte ich doch gewonnen!
If only I'd not said a thing to him!   If only I'd won!

256 Position of the parts of a separable verb

(a) The prefix of a separable verb is placed at the end of the sentence in the present and past tenses of simple statements and questions:

Der Zug fährt um 9 Uhr ab.
The train leaves at 9 o'clock.
Kommt der Zug um 11.30 Uhr an?
Does the train arrive at 11.30?

(b) The prefix of a separable verb is part of the infinitive in the future tense, and the infinitive is in the final position in both statements and questions:

Der Jet wird in Singapur auftanken.
The jet will refuel in Singapore.
Wird der Jet in Singapur auftanken?
Will the jet refuel in Singapore?

(c) The prefix of a separable verb forms part of the past participle in the perfect and pluperfect tenses, and the past participle is in the final position in both statements and questions:

Das ist nur einmal vorgekommen.
That has only happened once (before).
Ist das schon einmal vorgekommen?
Has that already happened before?

257 Position of the modal verbs in a simple sentence

(a) The modal verbs (**dürfen**, **können**, **mögen**, **müssen**, **sollen**, and **wollen**) are normally used with an infinitive.

(b) The modal verb which is mostly used as an ordinary verb is **mögen** (to like), and the form of the verb is then in the usual position, namely the second idea in a statement, or the first idea in a question:

Ich mag ihn.   Mögen Sie ihn?
I like him.   *Do you like him?*

(c) When a modal verb is used in combination with an infinitive, then the modal verb is in the usual position in statements and questions, and the infinitive is at the end of the sentence. For example:

Sie stottert. Ich kann sie kaum verstehen.
She stutters. I can hardly understand her.
Wollten Sie mit ihr sprechen?   Sie sollte langsam sprechen.
Did you want to speak to her?   *She ought to speak slowly.*

258 Order of verbs in multiple verb groups

There is a verbal group which includes (a) a form of an auxiliary
verb (**haben**, **sein**, **werden**), (b) a modal verb, and (c) the infinitive
of another verb. Not only is the word order unexpected, but so is
the form of the modal verb, in which the infinitive is used instead of
the past participle. Two examples will serve to show the structure:

Er hat gehen müssen.   Sie hätten es nicht tun dürfen.
He had to go.   *They ought not to have done it.*

The auxiliary verb is the second idea in the sentence, as expected.
Theoretically the past participles **gemußt** and **gedurft** of the modal
verbs should be used, but the infinitives **müssen** and **dürfen** are
used instead. The very last position is taken up by the infinitive of
the modal verb, and the infinitive of the main verb is in the position
before last. This structure is not often used.

259 Position of the passive verb in a simple sentence

The same principles apply to verbs in the passive as to verbs in the
active. The auxiliary verb is the second idea in a sentence, and a past
participle or an infinitive is in the end position of a main clause or a
simple sentence. For example:

Die Konferenz wurde auf unbestimmte Zeit verschoben.
The conference was postponed indefinitely.
Die Vorstandssitzung ist vertagt worden.
The committee meeting has been adjourned.

260 Position of the verb in expressing a hope or wish in the subjunctive

(a) There is one particular use of the subjunctive to express a hope or
a wish in which the verb is in the first position. Such a sentence can
often be turned round so that it begins with **wenn** (if) and follows
the normal word order for an adverbial clause of condition. For
example:

Wäre es nur möglich.   (Wenn es nur möglich wäre.)
If it were only possible.
Komme was wolle.
Come what may.   (This sentence cannot be used with **wenn**.)

(b) The same structure is more often found in complex sentences
which have subordinate clauses:

Würden wir eine neue Klubgarnitur anschaffen, könnten wir die
Nachbarn beeindrucken.
If we bought a new suite of furniture, we could impress the neighbours.

261 Position of the verb in a multiple sentence

A compound or a multiple sentence consists of a string of simple
sentences joined by a coordinating conjunction such as: **und** (and),
aber (but), **sondern** (but, after a negative statement), **oder** (or),
and **denn** (for, because). The word order in each simple sentence
within the compound or multiple sentence remains the same as in a
simple sentence. For example:

Er fuhr in die Stadt, und sie ging spazieren.
He drove to town, and she went for a walk.

Sometimes the subject is not repeated (ellipsis) if it is the same in
both or all parts of a multiple sentence:

Er fuhr in die Stadt, und (er) parkte im Parkhaus.
He drove to town and parked in the multi-storey car park.

262 Position of the verb in a relative clause

(**a**) The verb always comes at the end of the relative clause. For
example:

Der Wagen, den ich jetzt fahre, ist ein Gebrauchtwagen.
The car which I now own is a second-hand one.

(**b**) A separable verb used in the present or past tense is not separated
in a relative clause. For example:

Die Pfunde, die man im Training abnimmt, sind schnell wieder
zugenommen.
The pounds which one loses in training are soon put on again.
Das Trainingsprogramm, das der Trainer festlegte, war sehr
intensiv.
The training programme which the trainer laid down was very thorough.

(**c**) An auxiliary verb comes at the end of a relative clause. For
example:

Die Pfunde, die man im Training abgenommen hat, sind schnell
wieder zugenommen.
The pounds which one has lost in training are soon put on again.

263 Position of the verb in a main clause in which there is a relative clause

(**a**) A relative clause relates to a person or a thing, and is placed as
close as possible to that person or thing, because the clause extends
or defines the meaning. If the relative clause itself comes at the end
of the sentence, as in the following examples, then the verb in the
main clause is in its usual position, namely second place.

Ich kenne den Mann, mit dem Sie gesprochen haben.
I know the man (main clause) *with whom you spoke.*
Wir haben Gäste eingeladen, die Sie kennen.
We have invited guests (main clause) *whom you know.*

(**b**) The relative clause is often inserted directly after the subject, with the result that the main clause is split up. Then the verb in the main clause follows immediately after the relative clause, as in the following examples:

Das Haus, das abgerissen wird, wurde im Jahre 1900 erbaut.
The house (main clause) *which is being pulled down* (relative clause), *was built in the year 1900* (main clause).
Das Hochhaus, das man für diesen Platz plant, wird von der Gemeinde nicht genehmigt.
The tall block that they are planning for this spot will not be passed by the council.

264 Position of the verb in a subordinate clause

(**a**) The verb always comes at the end of a subordinate clause. For example:
Ich glaube, daß ich immer Glück habe.
I think (main clause) *that I'm always lucky* (subordinate clause).

(**b**) A separable verb used in the present or past tense is not separated in a subordinate clause. For example:
Er hofft, daß er durch das Training ein paar Pfunde abnimmt.
He is hoping that he will take off a few pounds through the training.
Er war enttäuscht, als er wieder zunahm.
He was disappointed when he put on weight again.

(**c**) An auxiliary verb comes at the end of a subordinate clause. For example:
Obwohl er viel Sport getrieben hatte, nahm er ständig zu.
Although he had played a lot of sport he constantly put on weight.

265 Position of the verb in the main clause of a complex sentence in which there is a subordinate clause

(**a**) A subordinate clause comes either before or after a main clause. If the subordinate clause comes first then it is treated as the first complete idea, and is followed immediately by the verb of the main clause, which is the second idea. For example:
Als er nach Hause ging, regnete es.
As he was going home (subordinate clause), *it was raining.*

Obwohl er einen Regenmantel trug, wurde er durch und durch naß.
Although he wore a raincoat he got wet through.

(b) If the main clause comes first, then the verb in the main clause is the second idea, and is in second place as usual. For example:

Es regnete, als er nach Hause ging.
It was raining when he went home (subordinate clause).
Er wurde durch und durch naß, obwohl er einen Regenmantel trug.
He got wet through, although he was wearing a raincoat.

266 Position of the modal verb in a subordinate clause

The modal verb (**dürfen**, **können**, **mögen**, **müssen**, **sollen**, **wollen**) comes at the very end of a subordinate clause, after the infinitive. In this respect a modal verb is like the form of an auxiliary verb (**haben**, **sein**, **werden**), which also comes at the very end of a subordinate clause. The following examples show the position of the modal verb when it combines with an infinitive:

Sie lief aus dem Haus, da sie ihre kleinen Kinder pünktlich vom Kindergarten abholen mußte.
She ran out of the house because she had to fetch her young children from the nursery school quickly.
Als sie aber abfahren wollte, sprang der Wagen nicht an.
When she wanted to drive off though, the car didn't start.
Sie lief zu ihrer Nachbarin, da sie dort mit dem Kindergarten telefonieren konnte.
She ran to her neighbour's house, as she could phone the nursery school from there.

The modal verbs **mußte**, **wollte**, and **konnte** in the above sentences are at the end of the subordinate clauses, after the infinitives.

267 Position of the modal verb in a multiple verb group which is used in a subordinate clause

The position of the modal verb in a multiple verb group used in a simple sentence or in a main clause is explained in para. 258.

The modal verb in a multiple verb group is used in exactly the same position in a subordinate clause, namely the end position. The infinitive comes immediately before the modal verb, and the auxiliary verb is first in the multiple verb group. For example:

Der Junge ist nachts mit einem brüchigen Floß über den See gerudert, obwohl er es nicht hätte tun sollen.
The young boy rowed across the lake on a rickety raft at night, although he ought not to have done so.

Er wollte das Floß heimlich ausprobieren, weil er es tagsüber nicht
hatte machen dürfen.
*He wanted to try out the raft secretly because he was not allowed to do it
during the day.*

268 Position of the verbs when a noun clause forms part of the sentence

(**a**) A noun clause may be the subject, object, or complement of a
sentence, or it may be used with a preposition. The verb in the noun
clause comes at the end of the clause. For example:

Ich weiß nicht, wer es gesagt hat.
I don't know (main clause) *who said it* (noun clause, object).
Das ist Wort für Wort das, was er damals sagte.
That is word for word (main clause) *what he said at the time* (noun
clause, object).
Er konnte sich nicht mehr erinnern, mit wem er gesprochen hatte.
He could no longer remember (main clause) *with whom he had spoken*
(noun clause after the preposition **mit**).

(**b**) Should the noun clause be in first position in a sentence, then the
word immediately following the noun clause is a verb. For example:

Was er damals sagte, war mir neu.
What he said then (noun clause, subject) *was new to me* (main clause).

(**c**) The words **daß** (that), **wie** (as, how), and **ob** (whether, if) are
used to form noun clauses in the following way:

as a subject:

Daß sie hübsch ist, steht fest.
That she's pretty (subject clause) *is a fact.*
Wie er zum Erfolg kam, weiß ich wirklich nicht.
How he became successful (subject clause in German) *I just don't know.*
Ob er viel Geld besitzt, ist zweifelhaft.
Whether he has much money (subject clause) *is doubtful.*

as an object:

Niemand bezweifelt, daß sie hübsch ist.
Nobody doubts that she's pretty (object clause).
Ich sah, wie er es machte.
I saw how he did it (object clause).
Ich weiß nicht, ob er viel Geld besitzt.
I don't know if he has much money (object clause).

as a complement:

Tatsache ist, daß sie hübsch ist.
The fact is she's pretty (complement clause).

Es ist, wie ich sagte.
It's just as I said (complement clause).
Die Frage ist, ob er spielen wird oder nicht.
The question is whether he will play or not (complement clause).

269 Position of the verbs in reported speech

(**a**) The opening words of reported speech always announce who
said what. The verb (e.g. **sagte**) is the second idea in the sentence.
For example:

Er sagte, ...
Meine Schwester sagte, ...
Der Professor, den Sie kennen, sagte, ...

(**b**) There are two ways of reporting what was said, either beginning
with the conjunction **daß**, or without using **daß**. The position of
the verb in the reported speech varies according to whether **daß** is
used or not. For example:

Er behauptete, er sei müde.
Er behauptete, daß er müde sei.
He maintained (that) he was tired.
Er erzählte mir, daß er einen besonderen Preis gewonnen hätte.
Er erzählte mir, er hätte einen besonderen Preis gewonnen.
He told me that he had won a special prize.

The trend is towards using the method without **daß**, whereby the
verb is the second idea in the speech reported. If **daß** is used,
however, then the verb, or the auxiliary verb if there is one, comes
at the end of the sentence.

270 Position of the verb in exclamatory sentences

The importance of the first position in a sentence has been stressed
in previous paragraphs. The beginning is a key position in the
communication of meaning.

Exclamatory sentences are, by their very nature, emotional
utterances in which a particular idea, thing, or person is stressed. It
is much easier to bring out a particular item in speech than in
writing. Loudness, the pitch of the voice, intensity, and length can
all be used in speech to achieve emphasis. In writing and in print
methods like underlining or the selection of a particular type serve
the same purpose. It is also possible, though, to show emphasis by
word order. For example:

Sie ist auf Nimmerwiedersehen verschwunden!
She's disappeared once and for all!

Verschwunden ist sie, auf Nimmerwiedersehen!
She's disappeared, (that's absolutely clear), once and for all!

The first sentence is a statement of fact, but the second sentence emphatically brings out the fact of the disappearance. The bringing of the verb (usually the past participle) forward to the first position in a sentence is not limited to situations in which strong emotion is felt or expressed. Mild surprise, for example, may be expressed by this method, as in the following short dialogue:

Wo ist Heinrich? Er wollte sich früh auf den Weg machen.
Where's Henry? He wanted to set out early.
Gegessen hat er. Das sieht man.
Well, he's eaten. You can see that.

The fact that Henry has eaten is the clue to his probable actions.

Students are advised to use this device sparingly, though, as its effect depends largely on the unusual nature of the word order. Whilst the device may occur from time to time in speech, it is only used occasionally for deliberate effect in writing.

271 Position of infinitive word groups in a sentence

Infinitive word groups, namely those formed with **zu**, **um . . . zu**, **ohne . . . zu**, **statt . . . zu**, and **anstatt . . . zu**, may form the subject the object, or the complement of a sentence. For example:

(**a**) as subject:
Seine Ausbildung zu vollenden, war sein vorrangiges Ziel.
His prime aim was to complete his training.

(**b**) as complement:
Sein Ziel war, seine Ausbildung zu vollenden.
His aim was to complete his training.

(**c**) as object:
Der Medizinstudent beabsichtigte, später eine allgemeinmedizinische Praxis aufzumachen.
The medical student intended to open a general practice later.

Infinitive word groups are mainly used, however, as parts of a sentence which may be loosely described as having an adverbial function. For example:

Er antwortete, ohne zu zögern.
He answered without hesitation.
Anstatt eine genaue Antwort zu geben, redete er um das Problem herum.
Instead of giving a precise answer he talked around the question.

Um ihre Unaufmerksamkeit zu verbergen, starrte sie auf den
Fußboden.
In order to cover up her inattentiveness she gazed at the floor.

272 Position of participial word groups in a sentence

Participial word groups either refer to a person or thing, or are
interposed in a sentence without forming part of the main flow of
thought.

(a) The use of a participial word group in the main flow of a
sentence is more likely to occur in writing than in speech, as it is a
compressed form of expressing an idea. For example:

Der moderne Bürger, wahlberechtigt und oft gut informiert, ist in
der Lage, seine Unzufriedenheit zu artikulieren.
*The modern citizen, with a vote and often well-informed, is in a position to
make clear his dissatisfaction.*
Er wechselt, vielleicht etwas zögernd, seine Parteizugehörigkeit.
He changes, hesitating perhaps somewhat, his party membership.

The participial word group may be formed around a present or a
past participle. In the above sentences the phrases **wahlberechtigt
und oft gut informiert** and **vielleicht etwas zögernd** could
equally well be replaced by relative clauses, but the participial word
groups are precise and clear.

(b) The other form of participial word group is a kind of
Denkpause – a break in the chain of thought either to give the
speaker time to think out the rest of the sentence or to add emphasis
to what is coming.

There are many such phrases, some practically meaningless and
some which give a particular turn to the meaning of what is being
said. The following examples illustrate the range:

genau genommen (strictly speaking), **streng genommen** (strictly
speaking), **im Grunde genommen** (basically), **besser
ausgedrückt** (better expressed), **besser gesagt** (or rather), **etwas
grob ausgedrückt** (somewhat coarsely expressed), **fein
ausgedrückt** (delicately expressed), **richtig gesagt** (correctly
speaking), **kurz gesagt** (briefly), **ehrlich gesagt** (honestly
speaking), **richtig gesehen** (correctly considered or viewed), **rein
praktisch gesehen** (seen from a purely practical point of view),
realistisch gesehen (seen realistically), **im großen und ganzen
gesehen** (seen by and large), **wohl bemerkt** (let it be noted),
allgemein betrachtet (generally considered), **realistisch
betrachtet** (considered realistically), **stilistisch betrachtet**
(considered from the point of view of style).

There are many variations of the above examples. Two sentences are sufficient to show the use of participial word groups:

Seine Wahlchancen, realistisch betrachtet, sind nicht sehr gut.
His election chances, realistically considered, are not very good.
Sie ist, fein ausgedrückt, keine Dame.
She is not, delicately expressed, a lady.

273 Order of words within a noun group

(a) The first word in a noun group may be:

(i)   a definite article (**der**, **die**, **das**)
(ii)   an indefinite article (**ein**, **eine**, **ein**)
(iii) a demonstrative pronoun (**dieser**, **jener**, **jeder**)
(iv)   a possessive pronoun (**mein**, **sein**, **ihr**, **usw.**)
(v)   an indefinite pronoun (**alle**, **sämtliche**, **einige**)
(vi)   an adjective (declined like type III para. 161)

The number (singular or plural), the gender (masculine, feminine, or neuter), and the case (nominative, accusative, genitive, or dative) of the noun can usually be determined from the form of one of the above words.

(b) The last word in a basic noun group is the noun.

(c) Between the first and last word of a noun group may come an adjective, or several adjectives, or an adjectival construction (see para. 118).

(d) A noun group may be extended by the addition of explanatory words which are loosely connected with it, but do not form part of the actual basic noun group. The above word order is therefore not affected. For example:

das alte Hause (basic noun group)
ein altes Haus (basic noun group)
das alte Haus (basic noun group) **dort drüben** (addition)
das alte Haus (basic noun group), **von dem wir gesprochen haben**, (addition)

274 Position of a noun group in the dative

(a) A noun group in the dative comes after the main verb, or after the auxiliary verb in compound tenses. For example:

Dieses Haus gehört meinem Vater.
This house belongs to my father.
Dieses Haus hat meinem Vater gehört.
This house once belonged to my father.

(**b**) If one noun group is in the dative, and one noun group is in the accusative, then the noun group in the dative comes first. For example:

Sie gab ihrer Mutter ein hübsches Weihnachtsgeschenk.
She gave her mother (dative) *a nice Christmas present* (accusative).
Das Publikum spendete dem Schauspieler viel Beifall.
The public accorded the actor (dative) *much applause* (accusative).

(**c**) If a pronoun is substituted for the noun group in the dative, then the pronoun, like the noun group, comes first. For example:

Sie gab ihr ein hübsches Weihnachtsgeschenk.
She gave her (dative) *a nice Christmas present* (accusative).
Das Publikum spendete ihm viel Beifall.
The public accorded him (dative) *much applause* (accusative).

(**d**) If, however, a pronoun is substituted for the noun group in the accusative, then the pronoun comes first. For example:

Sie gab es ihrer Mutter.
She gave it (accusative) *to her mother* (dative).

The second example in (**b**) and (**c**) does not lend itself to the use of a pronoun instead of **viel Beifall**, for the substitution of a pronoun does not always make sense in the accusative.

(**e**) Should two pronouns be used, then the accusative comes before the dative. For example:

Sie gab es ihr.
She gave it (accusative) *to her* (dative).
Ich habe es Ihnen schon gegeben.
I've already given it (accusative) *to you* (dative).

(**f**) The word order (dative before accusative) where two noun groups are concerned (see sub-para (**b**)) is not always followed in speech. Other factors, such as the order in which thoughts occur to the mind, or even the speed of speech, which does not allow quick grammatical analysis, may lead to spoken sentences such as:

Herr Bremsschneider gab den alten Wagen seinem Sohn.
Herr Bremsschneider gave the old car to his son.

Students are advised to keep to the word order in (**a**)–(**e**).

275 Position of the reflexive pronoun in a simple sentence

(**a**) The reflexive pronoun follows immediately after the main verb in a simple sentence. For example:

Er erinnerte sich oft an seine Jugendzeit.
He often remembered the time of his youth.

Ich freute mich über das Geschenk.
I was pleased with the present.

(**b**) If an auxiliary verb (**haben**, **sein**, **werden**) is used to form a
tense, then the reflexive pronoun follows immediately after the
auxiliary verb. For example:

Er hat sich oft an seine Jugendzeit erinnert.
He often remembered the time of his youth.
Ich habe mich über das Geschenk gefreut.
I was pleased with the present.

(**c**) If a modal verb is used with the infinitive, then the reflexive
pronoun follows immediately after the modal verb. For example:

Er kann sich gut an seine Jugendzeit erinnern.
He can remember the time of his youth very well.
Er kann sich wirklich über dieses teure Geschenk freuen.
He can really be pleased with this expensive present.

276 Position of the reflexive pronoun in a subordinate clause

It is the verb which is placed at the end of a subordinate clause and
not the reflexive pronoun with it. If one imagines that there is a gap
left when the verb is 'taken out' and placed at the end of the
subordinate clause, and that the gap is then closed up by moving all
the words to the left, then it is clear that the reflexive pronoun is
moved to a position next to the subject. In fact the word order of the
rest of the sentence, including the reflexive pronoun, remains
unchanged when the verb is moved. The following examples are
based on those in para. 275, and should be compared with them:

(**a**) Ich glaube wohl, daß er sich über das Geschenk freute.
    I really believe that he was pleased with the present.

(**b**) Er erzählte mir, daß er sich oft an seine Jugendzeit erinnert hat.
    He told me that he often recalled the time of his youth.

(**c**) Meine Frau meint, daß er sich wirklich über dieses teure
    Geschenk freuen kann.
    *My wife maintains that he can really be pleased with this expensive
    present.*

277 Position of certain prepositions

(**a**) As the word 'preposition' suggests, a 'pre-position' normally
comes before the noun, or at the head of a basic noun group. For
example: **ohne Worte** (without words), **in einem Wald** (in a
wood), **aus dem kalten Wasser** (out of the cold water), **auf dem
Lande** (in the countryside).

(b) Certain prepositions, however, (**entgegen**, **entlang**, **gegenüber**, **gemäß**, **zufolge**, **zugunsten**) may either be used before or after the noun group. The following examples show both uses. The case of the preceding or following noun is considered in more detail in paras. 235 (d) and 238, but examples are also given below, as the case varies with **entlang**, **zufolge**, and **zugunsten**:

(meinem Rat entgegen)	den Rhein entlang
entgegen meinem Rat	entlang dem Rhein
against my advice	*alongside the Rhine*
dem Hotel gegenüber	dem Programm gemäß
gegenüber dem Hotel	(gemäß dem Programm)
opposite the hotel	*according to the programme*
dem Gesetz zufolge	ihrem Konto zugunsten
(zufolge des Gesetzes)	zugunsten ihres Kontos
according to the law	*to the credit of her account*

(c) The following prepositions always come after a pronoun, and never before it:

mir entgegen	ihr gegenüber
towards me	*opposite her*

(d) Note: **meinetwegen** (for my sake), **seinetwegen** (for his sake)...

278 Position of certain conjunctions

(a) A conjunction is basically a joining word which links words, word groups, or clauses. For example the word **und**: **München und Hamburg**; **die bayrische Hauptstadt München, und die Freie und Hansestadt Hamburg**. The conjunction therefore normally stands between the words or word groups which it is linking.

(b) A conjunction normally comes at the beginning of a subordinate clause, even if the clause is in first position in the sentence. Note the position of the conjunction **als** in these sentences:

Es regnete, als ich nach Hause ging.
Als ich nach Hause ging, regnete es.
It rained (or was raining) as I was going home.

(c) Certain conjunctions, such as **aber**, **auch**, **doch**, and **nur**, can float away from their linking positions. For example:

aber das ist wahr	auch das ist wahr
das aber ist wahr	das ist auch wahr
das ist aber wahr	(das ist wahr, auch)
(das ist wahr, aber)	*that's also true*
that's true though	

It is not practical to try to formulate rules concerning these floating
conjunctions, nor can it always be assumed that all of those
conjunctions can be used in all positions. There is also some doubt
in German whether the words as used above are conjunctions or
adverbs.

(**d**) Certain conjunctions are used in pairs, such as **entweder . . .
oder** (either . . . or), **weder . . . noch** (neither . . . nor), **sowohl . . .
als auch** (not only . . . but also), **je (kleiner), desto (besser)** (the
(smaller) the (better)), **je (kleiner), um so (besser)** (the (smaller)
the (better)). These conjunctions precede the ideas which are being
contrasted.

(**e**) The infinitive conjunctions (**zu, anstatt . . . zu, statt . . . zu,
ohne . . . zu, um . . . zu**) often link an infinitive phrase to a previous
statement or question. The infinitive phrase then completes the
sense of the sentence, and comes at the end. For example:

Sie geht in die Stadt, Einkäufe zu machen.
She goes to town to do (her) shopping.
Er wäscht sein Auto, statt mit ihr zu gehen.
He is washing his car instead of going with her.
Sie fährt mit dem Bus, um schneller in die Stadt zu kommen.
She travels by bus to get to town quicker.

(**f**) An infinitive group may also form an independent idea, and be
the subject, complement or the object of a sentence. The position of
the infinitive group is then the same position as is normally
occupied by the subject, complement, or object of a sentence:

Das Problem als Ganzes zu erfassen (subject), war sehr schwierig.
Es war sehr schwierig, das Problem als Ganzes zu erfassen
(complement).
It was very difficult to grasp the problem as a whole.
Er versuchte, das Problem als Ganzes zu erfassen (object).
He tried to grasp the problem as a whole.

(**g**) The infinitive group may be in the first position in a sentence if
the sequence of events makes this necessary:

Ohne zu zögern, sprang er ins Wasser.
Without hesitating he sprang into the water.
Statt zu schießen, zögerte er, und verlor den Ball.
Instead of shooting he hesitated and lost the ball.

(**h**) It can be seen from the examples in (**e**)–(**g**) that an infinitive
group comes at the end or at the beginning of a sentence. Whilst the
middle position cannot be excluded, it is unusual.

279 Position of the adverb, the adverbial phrase, and the adverbial clause in a sentence

An adverb (or an adverbial phrase) has more possible functions in a sentence than any other part of speech, and it is hard to pin it down to any particular position in the sentence. Generally it may be said that an adverb comes close to the particular word or idea which it clarifies or modifies.

(a) An adverb, adverbial phrase, or an adverbial clause may be in the first position in a sentence. For example:

Gestern fuhr er nach Hamburg.
Vorige Woche fuhr er nach Hamburg.
Yesterday (last week) he drove to Hamburg.
Da er geschäftlich dort zu tun hatte, fuhr er nach Hamburg.
As he had business to do he drove to Hamburg.

(b) An adverb, adverbial phrase, or adverbial clause may be in the end position in a sentence. For example:

Ich traf sie gestern.
Ich traf sie vorige Woche.
I met her yesterday (last week).
Ich traf sie, als ich durch das Einkaufszentrum ging.
I met her as I was walking through the shopping centre.

(c) An adverb may also be used in the middle of a sentence provided that the rule of proximity is observed; that is to say that the adverb is close to the word which it is clarifying or modifying. It usually comes before the other word. A consideration of three adverbs, one of place, one of time, and one of manner will serve to illustrate the use of the adverb in the middle of a sentence. Note the position of the adverbs **überall** (everywhere), **heute** (today), and **besonders** (especially) in the following sentences:

Die Mondfinsternis war überall sichtbar.
The eclipse of the moon could be seen everywhere.
Sie war überall im Lande sichtbar.
It could be seen from all over the country.
Sie wurde überall genau beobachtet.
It was closely watched everywhere.
Wir fahren heute noch in Urlaub.
We are going on holiday later today.
Wir hätten eigentlich heute in einer Woche fahren sollen.
Actually we ought to have been going in a week's time.
Ich finde es besonders gut, daß das Buch als Taschenbuch erscheint.
I find it especially good that the book is appearing in a paperback edition.

Es ist, in der Tat, besonders preisgünstig.
In fact it is especially good value for money.

(**d**) To summarize (**a**)–(**c**):

(i) Adverbs, adverbial phrases, or clauses of time occur most frequently in the first or the end position.

(ii) Adverbs, adverbial phrases, or clauses of place occur most frequently in the end or the first position.

(iii) Adverbs or adverbial phrases of manner occur mostly in the middle of a sentence, usually before the parts of speech which they modify.

(iv) Adverbial clauses seldom occur in the middle of a sentence.

(v) The rule of proximity is followed.

280 Sequence of adverbial phrases

(**a**) Adverbs and adverbial phrases usually occur in one of the following orders:

(1) time	(2) manner	(3) place
(1) manner	(2) time	(3) place
(1) time	(2) place	(3) manner

For example:

Die Kinder fahren jeden Morgen mit dem Bus zur Schule.
Die Kinder fahren mit dem Bus jeden Morgen zur Schule.
Die Kinder fahren jeden Morgen zur Schule mit dem Bus.
The children travel to school by bus every day.

(**b**) It is unusual for all three (time, manner, and place) to occur in a single sentence. Time almost always occurs before place or manner. For example:

Die Kinder gehen jeden Morgen zur Schule.
The children go to school every morning.
Die Kinder fahren jeden Morgen mit dem Bus.
The children travel by bus every morning.

(**c**) Place and manner are interchangeable. For example:

Die Kinder fahren mit dem Bus zur Schule.
Die Kinder fahren zur Schule mit dem Bus.
The children travel to school by bus.

(**d**) If there are two expressions of time or of place, then the general comes before the particular. For example:

Sehen wir uns heute abend um 7 Uhr wieder?
Shall we be seeing each other again tonight at 7 o'clock?

Sie wartete im Park unter einem schattigen Baum.
She waited in the park beneath a shady tree.

281 Ellipsis and word order

Ellipsis refers to the deliberate omission of words from a sentence.
There are many reasons why this should happen, such as the
avoidance of unnecessary repetition, the desire to express an idea
quickly without irritating the listener or the reader, the fact that the
context is known fully to all concerned, or even stylistic grounds.

Briefly, ellipsis does not affect word order. Words are omitted, but
grammatically it is assumed that they are still there. The missing
'gaps' are simply closed up in order to keep the flow of the
language. A short dialogue, for example, might be:

Noch ein Stück?	(Möchtest du noch ein Stück Schwarzwälder Torte?)
Nein, danke.	(Nein, aber ich danke dir.)
Warum nicht?	(Warum möchtest du kein zweites Stück Torte?)
Diät!	(Ich lebe jetzt Diät!)

The dialogue on the left is a likely one between friends, whereas the
fuller version on the right would indeed be stilted. Ellipsis, then, is
the omission of words, but the word order is not affected.

Punctuation

282 Changing attitudes to punctuation

Language is always in a state of change, and change is probably most perceptible in the field of vocabulary, whereas movement in the fields of grammar, meaning, or punctuation is usually imperceptible in the day-to-day use of language. Attention has already been called in this book to trends in grammar, and it is now necessary to call attention to trends in punctuation.

The present position is that the German language is moving away cautiously – and sometimes incautiously – from rigid formality in punctuation.

283 The full stop

(**a**) The full stop is used at the end of any sentence which is not a question or an exclamation.

(**b**) It is used after an abbreviation. For example:
usw. (und so weiter), m. (männlich), w. (weiblich), s. (sächlich), dt. (deutsch), ev. (evangelisch), kath. (katholisch), z.B. (zum Beispiel).

(**c**) It is used after the ordinal number in dates:
am 1. Oktober, **zum 25. Geburtstag**, **1. Januar 1981**.

(**d**) It is also used between figures, for dates of birth, etc.:
9.9.61, 29.02.62

(**e**) Names of political parties, organizations, most measures, and points of the compass are, however, not normally followed by a full stop. For example:
CDU, **DGB**, **m**, **km**, **kg**, **SW**, **SSW**, **ARD**, **ZDF**

(**f**) The full stop, and not the comma, is used to separate the thousands.
For example: **1.000.000 or 25.850.000**
Sometimes a gap is used instead of the full stop. For example:
1 000 000 or 25 850 000

284 The colon

(**a**) In German the colon is used to introduce the actual words of direct speech. In English the comma is used for this purpose.

For example:

Tell sagte: ,,Durch diese hohle Gasse muß er kommen,
Es führt kein andrer Weg nach Küßnacht . . .''

(Schiller, Wilhelm Tell)

Tell said, '*He must come along this sunken lane,*
for there's no other way which leads to Küßnacht . . .'

(**b**) The colon is used to introduce items in a list, examples, details,
or an important statement. For example:

Die folgenden Abgeordneten wurden gewählt:
The following representatives were elected:
Zum Beispiel: (z.B.:)
For example: (e.g.:)
Ich sage euch: Wer glaubt, hat das ewige Leben.
I tell you, the believer possesses eternal life. (John 6.47)

(**c**) The colon is also used for stylistic effect near the end of a
sentence, when the foregoing thoughts are summarized:

Alles was der Mensch brauche, sei Klarheit des Denkens. Dies führe
zum dritten Grundsatz des Deismus: Vernunft.
All that mankind needs is clarity of thought. This leads to the third basic
principle of deism – reason.

(**d**) The colon is, however, not used in German for antithesis. This
device is used in English. Note the punctuation:

Der Mensch denkt, Gott lenkt.
Man proposes: God disposes.

285 The semi-colon

(**a**) The semi-colon marks a stronger division than a comma, but a
lesser one than a full stop. The semi-colon is therefore used to
separate part-sentences which could be expanded into full sentences:

Nach den Bestimmungen des Versailler Friedensvertrags im Jahre
1919 verliert Deutschland Elsaß-Lothringen und fast ganz Posen
und Westpreußen. Abstimmungen finden statt: im Saargebiet nach
15 Jahren (Bergwerke sogleich französisches Eigentum); in
Nordschleswig 1920; in Oberschlesien 1921; in Eupen-Malmédy
nach der Annexion durch Belgien.
According to the terms of the Treaty of Versailles in 1919 Germany loses
Alsace-Lorraine, and almost the whole of Posen and West Prussia.
Plebiscites are due to take place in the Saar after 15 years (coal mines
become French property immediately); in North Schleswig in 1920; in
Upper Silesia in 1921; in Eupen-Malmédy after its annexation by
Belgium.

(**b**) The semi-colon can be used in German, instead of a full stop, if
the two sentences have a common theme or a very close connection.
For example:

Das staatliche Leben in der Bundesrepublik spielte sich anfangs
vorwiegend in den Ländern ab; allerdings hatte Bundesrecht
Vorrang und konnte erzwungen werden.
*At first the political life of the Bundesrepublik ran its course mainly in the
Länder; nevertheless federal law had priority and could be enforced.*

(**c**) The semi-colon can be used in German, instead of the comma, if
it is felt that a stronger division of ideas is necessary. For example:

Und was herrscht in der Welt? Hunger und Not; Armut und Elend;
Brutalität und Krieg.
*And what predominates in the world? Hunger and need, poverty and
distress, brutality and war.*

286 Trends in the use of the comma

The comma in German has always been essentially an instrument of
grammar which is used to split up units such as phrases and clauses
within the sentence. There is a trend towards letting the language
flow freely without the breaks caused by commas. This depends
entirely on the sentence. A short sentence lends itself to this
treatment, whereas a break in a longer sentence may seem desirable.
Commas are now being inserted, as in English, where a pause for
breath, or a thought pause, seems necessary. Firm rules are
therefore no longer always applicable. There is also a difference in
usage by the older and younger generations arising as the strict
grammatical formality is relaxed in places.

287 The comma between words and phrases

The following points are for general guidance. Grammatical
necessity usually demands the use of a comma between groups of
words and phrases. The main uses are:

(**a**) The comma is always used to separate words, names, or items in
a list:

Beim Wiener Kongreß (1814–18) waren die Hauptunterhändler
Castlereagh (England), Metternich (Österreich), Hardenberg
(Preußen), Nesselrode (Rußland) und nach 1815 Talleyrand
(Frankreich).
*At the Congress of Vienna (1814–18) the main negotiators were
Castlereagh of England, Metternich of Austria, Hardenberg of Prussia,
Nesselrode of Russia, and after 1815 Talleyrand of France.*

(**b**) The comma is used to separate the details in a bibliographical reference by some publishers. For example:

Weisgerber, Leo, Die geschichtliche Kraft der deutschen Sprache, Pädagogischer Verlag Schwann, Düsseldorf 1959.

Other publishers have a colon after the name instead of a comma.

(**c**) The comma is similarly used to separate the details of an address, days and dates, or details in a catalogue:

Er wohnt Klausheider Straße 19, 4800 Bielefeld.
Die Konferenz ist vom Montag, 6. Januar, bis Samstag, 11. Januar.
The conference is from Monday, 6th January to Saturday, 11th January.
Quarz-Armbanduhr, superpreiswert, Monat, Datum, Jahr, Frontbedienung und Beleuchtung.
Quartz wrist-watch, super value, month, day, and year, front adjustment and illumination.

(**d**) Words in apposition are enclosed in commas:

Wilhelm I, König von Preußen, wurde 1871 als deutscher Kaiser anerkannt.
William I, King of Prussia, was accepted as German Emperor in 1871.

(**e**) Words of address to a particular person are followed (or enclosed) by a comma:

Inge, was meinst du dazu? Was meinst du, Inge, dazu? Was meinst du dazu, Inge?
What do you think about it, Inge?

(**f**) Descriptive words which are added, perhaps as an afterthought, are separated by a comma from the previous part of the sentence:

Sie wollte ihn nicht mehr sehen, und nun sitzt sie zu Hause, allein und verlassen.
She didn't want to see him again, and now she sits at home, lonesome and forlorn.

(**g**) An infinitive group at the end of a sentence is separated by a comma when it is a kind of afterthought:

Sie saß ganz still, ohne ein Wort zu sagen.
She sat quite still, without saying a word.

(**h**) An infinitive group, however, which is used as a subject, or an essential part of the sentence, is not separated by commas:

Sich selbst treu zu sein hat großen Wert.
To be true to oneself is of great value.
Dieser Spruch ist zu überdenken.
This saying is worth thinking about.

(i) A participial group may or may not be separated by a comma, depending mainly on the flow of words:

Sie wurde blaß, überrascht vom ganzen Rummel.
She turned pale, surprised at the whole uproar.
Sie kam weinend nach Hause.
She came home crying.

(j) A comma is used between contrasts formed with **nicht nur** . . . **sondern auch**, but not between those formed with **sowohl** . . . **als auch** or comparisons with **als** or **so** . . . **wie**:

Er ist nicht nur eigensinnig, sondern auch dumm dazu.
He is not only stubborn but stupid with it.
Sie ist sowohl hübsch als auch elegant.
She is both pretty and elegant.
Sie ist größer als er.   Er ist nicht so groß wie sie.
She is taller than him.   He is not so tall as her.

(Note: The English translations with 'him' and 'her', instead of 'he' and 'she' are common English usage, for which there is no satisfactory grammatical explanation.)

(k) There is no comma in German before the word **und** near the end of a list:

deutsche, englische, amerikanische und französische Flaggen . . .
German, English, American, and French flags . . .

(l) The comma is also omitted nowadays if it would disturb the flow or unity of a complete expression:

ein guter schwerer fränkischer Wein
a good heavy Frankish wine

(m) The comma is also omitted before conjunctions like **und** to ensure a smooth flow of words:

Die Außenministerkonferenz in Moskau 1947 erzielte keine Einigung über die deutschen Reparationen und über die Struktur eines künftigen gesamtdeutschen Staates.
The Foreign Ministers' Conference in Moscow (1947) was unable to achieve agreement on German reparations and the structure of a future all-German state.

(n) If a comma is used (instead of an exclamation mark) after addressing someone in a letter, then the first word of the text must begin with a small letter:

Sehr geehrter Herr Brinkmann,
vorgestern haben wir . . .

(o) The comma is used in German between two units of measurement, etc., whereas the 'point' is used in English:

Ergebnisse: Hochsprung 2,30 m; Weitsprung 8,10 m; Stabhochsprung 5,50 m

Results: high jump 2.30 m; long jump 8.10 m; pole vault 5.50 m

288 The comma between clauses

The comma is used grammatically to separate one clause from another. The use is most rigid in the separation of a main clause from a relative or a subordinate clause; the use is least rigid when a smooth flow of thought is desired, such as between main clauses or in short sentences. The following notes begin with the circumstances under which a certain rigidity is observed, and where students of the language are advised always to use commas.

(a) Commas are used to separate a relative clause from the parts of the main clause:

Die Weimarer Koalition von 1919, die aus SPD, Zentrum und Deutsch-Demokratischer Partei entstand, wählte Friedrich Ebert zum vorläufigen Reichspräsidenten.

The Weimar Coalition of 1919, which arose from the SPD, the Centre Party, and the German Democratic Party, elected Friedrich Ebert as provisional President.

(b) Commas are used to separate a subordinate clause from a main clause, especially if the subordinate clause comes first:

Als Deutschland 1926 in den Völkerbund eintrat, erhielt es sofort einen ständigen Ratssitz.

When Germany in 1926 became a member of the League of Nations she was immediately given a permanent seat on the Council.

(c) The main clause in indirect speech is separated from the following clause by a comma:

Churchill behauptete, daß die wirtschaftlichen Bestimmungen des Friedensvertrages (1919) so bösartig und töricht waren, daß sie tatsächlich nutzlos wurden.

Churchill maintained that the economic clauses of the Treaty (1919) were so malignant and silly that they obviously became futile.

(d) Commas are used to separate a detached thought within a sentence:

Die Weimarer Republik war, genau genommen, von Anfang an ein Unglückskind.

The Weimar Republic – basically – was born under an unlucky star.

A thought which is in parenthesis, such as **genau genommen**, is separated by commas in German, whereas dashes are often used in English.

(**e**) Commas can separate main clauses:

Ich kam, ich sah, ich siegte. (Cäsar)
I came, I saw, I conquered. (Caesar)

(**f**) Commas are not necessary between main clauses if a smooth flow of thought is felt desirable:

Er blieb zu Hause und sah sich eine Fernsehsendung an.
He stayed at home and watched a television programme.
Entweder gehen wir spazieren oder wir machen einen Waldlauf.
Let us either go for a walk or a run in the woods.

(**g**) A comma is not usual between two main clauses which share a common subject, and perhaps a common verb:

Die Weimarer Republik hätte sich auf eine sozialistische Mehrheit der Arbeiterschaft oder auf ein liberaldemokratisches Bürgertum stützen können.
The Weimar Republic should have been able to rely for support on a socialist majority from the working class or on a liberal democratic bourgeoisie.

(**h**) There is often no comma between two subordinate clauses if there is something in common between them and they begin with the same conjunction:

Er sieht ein, daß du schwer zu arbeiten hast und daß du dadurch reizbar bist.
He sees that you have to work hard and that you are therefore irritable.

289 The question mark

(**a**) The question mark is used after a direct question:

Was willst du?   Warum gehst du?
What do you want?   *Why are you going?*

(**b**) It is not used in reported speech to record the substance of a question:

Er fragte, warum ich gehen wollte.
He asked why I wanted to go.

(**c**) The question mark is used after question words such as:
Wie? Was? Wer? Wann? Warum nicht?

290 The exclamation mark

(a) The exclamation mark is used to indicate strong emotion, real or simulated:

Achtung! Paß auf!   Was für ein reizendes Kleid!
Mind! Look out!   *What an attractive dress!*

(b) It is often used to address a person in a letter. It is then followed by a capital letter at the beginning of the text:

Sehr geehrte Frau Brinkmann!
Leider ist es nicht möglich . . .

(c) It is used after single words to give emphasis:

Unmöglich!
Impossible!

(d) It is used after commands in which there is an emotional element:

Hör endlich auf zu weinen!
Now (for goodness sake) stop crying!

(e) It can be used instead of a question mark if the words express a wish or a kind of inner dialogue:

Wie oft habe ich das sagen müssen!
How often have I had to say that.

291 The hyphen

(a) In English, the hyphen joins: a dash separates. The German word for a hyphen, **der Bindestrich**, brings out the function of the hyphen. The following examples are taken at random from a mail-order catalogue:

Mädchen-T-Shirt, Safari-Look, Mokassin-Slipper, 3-Stück-Packung, Freizeit-Schuh, Kinder-Clog, Skateboard-Halbschuh, Jogging-Set.

This random selection reveals not only the use of the hyphen but also temporary fashions and the more permanent influence of English on the German language.

(b) If parts of a compound word are repeated almost immediately in another compound word, then the part of the word which is common is omitted. Sometimes it is the first part of a word, and sometimes the last. Note the position of the hyphens in the following examples:

bergauf und -ab (uphill and downhill), **Naturholz-Fenster und -Türen** (wooden window frames and doors), **vollwaschbare**

Tages- und Steppdecken (fully washable combined covers and quilts), **Ein- und Ausfuhr** (import and export), **ein- und ausatmen** (to breathe in and out).

292 The dash

(**a**) The dash is called **der Gedankenstrich** in German, which indicates that its function is to call attention to a particular thought, and not merely to separate, as in English. The normal way in German of indicating a thought in parenthesis is by using commas, but seldom dashes. The following sentence is to be preferred to one in which dashes are used:

Eine Regierungskrise, nach Meldungen aus der Hauptstadt, steht unmittelbar bevor.
A governmental crisis – according to reports from the capital – is imminent.

(**b**) The dash is used in German to separate single ideas clearly and distinctly, as for example in a title:

Machtpolitik – Aufrüstung – und dann?
Power-politics – rearmament – and then?

(**c**) The dash can indicate an unspoken word or a word which the writer considers unprintable:

Unerhört! Du –!
Scandalous! You –!

(**d**) The dash is used in German to introduce an afterthought:

Wien, Wien, nur du allein – du sollst die Stadt meiner Träume sein.
Vienna, Vienna, you alone – you shall be the city of my dreams.

(**e**) The dash is also used for an afterthought which is designed for effect:

Hinein in diese Menschenmasse – aber ohne mich.
(Forwards) into this mass of people – but without me.

(**f**) In spite of the remarks in sub-paragraph (**a**), dashes are occasionally used to mark off an important parenthetical thought:

Die Geschichte dieser Epoche – soweit sie schriftlich noch zugänglich ist – sollte sorgfältig erforscht werden.
The history of this period – insofar as it is accessible in written form – ought to be carefully revised.

293 Brackets

(a) Brackets are used in a sentence to include brief, explanatory information:

Anfang Februar 1945 legten in Jalta Roosevelt (USA), Stalin (UdSSR) und Churchill (Großbritannien) das endgültige militärische Vorgehen fest.
At the beginning of February 1945 in Yalta Roosevelt (USA), Stalin (USSR), and Churchill (Great Britain) laid down the final concerted military action.

(b) Brackets (often square brackets) are used to indicate that a letter or letters may be included or omitted:
hör(e) zu!   wasch(e) dich!   kämm(e) dich!

(c) A meaning may be included in brackets:
horizontal (waagerecht), vertikal (senkrecht)

294 Quotation marks (or inverted commas)

(a) Quotation marks are used to show the beginning and the end of the word or words quoted. In German, quotation marks are usually double, but the decision on this point may rest with the printer. The opening marks are on the line and below, whilst the closing marks are above the line as in English. For example:

Goethes ,,Götz von Berlichingen" ist ein Werk des Sturm und Drangs.
Goethe's 'Götz von Berlichingen' is a work of the 'Sturm und Drang' period.

(b) Should a newspaper such as **'Die Welt'** be quoted, and the noun and article be used in the dative case, then the changed article is used outside the quotation marks:

Ein Artikel über dieses Thema erschien vor kurzem in der ,,Welt".
An article on this subject appeared recently in 'Die Welt'.

(c) Quotation marks (inverted commas) are used to quote the actual words of a speaker:

Friedrich der Große sagte einmal zu seinem Freund d'Argens: ,,Es wird so viel über uns Könige, die wir Gottes Ebenbild auf Erden seien, gesprochen. Darauf habe ich mich im Spiegel betrachtet und habe mir gesagt: um so schlechter für Gott, wenn ich ihm ähnlich bin."
Frederick the Great once said to his friend d'Argens, 'There is so much said about us kings, that we are the very likeness of God on earth. So I looked at myself in a mirror, and said to myself, "So much the worse for God if I am like him".'

It should be noted from the above example that direct speech in German is introduced by a colon. If a quotation within a quotation is made, as in the example, then the colon is sufficient to indicate that there is a kind of direct speech within the direct speech. Note the colon after **gesagt**, and the fact that there are no additional quotation marks in German.

(**d**) If the quotation comes first in a sentence, then a comma separates the quotation and the explanation:

,,Es ist sehr wahr, daß, wenn man untersucht, was der Ruhm sei, dieser zu etwas sehr Geringem wird. Von Unwissenden beurteilt und von Dummköpfen geachtet zu werden, den eigenen Namen von einem Volkshaufen ausgesprochen zu hören, der ohne Verstand zustimmt, abweist oder haßt, darin liegt nichts, worauf man stolz sein könnte", so lauteten die bitteren Überlegungen des Alten Fritz gegen Ende seines Lebens.

'It is very true that if one begins to examine what fame is, then this becomes something very trifling. To be judged by those with no knowledge and to be esteemed by blockheads; to hear one's name spoken by a heap of people who agree, reject, or hate, without understanding; there's nothing in all that of which one might be proud', so ran the bitter reflections of 'der alte Fritz' towards the end of his life.

Glossary
of grammatical terms

This glossary lists and explains the technical terms of grammar as they are used in this book. The terms are given in full as they appear in the text, and are arranged alphabetically according to the first letter of the first word. The numbers in brackets refer to the paragraphs in which examples are to be found, or further explanations given.

The **accusative** or the **accusative case** is the form of the word used when it is (part of) the direct object of a sentence. In German the complement can also be accusative. (**137–8**) (**154**)

The **active** or **active voice** refers to a form of the verb used when the subject of the sentence is active, and not passive, that is to say when a person performs an action, or a thing sets something in motion. (**12**) (**60**)

An **adjective** is a word added to a noun to describe a person or a thing more fully. (**159**)

An **adjectival noun** in German is a word which is declined like an adjective, but has the function of a noun. (**170**)

An **adverb** is a word that modifies or qualifies another word, especially a verb, an adjective, or another adverb. (**197**)

An **adverbial clause** in a complex sentence has the same function as an adverb in a simple sentence. (**279**)

An **adverbial phrase** is a word-group expressing a relation to place, time, circumstance or manner. (**197**)

Agreement is a grammatical term used to refer to the matching of grammatical number, case, and person. (**143**)

An **allophone** is a variation of a phoneme as it is produced in actual speech. (**2**)

Nouns in **apposition** are noun groups which are adjacent or next door to one another by way of explanation, and which refer to the same person or thing, and which share the same verb. (**158**) (**168**)

An **article** in grammar is either definitive or indefinite, and is used before a noun. (**137**)

An **auxiliary verb** helps to form certain tenses. There are three verbs in German which may be used: **haben**, **sein**, and **werden**. (**14**)

A **cardinal number** is a whole number such as 5 or 15. (**179**)

A **case** in grammar refers to the form of the word which shows the function of a noun or a pronoun in a sentence. (**137–8**)

A **clause** is a distinct part of a sentence with a subject and predicate (including a verb). (**263**)

The **comparison of adjectives or adverbs** refers to the degree or extent of one of those words. The three degrees are simple or positive, comparative, and superlative. The comparative is used for the comparison of two persons or things, and the superlative for three or more. (**175**)

A **complement** in German grammar is the word (or words) used after verbs like **sein** and **werden** to complete the sentence. (**137**)

A **complex sentence** consists of one or more main clauses, and one or more subordinate or relative clauses. (**265**)

A **compound word** in German is a single word made up of parts, each of which could be a separate word on its own. (**8–10**) (**134**) (**203–4**)

The **conditional** or the **conditional form** of the subjunctive is used in German in connection with a so-called *if*-clause, when a condition or supposition is expressed. There are two forms of the conditional in German. (**68**) (**75–6**)

A **conditional clause** is one in which a condition is stated. The main clause gives the consequence or result. (**245(e)**)

The **conjugation** of a verb is the system of forms, including person, number, and tense. In German the endings and possibly the vowel of the stem are particularly affected. (**11–13**)

A **consonant** is a speech sound in which the breath is partially or almost completely obstructed. (**2**)

A **coordinating conjunction** in German links words, clauses, and even sentences in such a way that there is no change of word order. (**241–2**)

The **dative** or the **dative case** is the form of a word used when it is (part of) the indirect object. (**137–8**) (**156**)

Declension is the change in form which a noun, etc., undergoes according to its gender, number, and case, and which depends on its function in a sentence. (**152**)

The **definite article** is used with special reference to a particular noun. (**137**)

Demonstrative adjectives or pronouns are those which indicate, show, or point out. (**166**)

A **derivative** is a word which originates or arises from another word. (**4**)

A **diminutive** in grammar refers to smallness or youngness indicated in German by a special ending. (**127**)

A **diphthong** is a combination of two vowel sounds which are then heard as one sound of variable pitch. (**5**)

The **direct object** is the person or thing directly affected by the verb. (**137**)

A **double prefix** is one formed by the joining of two separate particles. (**124**).

The **du-form** in German, and also the **ihr-form**, are forms of the verb which are used to speak to children, to close friends, and to members of the family. (**212**)

Ellipsis refers to the deliberate omission of words from a sentence. (**281**)

Etymology is the science of the origin and history of words. (**136**)

The **first conditional** in German is the tense formed with **würde**, etc., plus the infinitive of the verb. (**75**)

A **fixed phrase** or **fixed expression** is one which never varies in form. (**7**)

The **future perfect tense** in German refers to something which will have been completed at a specific point in future time. As with the future tense, this is philosophically mere speculation, but optimism prevails. (**56–8**)

The **future tense** in German refers to a time or an event which is coming after the present. Philosophically this is mere speculation, but it is assumed grammatically that there is a future. (**51–5**)

The word **gender** refers in German to a grammatical grouping of nouns into masculine, feminine, and neuter. (**126**)

The word **generic** refers to the genus, kind, class, or group. (**137**) (**141**)

The **genitive** or the **genitive case** is the form of a noun or pronoun which indicates belonging to, or possession. (**137–8**) (**155**)

The German **Hochsprache** is the generally accepted theoretical standard pronunciation of the sounds of German. It is a theoretical set of norms. (**250**)

The **imperative** is the form of the verb used to give a command or an order. (**13–14**) (**99–102**)

Imperfect tense – see past tense. (**33**)

An **impersonal verb** is one which is used after an impersonal subject such as **es** (it). (**24**) (**84–5**)

An **indeclinable adverb** is one whose form does not change, and which cannot be expressed in the comparative or superlative. (**198**)

An **indefinite adjective or pronoun** is one whose meaning is vague or not clearly stated. (**172**) (**232**)

An **indefinite article** is used with a noun. There is no specific reference, but only generic reference, namely to the genus, kind, class, or group. (**137**)

The **indicative** or the **indicative mood** in German is used to state a fact, to make a declaration, or to ask a factual question. The mood or modus is shown by the form of the verb. It is in contrast to the subjunctive mood. (**12**) (**26**)

The **indirect object** refers to the person or thing indirectly affected by the verb. (**137**)

Indirect speech – see reported speech. (**69**) (**71**) (**269**)

The **infinitive** is the basic form of a verb as given in a dictionary. After the ending is removed the stem remains. (**13–14**) (**105–8**)

An **infinitive conjunction** in German is a word or words used to link the infinitive to the rest of the sentence. (**244**)

An **inseparable verb** in German is one which has a prefix before the basic verb, and which is never separated under any circumstances. (**8–10**) (**119**) (**122**)

An **interjection** is an emotional sound which does not form part of the grammatical flow of speech. (**248**)

The **International Phonetic Alphabet** is a set of symbols produced by the International Phonetic Association. Each symbol represents the norm of a particular sound. (**1**)

The **interrogative form** of a word is the question form, and an interrogative word is one used to ask questions. (**30**) (**229**)

Intonation is the contrastive variation in the pitch level of the voice in continuous utterance. (**3**)

An **intransitive verb** is one which does not take a direct object. (**61**)

An **irregular verb** in German is one which has the same endings in the past tense and past participle as a weak verb, but changes its stem vowel like a strong verb. (**12**) (**18**)

A **modal verb** is one which describes or indicates a mood. This may be a wish, an obligation felt, a liking, or a feeling of ability. There are six modal verbs in German: **dürfen**, **können**, **mögen**, **müssen**, **sollen**, and **wollen**. (**22–3**) (**80–3**)

Mood in German grammar refers to the distinction in meaning expressed by a particular form of a verb. The indicative mood expresses facts, and is used to ask questions and give orders. The subjunctive mood expresses wishes, uncertainty, etc. (**67**)

A **multiple sentence** consists of a string of simple sentences joined by coordinating conjunctions. (**261**)

A **multiple verb group** consists of three elements: an auxiliary verb, a modal verb, and the infinitive of another verb. (**258**)

The **nominative** or the **nominative case** is the form of a noun or pronoun when it is the subject of a sentence. In German the complement can also be nominative (or accusative). (**137–8**) (**153**)

A **noun** is a word used to name a person, place, or thing. (**127**)

A **noun clause** is one which replaces or does the work of a noun. (**268**)

A **noun group** is a cluster of words around a noun. (**273**)

The term **number** is used in grammar to distinguish between singular, which refers to one of a kind, and plural, which refers to more than one. (**12**) (**138**)

An **object** in German grammar is a noun, pronoun, or noun group governed by (following) a transitive verb or a preposition. In German it may be in the accusative case (direct object), in the genitive, or in the dative (indirect object). (**154–6**)

An **ordinal number** is used to place people or things in an arithmetic order, such as the fifth or the fifteenth. (**182**)

Parallel forms refer in German grammar to two adjectives which have the same endings. (**173**)

A **participial phrase or word group** is one in which the present or past participle is the key word, which in turn relates to a person, thing, or idea in the rest of the sentence. (**114**) There is a participial structure which is peculiar to German. (**118**).

A **participle** is a verbal adjective which retains some qualities of a verb, and qualifies a noun. (**105**) There are two forms of participle in German, the present and the perfect, whose form of the verb in English is known as the past participle. (**110–13**)

A **particle** is a minor part of speech such as an article or a prefix. (**4**)

The **passive** or **passive voice** refers to a form of the verb used when the subject of the sentence suffers an action. More accurately in German it is a form of the verb which is made up of a tense of the verb **werden** plus the past participle of the given verb. (**15**) (**60**) (**63**)

The **past tense** in German is used to describe the past as it is considered at the time by the speaker or the writer. (**37**)

The **perfect tense** in German is a combination of the present tense of **haben** or **sein** plus the past participle of the verb. The activity lies in the past, but there is usually a connection in the mind of the speaker or writer with the present. (**39–43**)

The term **person** is used in grammar to distinguish the form of the verb which is used. In German the **ich-form** is the first person, the **du-form**, **ihr-form**, or **Sie-form** is the second person, and the **er-form**, **sie-form**, **es-form**, or the plural **sie-form** is the third person. (**12**)

A **phoneme** is the smallest unit of sound which can be contrasted with another sound. A phoneme is represented by a separate symbol in the International Phonetic Alphabet. (**2**)

A **phrase**, as distinct from a clause, is a cluster of words without a verb with a tense. (**7**)

The **pluperfect tense** in German refers to the past before the past, to something which had already happened when something else occurred. (**46–50**)

Possessive pronouns used as adjectives are ones indicating belonging to someone or something, or possession. (**165**)

A **postmodifying adjective** is one which comes after a noun and yet relates to it. It is not declined. (**159**) (**160**)

A **prefix** is a syllable or a word placed in front of a word to add to or change its meaning. (**4**)

A **premodifying adjective** comes before a noun and modifies or describes it. In German a premodifying adjective also shows the function of a noun in a sentence (subject, object, etc.) and is declinable. (**140**) (**159**) (**161**)

The **present tense** of a verb in German is used mainly for activity at the present time, or that which begins soon, or for a habit, or a repeated activity. (**29**)

A **pronominal adverb** in German is a compound word with a meaning which is partly adverb and partly pronoun. (**203**)

A **pronoun** is a (short) word doing the work of a noun in naming a person or a thing. (**208**)

A **pseudoreflexive verb** in German is one which is used with a reflexive pronoun although there is no grammatical justification. The dictionary does not list the verb as reflexive. (**87**)

A **reflexive verb** in German is a verb which is always used in conjunction with a reflexive pronoun. (**25**) (**86–90**)

A **relative clause** is one which relates to a person or a thing mentioned in the main clause. (**262**)

A **relative pronoun** is one which relates or links a subordinate clause to a main clause. (**225**)

Reported speech is not the accurate word for word recording of a conversation between one person and a second person, but a report (which may or may not be accurate) given by a third person. Since there may be some doubt about the accuracy the subjunctive is (usually) used in German. (**69**) (**71**)

Glossary of grammatical terms

The **second conditional** in German is the tense formed with **würde**, etc., plus the past participle of the verb, plus the infinitive **haben** or **sein**. (**76**)
Secondary stress is minor stress, as compared with primary stress, which is major stress. (**4(e)**)
A **separable verb** in German is one which is a single word in the infinitive, but whose prefix may be separated from the basic verb under certain circumstances, such as in the present or past tenses. (**8–10**) (**119–21**)
Set phrase – see fixed phrase. (**114**)
The **stem** of a verb is the basic form left after the removal of the ending. (**11**)
A **simple sentence** is one in which there is only one main verb. (**250**)
Stress in phonetics is prominence. This is usually achieved by using extra force to pronounce a particular syllable. (**4**)
A **strong verb** in German is one which changes the vowel in the past tense and the past participle, and does not add **-t**, **-te**, **-ten**, etc. to the stem of the infinitive. (**12**) (**17**)
The **subject** of a sentence is a noun, pronoun, or noun group about which something is asserted or questioned. (**153**)
The **subjunctive** or the **subjunctive mood** is used in German to express uncertainty, possibility, a hypothesis, a condition, a hope, a wish, etc. The mood (Latin: **modus**) is shown in the form of the verb, and is often in contrast to the indicative. (**13**) (**26**) (**67**)
A **subordinating conjunction** links clauses, one of which is subordinate, or which depends for its full meaning on the main clause. In German there is a change of word order in the subordinate clause. (**241**) (**245**)
A **suffix** is a particle added to the end of a word to make another word. (**4(i)**)
The **superlative** in German refers to the form of an adjective or adverb when three or more persons or things are compared. (**177**) (**195**)

A **tense** is a form of the verb which shows present, past, or future time. (**12**)
A **transitive verb** is one which takes (or is followed by) a direct object. This may be a person or a thing. (**61**)

An **umlaut** is a vowel change indicated by two dots over the vowel. (**5**)

A **verb** is a word which asserts or questions an action or state concerning the subject of the sentence. (**11**)
A **vowel** is a sound made when the vocal cords are partially open and vibrating without audible friction. (**2**)

A **weak verb** in German is one which forms its past tense and past participle by adding **-t**, **-te**, **-ten**, etc. to the stem of the infinitive. (**12**)

Appendix

Some translation problems

This Appendix provides some suggested translations of certain English words which may need various renderings in German. It is only able to deal with the main points and does not replace a dictionary.

The Appendix should be used in conjunction with the Index. In some cases, reference back to German word entries in the Index will provide additional information.

about

clock / time

about 4 o'clock (either way)	um 4 Uhr herum/etwa um 4 Uhr
about 4 o'clock (or shortly before)	gegen 4 Uhr

concerning

laugh about	lachen über (+ acc.)
be anxious about	Angst haben um

= around

about ten marks per person	(etwa) um zehn Mark pro Person
walk about the streets	durch die Straßen wandern/gehen
(round) about Christmas	um Weihnachten (herum)

about to

he was about to say	er wollte eben sagen

approximately

about 5 kilometres	ungefähr/etwa 5 Kilometer
about as far as	ungefähr so weit wie

about time

it's about time that	es ist gerade Zeit, daß
	es ist aber Zeit, daß
	es ist an der Zeit, daß

ago

a week ago (today)	(heute) vor acht Tagen/vor einer Woche
long ago	vor langem/vor langer Zeit
that is ages ago	das ist schon lange her
not long ago	vor kurzem/vor kurzer Zeit
how long ago?	wie lange her?

as . . . as

as long as the weather holds	solange das Wetter hält
as soon as the post arrives	sobald die Post kommt/da ist
the cats as well as the dogs	die Katzen sowie die Hunde
	die Katzen und auch die Hunde
	die Katzen sowohl als auch die Hunde
as tall as	so groß wie
as good as done	so gut wie gemacht/getan

at

place

at school; at the station	in der Schule; am Bahnhof
at the baker's/the butcher's	beim Bäcker/Fleischer
to be at the university	auf der Universität sein/studieren
at the office	im Büro
at the bank	(sie arbeitet) bei der Bank
	(sie ist) in der Bank beschäftigt
at home	bei mir/bei ihr/bei uns zuhause
at table	am Tisch/bei Tisch

time

at 9 o'clock; at this time	um 9 Uhr; zu dieser Zeit/um diese Zeit
at Christmas/Easter, etc.	zu Weihnachten/Ostern, usw.
at once (= immediately)	sofort/sogleich
at the same time	zur gleichen Zeit/zu derselben Zeit
suddenly, all at once	auf einmal/plötzlich

with numbers

at 17 (years old)	mit 17 (Jahren)
four pairs at 5 marks	vier Paar zu 5 Mark/ 4 Paar zu (je) 5 Mark

price

at this price	zu diesem Preis

with verbs

be astonished/annoyed at	staunen/sich ärgern über (+ acc.)
look at the clock	auf die Uhr sehen/schauen
knock at the door	an die Tür klopfen
someone is knocking at the door	es klopft an der Tür

be

state

to be unhappy	unglücklich sein

be

position

to be in the corner	in der Ecke sein
to be on/under the table	auf/unter dem Tisch sein

identity

to be a teacher	Lehrer sein
to be French (nationality)	französisch sein
to be French (person)	Franzose/Französin sein

= become

to be (become) a teacher	Lehrer werden
to be (become) better	besser werden

in passive

to be injured in an accident	bei einem Unfall verletzt werden

been

*past part. of **be***

I have been ill	ich bin krank gewesen

=gone

he has been across the river	er ist über den Fluß gegangen
I have never been abroad	ich war nie im Ausland
	ich bin nie im Ausland gewesen

before

adv.

(on) the day before	am Tag zuvor
better than before	besser als zuvor/früher
I should have done it before	ich hätte es eher/zuvor machen sollen
he has done that sort of thing before	so etwas hat er schon einmal gemacht

prep.

time

before lunch/the war	vor dem Mittagessen/dem Krieg
he will be back before (= by) the end of March	bis/vor Ende März ist er zurück

place

1 km. before the turning	1 km vor der Abzweigung

conj.

before I could answer	bevor/ehe ich antworten konnte
it will be a long time before I finish it	es wird lange dauern, bis ich damit fertig bin

by

agent

stolen by a burglar	von einem Einbrecher gestohlen
a novel by Dürrenmatt	ein Roman von Dürrenmatt

cause

killed by lightning	vom Blitz erschlagen

means

by hard work	durch harte Arbeit
take someone by the hand	jemanden bei/an der Hand nehmen
by train; by ship (travel)	mit dem Zug/mit der Bahn; mit dem Schiff/per Schiff
(send goods) by ship	per Schiff senden
send by airmail (letter etc.)	per/mit Luftpost schicken

=near

by the window/river	am Fenster/Fluß

=beside

he sat by the president	er saß neben dem Präsidenten

=by way of

he got out by the emergency exit	er ist durch den Notausgang herausgekommen

=via

we travelled by Cologne	wir sind über Köln gefahren

time

by 20th March; by that time	bis zum 20. März; bis dahin
by tomorrow morning	bis/bevor morgen früh
by the time (that) he knew	bis (daß) er es wußte
by the hour	pro Stunde
by now (this moment)	bis jetzt

circumstance

by daylight	bei Tageslicht
by day and by night	bei Tag und Nacht

with verbs

know by sight	vom Ansehen kennen
lead by the hand	an der Hand führen
recognize by	erkennen an (+ dat.)
to walk by (someone)	(an jemandem) vorbeigehen

could

was able

she could not lift it	sie konnte es nicht (auf)heben

could

would be able

we could do it tomorrow   morgen könnten wir es machen

=might

that could be true   das könnte wahr sein

could have

would have been able

we could have seen him yesterday   wir hätten ihn gestern sehen können

=might have

they could have been in London   sie könnten in London gewesen sein/sie hätten in London sein können

few, a few

quantity

he had few friends   er hatte wenige Freunde

I have brought a few books   ich habe ein paar/einige Bücher mitgebracht

time

(for) a few days   (für) einige Tage/ein paar Tage

for (prep.) Usually **für**, but note also:

for Christmas/his birthday   zu Weihnachten/seinem Geburtstag

it (e.g. the weather) is too hot for me   mir ist es zu warm

for supper; for example   zum Abendessen; zum Beispiel

ready for; depart for   bereit; abreisen nach

jump for joy   vor Freude springen

for a holiday   auf Urlaub

for

time (past)

we have been here for three days   wir sind schon/bereits drei Tage hier

time (future)

we are going to Germany for a fortnight   wir reisen auf/für vierzehn Tage nach Deutschland

destination

to set out for Berlin   nach Berlin abreisen

the train for Munich   der Zug nach München

Appendix

from

from, in origin

he has just come from school	er ist gerade aus der Schule gekommen
she comes from Munich	sie stammt aus München
this piece is from the 18th century	dieses Stück ist aus dem 18. Jahrhundert

from . . . to

| from A to Z | von A bis Z |
| to drive from A to B | von A nach B fahren |

from (place)

the train is from Hamburg	der Zug kommt von/aus Hamburg
ten kilometres from Cologne	10 Kilometer von Köln (entfernt)
seen from above/below	von oben/unten gesehen

time

open from 8 a.m. to 8 p.m.	von 8 bis 20 Uhr geöffnet
from time to time	von Zeit zu Zeit
from now on	von jetzt an/ab jetzt
from 6 o'clock/from Monday	ab 6 Uhr/ab Montag
from day to day	von Tag zu Tag

source

| quotation from Goethe | Zitat von Goethe |
| wine is made from grapes | Wein wird aus Weintrauben gekeltert/gemacht |

have usually **haben**, but note also:

perfect tense

they have won (a prize)	sie haben (einen Preis) gewonnen
they have gone away	sie sind verreist/fortgegangen
I have succeeded	mir ist es gelungen

have

cause (to be done)

| have one's car repaired | sein Auto reparieren lassen |

obligation

| he has to go | er muß gehen |

action

| to have a walk | spazierengehen |
| to have a talk about or over | besprechen |

in, into usually **in**, but note also:

prep.

in the street; in this way	auf der Straße; auf diese Weise
he drove into a tree	er fuhr gegen einen Baum
how is it spelt in German?	wie schreibt man das auf deutsch?
translate into German	ins Deutsche übersetzen
in writing; in a loud voice	schriftlich; mit lauter Stimme/laut
in your place I would say nothing	an Ihrer Stelle würde ich schweigen/nichts sagen
to have something in common	etwas gemeinsam haben
be interested in	sich interessieren für
in the town/in the country	in der Stadt/auf dem Land(e)

adv.

go in; come in	hineingehen; hereinkommen
is anyone in?	ist jemand da?
is everyone in (e.g. the car)?	sind alle drin?

state/condition

in good health/in a good mood	bei guter Gesundheit/bei guter Stimmung/Laune

conj.

she was right in that she …	sie hatte Recht, indem sie …

just

at this/that moment

he has just come in	er ist gerade/eben hereingekommen
just as he came in	gerade, als er hereinkam

precisely

that is just what I had in mind	das ist genau, was ich im Sinn hatte/eben das hatte ich im Sinn
it is just 4 o'clock	es ist genau 4 Uhr
just as tall as	eben/genau so groß wie
just enough/just there	eben genug/genau dort/da
that is just right	das ist gerade recht/das ist genau richtig

barely

we've got just enough time	wir haben gerade genug Zeit

last

previous

it happened last Tuesday	es ist letzten/am vorigen/am vergangenen Dienstag geschehen

last

previous
last night — gestern abend

final
the last train — der letzte Zug
the last day of the month — der letzte Tag des Monats

phrases
to the last — bis zum Ende
last but one — vorletzt...
last of all — zum Schluß/zuletzt

like (vb.)

I like him — ich habe/mag ihn gern/er gefällt mir

I like this play (very much) — dieses Stück gefällt mir (gut)
I like chamber music — ich habe Kammermusik gern/ ich höre gern Kammermusik

I like cheese/wine — ich esse gern Käse/trinke gern Wein

I like riding — ich reite gern
I should like to come too — ich möchte (gern) mitkommen
(vb.)
like (=prefer) this more than that — dies dem anderen vorziehen
I will go with you, if you like — ich werde mitgehen, wenn/falls Sie es (haben) wollen/gerne möchten

may have

possibility
he may have been ill — er kann krank gewesen sein

indirect speech
I fear he may have missed the train (fairly certain) — ich fürchte, er hat den Zug verpaßt
I fear he may have missed the train (possibility) — ich fürchte, er könnte den Zug verpaßt haben

might, might have

possibility
they might be away — sie könnten/dürften verreist sein
she might have lost it in the hotel — sie könnte es im Hotel verloren haben

or — sie hat es vielleicht im Hotel verloren

might, might have

indirect speech

I fear he might be dead	ich fürchte, er könnte tot sein
I thought she might have found it	ich dachte/glaubte, sie könnte es
(would have been able to *or*	gefunden haben
ought to have been able to)	*or* ich glaubte, sie hätte es finden
	können

hesitation/diffidence

might I make a suggestion?	darf/dürfte ich einen Vorschlag
	machen?

obligation

you might at least help	du könntest wenigstens mithelfen

nor, not ... nor

neither the ones nor the others	weder die einen noch die anderen
he's not coming, nor am I	er kommt nicht (mit), ich auch
	nicht
nor do I know the neighbours	die Nachbarn habe ich auch nicht
	kennengelernt/weder kenne ich
	die Nachbarn
not a sound, nor a sign of life	weder Ton noch Lebenszeichen

of usually **von**, or genitive, but note also:

I must think of the cost	ich muß an die Kosten denken
what do you think of my plans?	was denkst du über meine Pläne
remind of	erinnern an (+ acc.)
be afraid of	Angst haben vor (+ dat.)

of

of his (her) own	aus eigenem Antrieb
of an afternoon/of a Sunday	an einem Nachmittag/sonntags
(a wooden table	ein Tisch aus Holz)
a sheet of paper	ein Blatt Papier

on, onto

horizontal surface

put the cups on the table	die Tassen auf den Tisch setzen/
	stellen
to lie on the floor	auf dem Boden liegen

vertical surface

write on the wall	an die Wand schreiben
be hanging on the wall	an der Wand hängen

on, onto

place

on the bus/train	im Bus/Zug

time

on Sunday/Sundays	(am) Sonntag/sonntags
on arrival	bei der Ankunft

idioms

the light is on	das Licht ist an
turn on a tap	einen Hahn aufdrehen
agree on	sich einigen über/auf (+ acc.)
reflect on; live on (e.g. fruit)	nachdenken über; leben von
to talk on and on	immer weiter reden
later on/and so on	später/und so weiter
what's on?	was gibt's?
have you money on you?	hast du Geld bei dir?
on the first of April	am ersten April
on no account	auf keinen Fall
on good authority	aus guter Quelle
a house on the main road	ein Haus an der Hauptstraße
on business	geschäftlich
he has gone on holiday	er ist in Urlaub gegangen/gefahren
he is on holiday in Berlin	er ist auf Urlaub in Berlin

only

adv.

not more than

only two of them came	es kamen nur zwei (davon)
it is only 6 o'clock	es ist erst 6 Uhr
one can only hope	man darf/kann nur hoffen

no longer ago than

only recently/last Friday	erst kürzlich/neulich/letzten Freitag

not before

he is only coming tomorrow	er kommt erst morgen
only when we get some rain	erst wenn wir Regen haben

adj.

the only spectator	der einzige Zuschauer

conj.

I will do it, only not today	ich tue es, nur nicht heute
he will do it, only if	er wird es tun, nur wenn

ought, should

I ought to/should do it	ich sollte/mußte es machen
you ought not to/should not smoke so much	du sollst/solltest nicht so viel rauchen
we ought to/should have started earlier	wir hätten früher anfangen sollen
he ought not to/should not have spoken like that	er hätte sich nicht auf diese Weise äußern dürfen/sollen

shall, should

future

in June I shall be abroad	im Juni werde ich im Ausland sein
we shall have spent more than 400 marks	wir werden mehr als DM 400 ausgegeben haben

idioms

what shall we do?	was sollen wir machen?
shall we go into the town/take a boat trip	wollen/sollen wir in die Stadt gehen/eine Bootsfahrt machen?
it shall not happen again	es soll nicht wieder vorkommen
if it rains, I should stay at home	wenn/falls es regnet, würde ich zu Hause bleiben
I should have bought it	ich hätte es kaufen sollen

so

advb.

it is so big	es ist so groß
he said so	er hat es gesagt
I think so	ich glaube (es)

conj.

=therefore

it was already late, so we had to hurry	es war schon spät, deshalb/also mußten wir uns beeilen

so as to

he paid in advance so as to get a rebate	er zahlte im voraus, um einen Rabatt zu erhalten

so that

purpose

they divided it in four so that everyone should have enough	sie teilten es unter vier auf damit alle genug hatten/hätten

Appendix

so

result

there has been no rain since March, so that our stream has dried up

seit März hat es nicht geregnet, so daß unser Bach ausgetrocknet ist

condition

this part is good for tourism so so long as one avoids main roads

dies Gebiet ist gut für Tourismus wenn man nur/vorausgesetzt , daß man die Hauptstraßen vermeidet

phrases

he speaks German and so does his brother

er spricht Deutsch, genau wie/ ebenso wie sein Bruder

so to speak

sozusagen

some

vague amount

take some

nimm (etwas) davon!

he ate some of the fruit

er aß vom Obst

I'll buy some meat

ich kaufe etwas Fleisch/ich werde etwas Fleisch kaufen

small amount

he has some experience

er hat einige Erfahrung

after some thought

nach einiger Überlegung

we have some friends who will help

wir haben (einige) Freunde, die mithelfen wollen

some (people) were quite horrified

einige waren ganz entsetzt

longer time

for some time

eine Zeitlang/seit einiger Zeit

=*roughly*

some 50 years ago

etwa/ungefähr vor 50 Jahren

some 10 kilometres

etwa 10 Kilometer

vagueness

at some flat in Frankfurt

in irgendwelcher/irgendeiner Wohnung in Frankfurt

in some book or other

in irgendeinem Buch

words/phrase

somehow; somewhere

irgendwie; irgendwo

at some time or other

irgendwann

there is, there are

be present, exist, occur

there are oases in the desert	es gibt Oasen in der Wüste
there is a good reason for it	es gibt einen guten Grund dafür
there was an accident yesterday outside my house	gestern gab es einen Unfall vor meinem Haus
there is a man who...	es gibt einen Mann, der...
there are two men who... (specifically)	es sind zwei Männer, die...

existence

there are five people in the waiting room	es sind fünf Personen im Wartezimmer
is there a letter for me?	ist ein Brief für mich da?

idioms

today there is strawberry or vanilla ice for dessert	heute gibt es Erdbeer- oder Vanilleeis zum Nachtisch

another verb used

there was a nun standing on the doorstep	es stand eine Nonne vor der Tür
there has been a burglary next door	nebenan ist eingebrochen worden
last year there were a lot of tourists coming to England	letztes Jahr kamen viele Touristen nach England
there is an engraving on the wall	es hängt ein Kupferstich an der Wand
there is a cupboard in the corner	es steht ein Schrank in der Ecke

N.B. the 'other verb' construction, as above, is more frequent in German than in English

till, until

prep.

till now; until last Monday	bis jetzt; bis letzten Montag
from now till/until 12th August	von jetzt bis zum 12. August
there are no trains till Saturday	es fährt kein Zug vor Samstag
he is not coming back till/until next week	er kommt erst nächste Woche wieder

conj.

we shall wait till he comes	wir wollen warten, bis er (an)kommt
don't set out until your passport arrives	reise nicht ab, bevor dein Paß da ist!

time

occasion

this time I will let it pass	dieses Mal/diesmal lasse ich es durchgehen
try again another time	versuch es ein anderes Mal (wieder)

multiplier

six times seven	sechs mal sieben

period of time

that takes a lot of time	das nimmt viel Zeit in Anspruch/ das braucht viel Zeit
he talks all the time	er redet die ganze Zeit

moment or period (in time)

now is the right time	jetzt ist die richtige Zeit
time for lunch	Zeit zum Mittagessen
at this time (=hour)	zu dieser Stunde
at this time (=period)/at that time	um diese Zeit/zu der Zeit
at the time of the Thirty Years War	zur Zeit/zu Zeiten des Dreißig-jährigen Krieges
at all times; in the nick of time	stets/immer; im richtigen Augenblick/gerade zur rechten Zeit

clock time

what is the time?	wieviel Uhr ist es? wie spät ist es?
British Summer Time	britische Sommerzeit
the train is behind time	der Zug ist verspätet
it arrives ahead of/on time	er kommt vorzeitig/pünktlich an

phrases

have a good time!	viel Vergnügen!
to have a good time	sich (gut) amüsieren
to last a long time (while)	eine lange Weile/Zeit dauern
there is no time to lose	es eilt
for the time being	vorübergehend
to work against time	gegen die Uhr arbeiten

to

dative

show it (to) me	zeig es mir!
I shall say nothing to him	ich sage ihm nichts
it seemed to me as if...	mir ist vorgekommen, als(ob)...

implies 'into'

go to the office/the theatre	ins Büro/ins Theater gehen

to

implies 'into'

go to the forest/the mountains   in den Wald/in die Berge gehen

go to town/one's room   in die Stadt/in sein Zimmer gehen

alongside

go to the table/one's place   an den Tisch/an seinen Platz
       gehen

go to the door/the window   an die Tür/ans Fenster gehen

go to the bus-stop   an die Bushaltestelle gehen

come to the river/the beach   an den Fluß/an den Strand
       kommen

get to the frontier   die Grenze erreichen

as far as, up to, destination

does this bus go to the terminus?   fährt dieser Bus bis zur Endstation?

4 to 6 kilometres away   4 bis 6 Kilometer entfernt

from beginning to end   von Anfang bis (zum) Ende

soaked to the skin   bis auf die Haut durchnäßt

a single ticket to Cologne   eine einfache Fahrkarte (bis) nach
       Köln

geography

go to America/Belgium   nach Amerika/nach Belgien
       fahren

go to Switzerland/Paris   in die Schweiz/nach Paris fahren

idioms with nouns

go to the toilet/the market   auf die Toilette/zum Markt gehen

go to the country/the bank   auf das Land/zur Bank gehen

go to (the) university   auf die Universität gehen

idioms with verbs

contribute to; point to   beitragen zu; weisen auf (+ acc.)

come to an end   zu Ende gehen

refer to (=relate to)   sich beziehen auf (+ acc.)

refer to (=speak of)   sprechen von

compare to/with   vergleichen mit

to speak to (=address) someone   zu jemandem sprechen

to speak to (=converse with)   mit jemandem sprechen
   someone

he listened to the speech   er hörte der Rede zu

he wouldn't listen to my advice   er wollte nicht auf meinen Rat
       hören

I like listening to music   ich höre gern Musik

to turn to someone for help   sich an jemanden um Hilfe
       wenden

to turn to the right   sich nach rechts drehen/nach
       rechts abbiegen

to

idioms with nouns

to write to someone/to the
  management

an jemanden/an die Leitung
  schreiben

what

thing

what is that?

was ist das?

idioms

what is your name
what is the price
what is the best way to do it?
it is not what I wanted

he gave what he had

wie heißt du?
wieviel kostet es?
wie macht man das am besten?
es ist nicht das, was ich haben
  wollte
er gab alles was er hatte

what kind of

what car have you (got)

was für en Wagen hast du?

yet

advb.

we must wait two hours yet

wir müssen noch zwei Stunden
  warten

it has not yet appeared
that is the best yet
we have had no reply as yet
to write yet more/yet again
has he come yet?

es ist noch nicht erschienen
das ist bisher das beste
bis jetzt haben wir keine Antwort
noch mehr/nochmals schreiben
ist er schon angekommen?

conj.

we often meet, yet we don't say
  much

wir treffen uns oft, doch reden
  wir nicht viel